ROUTLEDGE LIBRARY EDITIONS: RITUAL

I0131230

Volume 5

RITUAL, IDENTITY, AND THE MAYAN DIASPORA

RITUAL, IDENTITY, AND THE MAYAN DIASPORA

NANCY J. WELLMEIER

Routledge
Taylor & Francis Group

LONDON AND NEW YORK

First published in 1998 by Garland Publishing, Inc.

This edition first published in 2020
by Routledge
2 Park Square, Milton Park, Abingdon, Oxon OX14 4RN

and by Routledge
52 Vanderbilt Avenue, New York, NY 10017

Routledge is an imprint of the Taylor & Francis Group, an informa business

© 1998 Nancy J. Wellmeier

British Library Cataloguing in Publication Data
A catalogue record for this book is available from the British Library

ISBN: 978-0-367-43594-3 (Set)
ISBN: 978-1-00-300665-7 (Set) (ebk)
ISBN: 978-0-367-43902-6 (Volume 5) (hbk)
ISBN: 978-0-367-43906-4 (Volume 5) (pbk)
ISBN: 978-1-00-300638-1 (Volume 5) (ebk)

Publisher's Note
The publisher has gone to great lengths to ensure the quality of this reprint but points out that some imperfections in the original copies may be apparent.

Disclaimer
The publisher has made every effort to trace copyright holders and would welcome correspondence from those they have been unable to trace.

RITUAL, IDENTITY, AND THE MAYAN DIASPORA

NANCY J. WELLMEIER

GARLAND PUBLISHING, Inc.
A MEMBER OF THE TAYLOR & FRANCIS GROUP
NEW YORK & LONDON / 1998

Library of Congress Cataloging-in-Publication Data

Wellmeier, Nancy J., 1942–
    Ritual, identity, and the Mayan diaspora / Nancy J.
Wellmeier.
        p.   cm. — (Native Americans)
    Includes bibliographical references and index.
    ISBN 0-8153-3117-7 (alk. paper)
    1. Kanjobal Indians—Social conditions. 2. Kanjobal
Indians—Rites and ceremonies. 3. Kanjobal Indians—Florida—
Indiantown. 4. Indiantown (Fla.)—Social conditions. I. Title.
II. Series: Native Americans (Garland Publishing, Inc.)
F1465.2.K36W45 1998
305.897'415—dc21
                                                        98-21606

Printed on acid-free, 250-year-life paper
Manufactured in the United States of America

For my parents, Martha and Alvin

Contents

List of Illustrations

TABLES

FIGURES

My Involvement

My involvement with the Maya people started with Juana. When she first approached me in 1985 at the rural Catholic parish where I was working, I knew only that she needed help in finding a place to live. But little by little, I discovered that Juana was fleeing violence in her home town in Guatemala, that she spoke Q'anjob'al Maya much better than Spanish, and that she had no acquaintance with telephones, wash machines, or hospital delivery rooms. Slowly, as the trust between us grew, I learned more about the political situation in Guatemala and met other refugees. Juana introduced me to the migrant way-station known as *La Huerta* where I saw a steady stream of Maya people headed for Florida. In my new job with an agency that provided services to Central American refugees, I visited *La Huerta* weekly from 1988 through 1991 and became thoroughly intrigued with both the origin of the Mayan refugees and their Florida destination.

I wondered what in the life of the highland Mayas could have prepared them to travel so far and to live and work in such unfamiliar surroundings. At first glance, it seems improbable that they should have come at all. Much studied in Mesoamerican ethnographic work, the Maya corn farmer is usually described as a peasant with a mystical attachment to his land. "For the Mayan peasant, land and corn form the basis of his self-identification, his community identification, and his concept of the universe" (Early 1982:74). Removal from the land is said to undermine the basis of psychological consciousness of self and sense of belonging. Moreover, the isolation and limited educational opportunities in the highland communities would seem to preclude both the skills needed for successful migration and the information required to undertake such a venture (Dagodag 1975, Diaz-Briquets 1989).

I wondered as well if the reports of a Maya town of over five thousand people in central Florida could be true, and if they really did celebrate their famous saints' fiestas there. Conversations in *La Huerta* revealed that Guatemalan Mayas had settled in nuclei in Los Angeles and San Diego, Houston, Portland, and in other Florida cities. Ethnographic research about Maya refugees was available only for Florida; Allan Burns and his students at the University of Florida had found that the Indiantown Mayas are self-consciously attempting to establish their external and internal identity and to preserve their traditions through key symbols (Miralles 1987; Burns 1988b, 1989a, 1989b). This research also confirmed that the Indiantown Mayas celebrate a yearly festival in honor of St. Michael, the patron saint of San Miguel Acatán. However, the emphasis in Burns' work was not on the ritual and told little about its Guatemala counterpart. Finding myself in the middle of an unbelievably long migration route, I wanted to see both ends, and I wanted to understand why a religious ritual was involved.

A two month long visit to Huehuetenango in the fall of 1991 and a reconnaissance trip to Indiantown, Florida, in January of 1992 convinced me that the situation was far more complex than I had imagined but that it was a unique research opportunity. The study of a refugee community affords a sort of speeded-up view of rapid, on-going cultural change. The boundaries that are crossed and re-crossed are not just political ones, and the effects are not all on one side of the political borders. Linking research about the places of origin, the migration process and the place of ritual in the establishment of a sense of place and peoplehood in the new setting seemed to hold promise for an enhanced understanding of both ethnicity and religious ritual. Kearney's formulation of the "Articulatory Migrant Network" is a helpful model of what I intend here. The sending community is a distinct corporate settlement with a well-developed identity; together with the daughter communities formed by its migrants, it forms the Articulatory Migrant Network. The totality of changing internal and external relationships constitutes the developmental life-cycle of the network. Persons, information, goods, services, and economic value flow through the network, and changes can be seen as due to individual and collective actions taken to minimize negative flow, or loss. This can be analyzed over time and on the social and cultural level as well as the economic one (Kearney 1986:353-355).

This book is the result of research I undertook in order to understand both how and why the indigenous Mayan refugees in the United States have rapidly organized themselves around their religious rituals and what this has to do with the growing "indigenism" movements and self-conscious symbolization of identity among the Mayas within and outside of Guatemala.[1] The persistence of ethnicity and ethnoregenesis are puzzling issues worldwide. The failure of technology to homogenize world culture, the phenomenon of the "Balkanization" of many modern nation-states into ethnic territories or enclaves, and the growing strength of the voices of indigenous peoples in world fora all call for analysis and explanation. In the case of the Mayas, Manning Nash notes that three million Mayas living in nearly the same places as they did five hundred years ago is a puzzle to environmental and technological determinists and to cultural materialists. "The 500 year persistence of a cultural tradition under adverse pressures from the Euro-American world clamors for a tidy explanation" (M. Nash 1989:92). Of course this need is exacerbated by the discovery that many elements of the cultural tradition persist under the even more hostile conditions of migration to the United States.

Findings show that in highland Guatemala, indigenous Maya peasants are far more familiar with organizing themselves for religious purposes than a reading of the Mesoamerican fiesta system literature would prepare one to suspect. Explanations based on symbolic interpretations of the rituals themselves (Gossen 1974, Vogt 1976, B. Tedlock 1982, Ingham 1986, Watanabe 1990a) have failed to deal with the social implications of organizing large-scale public events in rural communities. Economic and political explanations of the famous cargo systems and patron saints' fiestas (e.g. Cancian 1965, 1967; Annis 1987) have not, for the most part, indicated the importance of the organizational praxis that surrounds and enables these ritual displays. Several ethnographers (Collier 1975, Carmack 1981, Farriss 1984,

Greenberg 1990, Stoll 1990) point out that the traditional colonial and post-colonial religious practice of the highland Mayas contained the seeds of self-conscious protest against the dominance of the nation-state, in that it was autonomously organized and led. But most of the studies do not connect this tradition of autonomous organization for ritual to the modern religious practice of the majority of the highland Mayas. For exceptions see Earle (1990a) and Watanabe (1992).

This research shows that the renewal of official Catholic church attention to the Maya communities, beginning in the 1940s with the arrival of United States missionaries, [2] enabled the Mayas to use their organizational tradition in church-sponsored activities including, but not limited to, public ritual, and to articulate with the church's regional, multi-ethnic organization. The present generation of indigenous clergy has opened up even more space for the operation of intense autonomous organization. This popular Catholic ritual system is the locus for the rise of a native modern Catholic lay leadership which derives its authority from the traditional ethic of self-sacrifice for the good of the community and its legitimacy through its connections with the church.

When the same Maya people who have exercised leadership within their Catholic church setting in Guatemala migrate to the United States, they use the organizational aspects of religion and particularly religious ritual as a focal point around which to mobilize their ethnic community as a way of maintaining their identity and their ties with their home communities. The church experience of the leaders and the categories and expectations of the followers combine, in places where there are sufficiently large Maya settlements, to create a self-conscious transnational ethnic group. In Indiantown, as in other Maya diaspora communities, a fiesta cycle which epitomizes these processes is being elaborated. The contribution of this research is to open up to public view what goes on behind the scenes in the organization of a cycle of public ritual events, and to show how this backstage arena is where leadership is consolidated and conscious choices are made about the symbolization of ethnicity.

Subsistence agriculturalists until the middle of this century, Maya corn farmers have approached religious practice in the same way they approach life in general: they always have been and continue to be, producers rather than consumers. Religious ritual and practice are not something to be received, bought or consumed, but produced by oneself and one's community. This stance toward religious practice characterizes Maya fiestas in Guatemala and has been successfully transferred to the exile situation.[3] There is also continuity with the chief moral principle of highland Maya religious ritual, self-sacrifice for the good of the community.

Bringing together, then, and building upon studies of the Mesoamerican fiesta systems, religious ritual in general, and migration, this study shows how the Mayas in the United States use their tradition to maintain and enhance their sense of ethnicity, turning it into an advantage in their exile situation. The importance for the Mayas of their community identity, concretized by their frequent contacts with their villages of origin, their taking on responsibility for improvement projects in those villages, and their adherence to traditional religious practice with its ideology of self-sacrifice, will be apparent in the details of everyday life in exile described here. Through these strategies, the Maya people not only cope materially and spiritually with the chaotic and liminal experience of uprootedness, but struggle to strengthen those aspects of their identity which they perceive as advantageous in the United States and beyond.

The larger issues that are implicit in this process touch on some of the problems that bedevil our world today: the need to explain and find channels for the surprising re-awakening of ethnic loyalties, which has irrupted into the consciousness of nation-states, prompting international discussion of "multiculturalism"; and the need to minimize the suffering caused by large scale mass migrations, forced and voluntary, that characterize our world. The Maya refugee community in the United States may hold the key to these vexing problems, by showing how autonomy and connectedness can continue to exist in exile, and giving us clues about the rewards of maintaining ethnic identity within or across borders.

As I noted above, my introduction to Maya immigrants activated my curiosity about both their point of origin and their destination. For that reason, my field of research had, in some way, to encompass both ends of the exiles' journey, and my choices of field sites were guided by the hundreds of conversations with the temporary residents of *La Huerta* over a period of years. Most often mentioned were the rural *municipios* of northern Huehuetenango in Guatemala, and the towns of Indiantown, Immokalee and West Palm Beach, in Florida. Since the focus of the research was to be the process of transplanting the saints' fiestas, and the one apparently successful transplant I knew about was the annual Fiesta de San Miguel in Indiantown, it seemed obvious to connect with San Miguel Acatán, in Guatemala, and to Indiantown. I witnessed the patronal fiesta in San Miguel Acatán in September 1991, visiting there for a week. I also visited a week in nearby San Rafael la Independencia, and lived for over two months in Santa Eulalia, in the same region, during 1991 and 1992. At the other end of the journey, I lived in Indiantown, Florida, from May, 1992 to February, 1993.

The problem of choosing a unit of study which would work both in Guatemala and in Indiantown was a thorny one. Two have been used: the household and the parish. Migration affects the household at both ends of the path in terms of its structure and its survival strategies. For example, Gonzalez finds that among the Garifuna, most men ages twenty-one to fifty are absent from their homes, that the nuclear family unit may be scattered among several households, and that a household may not be based on a conjugal pair (Gonzalez 1969:56, 84). This is certainly true of Guatemalan immigrant families. In Indiantown, intact families are almost non-existent; the household proved a more useful unit. The parish, as a semi-voluntary social unit, was used successfully by Van Oss (1986); it is appropriate in this context because in both Guatemala and Indiantown, the parish community, either official or *de facto*, is the group out of which fiesta organization arises. Van Oss notes that the parish is the smallest unit of public Catholic practice (Van Oss 1986: xiv, 51). In Catholic church law ("canon law") the parish is a territorial bounded unit, and includes in its *de jure* membership all who reside within. In actual fact, only those who attend services and receive baptism are thought of as members. The Catholic parish, usually named for a saint, is co-terminous with *municipio* boundaries in rural Huehuetenango. There is some evidence that these units were also more or less natural geographic, language, and cultural units. See Recinos

1954:5,6; Acosta 1985:77; Earle 1990a:123. In Indiantown, the Catholic parish serves the town and the rural area surrounding it.

Chapter I is a brief description of both the Huehuetenango *municipios* and the South Florida area around Indiantown which will give the reader the setting for the focus on the Mayas of Indiantown and their religious practices in exile. Chapter II analyzes the contexts in which the Mayas live their lives, both in Guatemala and in the United States, from historical, anthropological and religious standpoints. Chapter III narrows the focus to the Mayas of Indiantown, concentrating on household structure and gender issues. This sets the scene for Chapter IV, which is a finer-grained portrait of the religious practice of the Indiantown Mayas. Chapter V shows how the organizational aspects of the religious practice are used to create power for the Maya people in exile. In Chapter VI, the lens widens again, tracing the processes by which a transnational ethnic group is formed and ethnic identity is imagined, realized and sustained. Chapter VII looks to the future, envisioning the possible theoretical and practical implications and applications of this research.

Here it only remains to indicate briefly what I think the reader needs to know about my own biases and beliefs in order to be aware of the strong subjective component that inevitably informs any ethnographic research. In the first place, I consider the ends of all science, including social science, to be the improvement of human life. As such, scientific knowledge, however partial and inconclusive, serves as part of the hermeneutic circle, a method of interpretation that sees new questions continually being raised to challenge older theories by the force of new situations (Holland and Henriot 1983:7-9). This method is sometimes called praxis. I understand praxis to be practical action based on reflection, informed by knowledge of the world, of human nature and culture, and by the results of previous action.[4] The ethnographic enterprise, then, contributes by providing knowledge about human culture and about the effects of past action on that culture. This orientation to action will no doubt account for some of my conclusions in Chapter VII.

By human culture I mean the knowledge, beliefs, norms, and customary behaviors which humans acquire by virtue of their membership in society. It has both cognitive and behavioral dimensions and varies across human groupings. Ethnic groups I take to be self-defined, that is, people who identify themselves with a given group are those who belong to it.[5] Ethnicity is problematic in our day as never before, partly because of the non-congruence of nation-states and ethnies, partly because of the mass movements of people across political and ethnic boundaries, and partly because of the growing self-conscious, even self-creating nature of ethnicity today (Yinger 1985:159; Ferris 1987:143). A more extensive discussion of ethnicity will be found in Chapter II.

Religion, which will be the focus of this work, I define according to the suggestion given by Peter Williams: a system of symbolic beliefs and actions, myth, rituals and creeds, and their supporting social structures, which provides its adherents with a coherent interpretation of their universe and their ultimate concerns (P. Williams 1989:9). This definition encompasses both societal and individual dimensions, belief and action, institutional structures and the person, and psychological and social needs. It also includes the relativity which permits a critique, suggesting that the coherency may fail; and while it focuses on the observable elements of religion, that is, action, ritual, creeds and social structures, it does not insist that these elements exhaust the content of religion.

Some obvious pitfalls line the path of the earnest ethnographer. Among them is the danger of accepting as spokespersons for a community those who offer themselves as such. These people can detour the research away from those quieter and less obtrusive folk who also have valuable insights into what is going on. I have attempted to avoid this pitfall by establishing communication with members of the opposite sides of every religious dispute and leadership struggle in Indiantown, as well as with people not involved in the religio-politics of Mayan ritual. I have also paid attention to the Mayan women, who, largely invisible in ritual, are sidelined in public social interaction (CTGAC 1987:4).

Another problem is the continual temptation to commit the sin of "essentialism"—to treat the community as a homogeneous whole with "a" culture, or even as, in this instance, a perfect crystallization of Maya belief and practice. This perspective would consider any deviation from specifically defined "Maya" cultural traits or practices to be a loss of

Mayanness.[6] Variation within a culture and within every residential community has always to be recognized, even as we try to pinpoint what it is that seems so "other" in the other.[7]

It is also important, at the outset, to recognize that in writing about religious practice, one necessarily concentrates on the adepts, those who are the most involved and commit the most resources to the ritual, but that there are many levels of adherence to creeds or participation in rites in any community. In Indiantown, the Maya people exhibit this same pattern of concentric circles, some distancing themselves a little from religious practice, others not involved at all. But the public practice of religious ritual is still striking for the numbers involved and the time and energy invested in it; otherwise it would not merit comment. It will also be argued here that the ritual organization of Indiantown has a wider circle of influence than just the participants or the local community.

Although the point of view, the errors and the shortcomings are mine alone, this book owes its beginning, middle and end to a whole host of others who facilitated, encouraged, prodded and otherwise made it possible. My parents passed on to me their love of travel and curiosity about " how people really live." My religious congregation, the Sisters of Notre Dame de Namur, Ohio Province, sustained many of the costs of six years of study and research. The Cushwa Center for the Study of American Catholicism provided a dissertation fellowship in the History of U.S. Hispanic Catholics. My teachers at Arizona State University, especially professors John Aguilar and John Chance in the Department of Anthropology and Tod Swanson in the Department of Religious Studies were unfailingly both supportive and challenging. Drs. Allan Burns, Duncan Earle and James Loucky have generously shared their unpublished observations about the Mayas in the United States. Father David López, pastor of Santa Eulalia, introduced me to the highland communities of Huehuetenango. But more than anyone, I need to thank the people of Indiantown, Florida, who accepted me as their " Sister," allowing me to intrude, ask rude questions, get in the way, and take their pictures at inconvenient moments. I will not forget any of them.

NOTES

1. Nancy Gonzalez outlined signs of this movement in her presentation at the 1992 American Anthropological Association annual meeting, "The Rise of the Not-So-Ancient-Maya" (Gonzalez 1992) See Kearney (1992) and *El Regional* 13-19 June 1993:14) in which a paid advertisement demands that the Guatemalan government recognize the Permanent Assembly of Maya Peoples.

2. A visit in March 1991 to the archives of the Maryknoll Order in Ossining, New York revealed the availability of journals, parish censuses, letters, diaries, directives from official Church authorities, and printed programs of religious and civic events, all collected by the missionaries over the time of their service in Huehuetenango from 1943 to 1980. See also Comité de Vecinos (1969:65) for an account of the missionaries' efforts from the native point of view, and Grollig (1959) for an intimate description of life in the Huehuetenango area parishes staffed by Maryknoll missionaries.

3. As Oliver La Farge says: "Each family head is a priest in a small way" (La Farge 1947:23).

4. The concept of praxis was developed by Paolo Freire in his classic *The Pedagogy of the Oppressed*, 1970. The hermeneutic method is explored in Juan Luis Segundo, *The Liberation of Theology*, 1976.

5. As John Hawkins puts it; ethnicity is subjective, "a meaning system based on belief" (Hawkins 1984: 14).

6. See Watanabe (1992:253) for a discussion of cultural essentialism and its dangers. See also T. Schwartz (1978) for a model of culture as a distributive phenomenon, which explains both diversity and commonality.

7. Ruth Behar discusses this point elegantly: "Clearly, any ethnographic representation—and I count my own, of course—inevitably includes a self-representation. Even more subtly, the act of representing almost always involves violence of some sort to the subject of the representation, using as it must some degree of reduction, decontextualization, and miniaturization. Yet I think there is hope insofar as we realize that ethnographic work is inherently paradoxical, being 'a process by which each of us confronts our respective inability to comprehend the experience of others even as we recognize the absolute necessity of continuing the effort to do so'" (Behar 1993:271).

CHAPTER I

Meeting the Mayas

Francisco[1] consulted the sky, as much of it as he could see from beneath the thick leaves of the orange tree. The sun was beginning its descent. About time, he figured, to start his walk down the sandy road between citrus trees that would take him to where he would be served his only meal of the day. Maybe today he would get lucky and succeed in bringing back a blanket to his camp under the tree. The January nights were cold, his shirt thin. Shoes too, maybe, although the shoes the church people brought were almost all too large for his feet. He had worn out his shoes, and his feet as well, on the three-day walk across the Sonora desert. But he had come a long way, and was excited to be in *Los Estados*, the United States, where he hoped to find work as quickly as possible. Perhaps tonight he and his three companions, who had traveled together all the way from San Miguel Acatán, deep in the mountains of Huehuetenango, Guatemala, would find a ride to Florida. He had heard of a place there called Indiantown, where other Maya people from his hometown lived and worked and even held an annual fiesta for their patron, San Miguel. Francisco found that hard to believe, but maybe in *Los Estados* anything was possible. Meantime, he was hungry.

Since the early 1980s, the citrus groves around the periphery of Phoenix, Arizona have been a collection and distribution point for groups of indigenous Maya people coming into the United States from Guatemala.[2] In one particular grove, known from the Maya homeland to Canada as *La Huerta*, the orchard, from fifty to two hundred

3

Guatemalans, mostly young men, arrived every week, on their way to connect with relatives and friends and to find work. Women and children sometimes accompanied the men. During their stay in *La Huerta*, they lived and slept hidden under the thick foliage of the orange and grapefruit trees, venturing out only for the daily meal provided by local church volunteers or to use the telephone and mail facilities at a nearby general store. To go farther, without the protection of the night, or of a vehicle, would be foolhardy; it would be to risk losing all the investment of time, money and physical effort required to reach this point. The *migra*, the United States Border Patrol, would escort them to the border and the whole difficult crossing would have to start over.[3]

Every day, between 4 and 5 P.M., several vans and cars pulled up to a central clearing deep inside *La Huerta*. Quickly, volunteers hauled out huge pots and tubs of steaming beans and stew, sandwiches, sweet rolls, coffee and clean water. The hungry travelers stepped up to the table to receive a plate piled high with food. Then the clothing, blanket, and shoe distribution began. On some days, there were toilet kits; other days a volunteer doctor was available for examinations and to dispense medicine.

This scene was repeated daily without fail from 1986 through 1997.[4] Although statistical information is non-existent, the informal coalition of church volunteers agreed with the estimate made by a supervisor of the citrus ranch: five thousand Guatemalans per year, minimum, probably more during 1987 and 1988.[5] The great majority were young men between the ages of fourteen and thirty-five; about half were single and the other half had left wife and children behind. They spent from two days to two weeks in *La Huerta*, dependent upon the availability of the "coyotes" or clandestine transportation providers, to take them to their destination. The most often mentioned places of origin were the departments of Huehuetenango and San Marcos in northwestern Guatemala, the home of the Q'anjob'al, Mam, Chuj and Jakaltek Mayas.[6] Occasionally there were immigrants from other areas of western Guatemala, such as Quetzaltenango, El Quiché, or Totonicapán. After 1990, there were also groups of Maya and Mixtec people from Chiapas and Oaxaca in southern Mexico. Their destination was almost always the same: Florida.

POINTS OF ORIGIN IN GUATEMALA

Guatemala is a relatively unknown country, in terms of its geography, history and culture. Small in size, it is dwarfed by its large northern neighbor, Mexico. It boasts a cosmopolitan capital with colonial charm, and many colorful tourist destinations where visitors can see evidence of the high achievements of the Mayan golden age: temples, pyramids and ball courts. One is left with the impression that the Mayas exist only in memory and artefact. Yet the majority population in Guatemala descended from those ancient temple-builders.

In what follows, the reader is introduced to the living Mayas, some of the areas they inhabit in Guatemala and in the United States, and their life-style at the end of the twentieth century.

San Miguel, San Rafael and Santa Eulalia are three municipalities high in the Cuchumatán mountains of northern Huehuetenango, Guatemala. Each township includes a *cabecera*, or head town, with around fifteen hundred to two thousand inhabitants, which serves as a political, market and religious center for the surrounding *aldeas* or hamlets, home to twelve to fifteen thousand more residents. The population of these *municipios* is 98% Q'anjob'al Maya, with some differences in vocabulary, style and cultural emphases among the three (see Figures 1 and 2). The relative inaccessibility (five to eight hours' drive from the departmental capital, on a one-lane gravel road that twists through and clings to the sides of the highest mountains in Central America), the altitude (over eight thousand feet) and the precipitous terrain have made it a classical "refuge region" where indigenous people were ignored by church and state for long periods after the initial conquest in 1524 by Pedro de Alvarado.[7] Although it is not good corn land because of thin soil, steep inclines and cold weather, corn farming is what almost everyone in the region does. However, the corn produced is not sufficient to last the typical family of six for a year, so other strategies are employed: selling the produce of vegetable gardens, long-distance labor migration to the coffee, cotton and sugar cane fincas (plantations) near the southern coasts of Guatemala and Mexico, and some commerce in the form of trucking, money changing, selling

Figure 1. Central America and Guatemala

Figure 2. Huehuetenango, Guatemala

supplies to isolated villages on both sides of the border, and raising of chickens, turkeys and pigs.

People live in block, stone, or cane houses with corrugated tin or thatched roofs, and dirt floors. They cook at indoor fireplaces with wood, eat their meals at tables on plastic or china dishes, wash clothing in cement sinks or water holes, bathe frequently in the family *chuj* or steam bath house, and send their children to school, at least on the days when the teacher shows up. Those who live in the *cabeceras* enjoy streets paved with stone, weekly markets, electricity, and often, satellite TV and video cassette players. They travel extensively, and for many reasons. Bus travel to the departmental capital or to Guatemala City is neither unusual nor infrequent. Sports teams, political committees, church leaders, teachers, secondary school students, and individuals and families visiting each other fill the old Bluebird buses inching their way up and down Cuchumatán Highway 9 in first gear.

All Huehuetenango *municipios* are governed politically by an *alcalde* (mayor), three *síndicos* (trustees), and a town council of five, elected by their townspeople. The candidates are usually aligned with one of the several national political parties, but recently a movement by local committees to sponsor candidates is gaining ground (*El Regional* 23-29 May 1993:14-19).

Religious practice can be divided into three types: traditional Maya-Catholic, evangelical Protestant, and modern Catholic. The first type is represented by the *alcalde rezador* (prayer leader) and his wife, who are appointed by the elders for service to individual townspeople when traditional Maya rituals, prayers or sacrifices are requested. These prayer leaders may or may not practice orthodox Catholicism in addition to their Maya religion. What is more important is that they know how to pray and make sacrifice to the spirits who govern rain, crops, and other forces of nature, as well as perform divination based on the ancient Maya calendar. In Santa Eulalia the office also includes a yearly divination in the cave of *Jolom Conob*, under the town, and the announcement of the agricultural fortune for the incoming year to the surrounding region (Siegel 1941, La Farge 1947, Recinos 1954, Grollig 1959).

The evangelical groups are notable chiefly for their loudspeakers, which broadcast lively hymns and thundering sermons from largely empty churches in the town centers. Several denominations sponsor private elementary schools which are popular with parents more for the constancy of their teachers than for their Christian content. In general, the evangelicals in this part of Huehuetenango have only a small following, perhaps strongest in San Miguel, than in other areas of Guatemala, where some figures place Protestant adherents at 21% of the population.[8]

The Catholic church received an infusion of new energy from Maryknoll missionaries who assumed responsibility for the Huehuetenango diocese in 1943 (Maryknoll archives; see also Comité de Vecinos 1969:65). They brought organizing techniques, an emphasis on what they called "human promotion" (education for the laity and training into church leadership roles) and contact with the outside world. They established a school and medical clinic in each *cabecera* and promoted cooperatives, colonies in the Ixcan jungle and training for health promoters, lay ritual leaders, youth group organizers and teachers of doctrine. This "human promotion" only intensified after the second Vatican Council went on record promoting lay involvement in the church. Maryknoll missionaries lived and worked in San Miguel, San Rafael, and Santa Eulalia and many other Huehuetenango municipalities until around 1980, when both the increasing state repression in the area and the availability of a sufficient number of priests native to the area made it seem like a good time to leave. The young clergy, largely indigenous, many of them Maryknoll protégées, inherited their methods and spirit, as well as the infrastructure of clergy residences, schools, and parish meeting halls. At the present time, there is a resident native Catholic pastor in San Miguel and Santa Eulalia; San Rafael remains a *visita* or mission of San Miguel.

Each parish has several *animadores de la fe* (faith animators) who lead services when the priest is not present, translate all the prayers, songs, Bible readings and instructions of the Catholic rituals into the local version of Q'anjob'al, and generally serve as priest substitutes. There is also a corps of *catequistas* (doctrine teachers) for each section of the town (*cantón*) and each *aldea*, who hold weekly services and monthly instructions for the entire Catholic population of each unit. Their work is supplemented by the efforts of a parish council and its committees on youth, education, culture and social work. All of these leaders receive training, some of them attending several week long courses each year in Huehuetenango, along with others from other *municipios*. The health promoters receive training in the former Maryknoll hospital in Jacaltenango. The celebrations of major and minor fiestas of the church year are planned and carried out, insofar as their church-related aspects are concerned, by these lay leaders. Physical work of plant maintenance and any construction is done by volunteers donating a day or two per month, together with others from their *aldea* or *cantón*. This remarkable organization which involves hundreds of people in each *municipio* has operated for many decades, and can even be said to be "traditional," a term heretofore reserved for the colonial and post-colonial *cofradía* and cargo system organization (Wagley 1949:79-104; Comité de Vecinos 1969:68; Earle 1992:386; Watanabe 1992:194-199). Through the church organization, Catholic people are brought into frequent inter-*municipio* contact, are chosen by their communities as delegates to attend meetings, and receive consistent long-term support for taking on the responsibilities of the church community. They also learn methods and techniques of planning and leading a meeting, achieving a consensus, planning an event, and evaluating the results of their efforts. It is this knowledge that enables them to rapidly organize themselves as Maya people in exile in the United States.

In Florida, the Mayas have found a new home in Indiantown. Indiantown is thirty miles inland from West Palm Beach, near the large freshwater Lake Okeechobee. (See Figures 3 and 4). The name Indiantown comes from the early inhabitants, the Seminole Indians, who used the oak-covered plateau as a seasonal camp long after they were defeated militarily by United States forces in 1837. The settlement became an orange and cattle producing area in the 1890s and then a stopover on both the Seaboard Air Line railway and the Okeechobee Waterway.[9] But these transportation connections have failed to make the town any more than a wide spot on the highway, a small, mostly poor and unincorporated population concentration in Martin County.

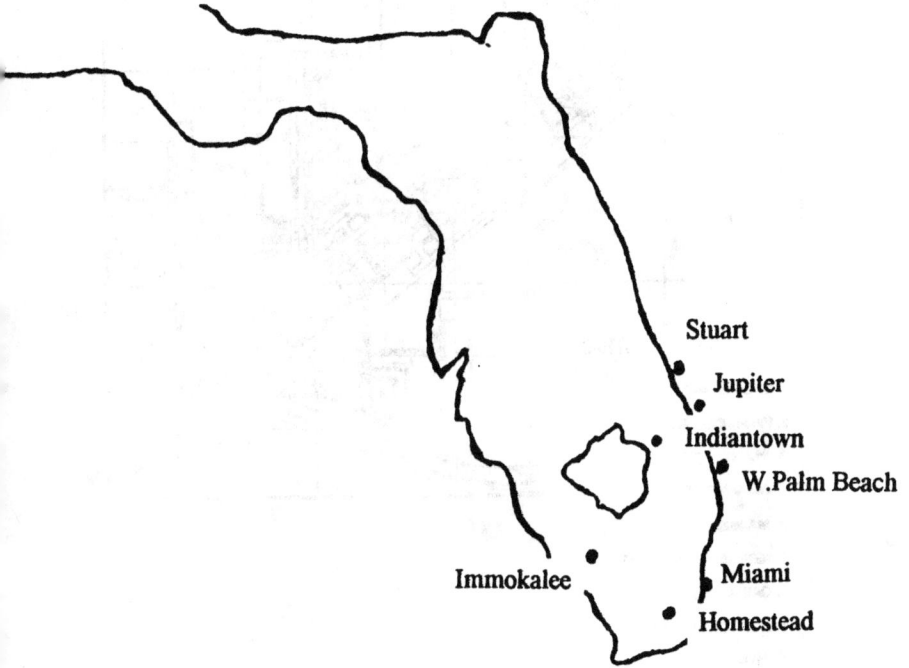

Figure 3. Florida

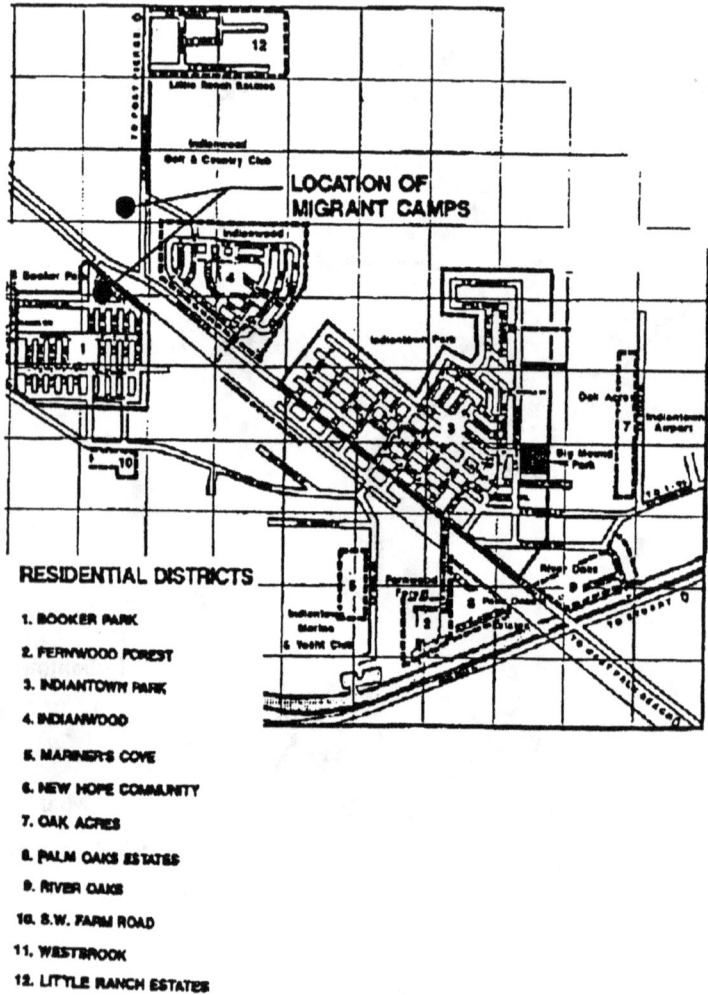

RESIDENTIAL DISTRICTS

1. BOOKER PARK
2. FERNWOOD FOREST
3. INDIANTOWN PARK
4. INDIANWOOD
5. MARINERS COVE
6. NEW HOPE COMMUNITY
7. OAK ACRES
8. PALM OAKS ESTATES
9. RIVER OAKS
10. S.W. FARM ROAD
11. WESTBROOK
12. LITTLE RANCH ESTATES

Figure 4. Indiantown, Florida

Indiantown has a fluctuating habitation of 5000 to 9000, due to the seasonal agricultural employment available in the area. Long-established white ranching families, and black, Mexican and Puerto-Rican agricultural workers were joined in the early 1980s by refugees from both Haiti and Guatemala. The Guatemalan Maya population has now become the majority, numbering from 3000 to 8000 (Rohter 1991: A-18; Hahn 1990:5). Many of them live in Indiantown year-round and work in golf course maintenance, plant nurseries, juice processing and landscaping. Others spend the months from September to May there, employed in picking vegetable and fruit crops, and then moving North to other States for summer harvests. Housing is in short supply and most rental units are overcrowded and overpriced. Life in Indiantown is tranquil and slow-moving for the most part, occasionally punctuated by inter-ethnic crimes of assault and robbery. The busiest places are the post office, the basketball courts and soccer fields, the grocery store, and the churches.

Government is by the Board of Commissioners of Martin County at the county seat in Stuart, twenty miles away on the Atlantic coast. One commissioner has responsibility for Indiantown and has a representative present in the community. There are several medical clinics, a bank, an elementary and middle school, a post office, library, sheriff's substation, and a fair assortment of commercial establishments and a proliferation of churches.

The Baptist Church, the Jehovah's Witness congregation and the Church of God are the largest and oldest Protestant groups, but there are many store-front churches and groups which meet in public spaces as well. There is also a Catholic parish which operates a private elementary school, a thrift store, a legal services center and a garment manufacturing cooperative. Many of the churches, including Holy Cross Catholic Church, offer separate services in English and Spanish each week. The Maya people in the town have become the majority in several congregations; in others, they constitute a group large enough to warrant a special service. In some cases, they have assumed leadership of some aspects of the established congregations, and in the Catholic parish, this includes the organization of fiestas for the patron saints of their Guatemalan hometowns/parishes/*municipios*.

The residents of Indiantown travel often to Stuart for most commercial purposes; they go to West Palm Beach for legal, medical or civic reasons. There are scattered colonies of Maya people in each of these cities and contact is frequent between them and the Indiantown Maya. The lonely, swamp-lined highways to these two metropolitan areas are also traveled by the farm labor buses and the Border Patrol (Earle 1990b). Trips are also made to Miami, usually to consult immigration attorneys or to meet someone at the airport, from which it is only a two and one half hour flight to Guatemala.

These two areas, the origin and the destination points of the immigration trail, have profoundly influenced each other through a reciprocal cultural exchange that is remarkable in its scope.

NOTES

1. The personal names used here are fictitious, and some places in the United States are indicated only in general terms, to protect the security of the Maya people who have shared their stories with me They are threatened with both deportation from the U.S. and retaliation against their families in Guatemala.

2. Although the Maya people who come to the United States often come for different reasons than the Mexican migrant field workers, they have inherited their pattern of trails, connections, and contact points The citrus grove described here was a collection and distribution center for Mexican migrant field hands long before 1980. Thus historic patterns of economic migration from Mexico and Central America to the United States have had a great influence on the later "conflict migration." See Aguayo 1986:109,115 and Ferris (1987:9). This means the infrastructure of migration, including safe houses, smugglers, rest and collection points, and providers of false documents, as well as the increase in provision for social services in Spanish in the public sector, have benefitted the later wave of Central American refugees. Guatemalan Mayas have also benefitted from immigration legislation which in 1986 provided an opportunity for most undocumented Mexicans who had lived in the United States for many years to acquire legal standing and move into better employment in the visible economy. This left open the underground employment sector: agricultural piece work, sweat shops, day labor in construction, etc., for the new immigrants to fill. Many moved right into the traditional agricultural migrant stream that most Mexicans were simultaneously abandoning (Ashabranner 1986:4,7; Miralles 1987:12; Burns 1988a:41; Burns 1989a:12; Burns 1989b:46).

3. They would be taken to the Mexico-United States border if they succeeded in "passing" as Mexican If discovered to be Guatemalan, they are detained and sent by planeload to Guatemala City. The Border Patrol uses investigation techniques based on vocabulary differences to discover national identity; for example, the voceo or use of the *vos* form of familiar address in Spanish; and the Guatemalan slang word for money, *pisto*, which means liquor in Mexico.

4. In July of 1997, an intense campaign by the Border Patrol was carried out with almost twenty-four hour presence in the area of *La Huerta* over a period of three months This forced changes in the collection point strategy; some reintegration of the stream of migration was apparent by November, although the volunteer "soup line" had not been reactivated.

5. Those who provide health services in this orchard have occasional coordinating meetings; the handout of the April 18, 1993 meeting tabulates the following numbers of "farm workers passing through the orange groves" during the period January 1 to April 15, 1993: men: 2905, women: 40, children under eight: 58. The majority were said to be Guatemalan Maya people. The tabulator cautions that he missed some days and knows that some travelers left the same day they arrived, so the actual count is higher (Franco 1993).

6. There are some 23 Maya languages in Guatemala The *Academia de Lenguas Mayas* is attempting to standardize orthography and produce grammars, as well as eliminate Spanish loan words. This movement is part of the Mayan cultural revitalization discussed later in Chapter VI and has resulted in a high demand for written material for newly literate Mayas. An example of this is the weekly newspaper *El Regional*, produced in western Guatemala in Spanish and several Maya languages. Although the Indiantown literature uses the spelling Kanjobal or K'anjobal, the spelling used in Guatemala by members of this language group is Q'anjob'al or Q'anjobal. This is according to the prescriptions of the *Academia*. See Maxwell 1992.

7. The concept of "refuge region" was proposed by Aguirre Beltrán in *Regiones de Refugio* to designate marginalized areas of nation-states. Many of the characteristics he proposed (lack of integration into the market system, absence of communication) are clearly not appropriate in this instance (Aguirre Beltrán 1967:129). See also Jonathan D. Hill (1989:34).

8. Bastien (1993:41). For a discussion of Protestantism in Latin America in general see Stoll (1990).

9. This history was gleaned from the Indiantown Chamber of Commerce brochure (Indiantown Chamber of Commerce, n.d., Indiantown Florida), and the Indiantown telephone directory (Indiantown Company, 1992, Indiantown, Florida).

CHAPTER II

Contexts

Anthropologist and Maya exile Victor Montejo is speaking to a group of Maya people in Indiantown.

Montejo: When Christopher Columbus arrived in the isles of the Caribbean, he did not know the indigenous languages spoken in those places. Two days after sighting land, he wrote in his diary, "All the natives began to shout that we were gods and that we came from heaven." Two days after touching land. Let us take this apart to understand the ideology within it. Then we will realize that it is a lie, that the people immediately took them for gods. But the Spaniards could say what they wished because they wrote the history. We did not write it. How do we appear in their history? As the vanquished, as savages, as idolators and cannibals. So the problem, the conflict, comes from that moment. During the colonial period, there were times when our people were massacred, destroyed, but they kept on insisting on their culture. Now we see ourselves conquered again, expelled again from our own land, living in exile. The Maya culture is very old. But it has not died. It exists and it expresses itself in each one of us.. We are here because we want to revitalize, reanimate our culture and begin to spread it in a more profound way.

Member of audience: But where did the Maya go and why did they decide to end their culture?

(Field notes 1992)

Some things have changed. But that does not mean the journey is over. It
is our children, I am afraid, who will have to continue the fight for justice
and respect in our land.

(Rigoberta Menchú,1992:14A)

500 YEARS OF CONQUEST

Modern Mesoamerican ethnography[1] began with a paradigm that tended
to describe institutions in rural communities considered to be static,
bounded and closed entities. The move toward recognizing conflict,
urbanization, and change during the late 1960s and 1970s, and the
subsequent emphasis on political and economic factors, tended to relegate
culture to a secondary position in the analyses of customs and behavior
patterns (Schwartz 1983:342). Research in that vein tended to reduce the
causal efficacy of culture or ignore its role, even as it made ethnic
groupings less distinctive. The response has been, in subsequent work, a
defense of native traditions presented as dynamic and self-protective
responses to the outside environment. Culture once again became part of
the explanation (Chambers and Young 1979, Schwartz 1983). Present
trends include studies in gender issues, ethnicity and class, urban
migration, and war/crisis issues. Historical and comparative depth in
community studies is now more the rule than the exception, as linkages
with state, nation and global systems are explicated. Other trends are the
"actor-oriented" or decision-making model, and a move to symbolic and
semiotic analysis (see Tax 1983:xiii).[2] This study builds on the rich
anthropological tradition of focus on microsocial units and integrates this
with the "world-systems" approach. It describes and analyzes the real
choices made by real people on the local level within the context of their
larger environment. In the research presented here, this means that the
Maya refugees of Indiantown operate within a force field that includes
historic migratory trends, recent conflict, public debates about
immigration and ethnicity in the United States, and an ancient tradition
of popular religious ritual influenced by twentieth-century church
policies. They are also the heirs of five hundred years of conquest and
domination.

Indigenous voices in all of the Americas, raised in protest of the "celebration" of five hundred years of "discovery" in 1992 unleashed a global-level consciousness-raising movement of indigenous peoples everywhere. The choice of a Maya Indian woman, Rigoberta Menchú, to receive the 1992 Nobel Peace Prize ushered in the International Year of the World's Indigenous Peoples in 1993, proclaimed by the United Nations Working Group on Indigenous Populations. This group has the participation of 315 indigenous organizations, including ninety-two in North America, thirty-nine in Central America and the Caribbean, and seventy-nine in South America (UNDPI 1993). Guatemala alone is represented by twelve entities, among them the Council of Maya Nations of Guatemala, the Solidarity Movement of Maya Aid and Action, and the Indigenous Parliament of America. There are many more examples of the growing momentum of this phenomenon; some are detailed in Chapters V and VI of this monograph.

The global nature of the movement raises questions about ethnicity and national boundaries; when these are non-congruous or when indigenous peoples migrate across borders, the very basis of what constitutes a "people" is shaken. The United Nations defines indigenous peoples as the "descendants of the first known peoples in their regions, strikingly different in their cultures, religions and patterns of social and economic organization from more recent immigrants, colonizers, and modernizers." The over three hundred million indigenous people in more than seventy countries are no longer remote and isolated but are often treated as outcasts and subject to forced relocation (UNDPI 1993). The agenda of the new indigenous groups aims at participation without discrimination in the life of their states, control of their traditional lands and resources, maintenance of their own languages and legal systems, compensation for lands, protection of treaty rights in international law, and protection against exploitation of their traditional knowledge, sacred sites, and other cultural property (UNDPI 1993). Often the traditional lands are situated in more than one political entity.

In the ambience of raised consciousness, contemporary researchers studying indigenous peoples tread carefully to avoid the errors of the colonizers, repressive modern nation-states, and patron-ising anthropologists throughout the years, yet recognize that our own historically-grounded biases influence our view of the "other." This is a recognition of the dialectical nature of research, in which the insights of today are often built on the shortcomings of yesterday, and reaction to one set of assumptions leads to new starting-points, perhaps more precise and less colored by our own filters. Nevertheless, "however wise we are, we never learn the whole truth about another culture, or for that matter, about our own" (Bunzel 1952:xxiv). With this caution in mind, I turn to dialogue with current research on migration, ethnicity, and Mesoamerican popular religion.

MIGRATION AND ETHNICITY

"Like death, migration only exists after it has taken place" (Robinson 1990:5). This fact means there are inherent limits in the possibilities of analysis: the use of a control group of those who considered migration to a given place but did not would be operationally difficult, and reliance on census data necessitates accepting the paradigm of the census-taking institution. Migration is only recorded when it takes place across some recognized boundary, and traditional migration studies are limited by assuming migrants are individual actors who have only one home, leaving out the household or family as a unit of analysis, and discounting the possibility of multilocal residence (Goldsten 1981:337).

Etically defined as the movement of people through geographic space, migration pertains to the domain of demography. Anthropological studies, on the other hand, concentrate on connecting movement with other issues, usually having to do with development, such as urbanization and industrialization, or with family structures, gender and decision-making. The main theoretical orientations of anthropological migration studies have been influenced by successive models in development theory: modernization, dependency and articulation constructs (Kearney 1986:332-345). Redfield's idea of a folk-urban continuum informed early migration research. It concentrated on such processes as adaptation, assimilation, and adjustment which were thought to denote progress. As it became apparent that high urban unemployment did not favor "development," migration began to be seen as a problem of underdevelopment rather than the solution.

Dependency theory conceptualized migration as part of the flow of economic surplus from the periphery to the core within a single world capitalist system with an international division of labor. This migration, domestic or international, leads to greater "underdevelopment." "International migrations both reflect and contribute to the imbalance of nations inserted in unequal positions in the contemporary world economy" (Portes 1985:18). Migration is a process internal to a single global system.

Articulation theory uses the idea of the world system, but suggests that dependency is not only the result of unequal exchange, but of the exploitation of non-capitalist relations of production and reproduction by the capitalist sector. Capitalism coexists with and strengthens the non-capitalist modes of production; labor migration links the two systems. The focus shifted to studies of how households and communities reproduce themselves by participating in two spheres of production. Migration, in other words, articulates the domestic community with world capitalism, especially temporary labor migration, which preserves and exploits the domestic economy (Kearney 1986:341-344; see also Meillassoux 1981).[3] Articulation research uses intermediate units of analysis, households and networks, at both ends of migration; the sending and receiving communities. Kearney's work with Mixtec migrants in Baja California, using his concept of an "Articulatory Migrant Network" shows that the Mixtec are "intentionally elaborating a collective identity" based on their common ethnic heritage. He sees this heightened ethnic identity as their way of consolidating the network on which their survival depends (Kearney 1986:353-355).

Earlier, Arizpe proposed that migration ethnography study both the rural community of origin and the urban migrants as a single unit of analysis (Arizpe 1978:10,12-13). She points out that the fact that not all people migrate rules out any unicausal explanation, and postulates that immediate, personal causes and economic or structural causes are complementary; the latter is necessary but only the former, often a specific event which is the "last straw," is sufficient to trigger migration. She claims only anthropological micro-studies can get at these "sufficient causes" (Arizpe 1978:38,41,42). This approach is especially useful when considering the case of the Mayas, many of whom experienced a crisis event that triggered flight. Both Kearney's and Arizpe's insights regarding the need to link place of origin with receiving community in migration studies have been key to this analysis.

Recent attention to temporary, or "return" migration has led to several interesting typologies of the process. In one study, a "four stage" pattern is found. In the first stage, young single male workers migrate into marginal, insecure, urban jobs and quickly return to their place of origin. The second stage sees married workers joining the flow, but without their families. They stay slightly longer and return home less frequently, but their returns diffuse the message about the possibilities. This leads to the third stage, in which married workers send for their spouses, and at this point, the process becomes "self-feeding," that is, the increasing number of migrants generates more possibilities for migration, In the fourth stage, the appearance of all the accoutrements of an ethnic enclave, such as ethnic shops, employers, secular and religious leaders, encourage longer stays and permanent settlement (Böhning 1974:61-17; King 1986:10-11).

Another more psychologically-oriented way of looking at this process considers the first stage to be located in the potential migrants' perception of the possible gains of migrating and the ease of reentry into his/her identity-bestowing village and kinship structure. The second stage is recruitment by the first successful migrants of others to join them, and the creation of informal networks of job information and kinship aid. In the third stage, the migrants move into occupational specialization as an origin group and form intragroup associations. This can eventually lead to an ethnic enclave, since people are concentrated by employment and their need to live together to economize. They soon begin to celebrate their native culture in food and festival, language and custom, and are encouraged to do so by the discriminatory reactions of the host society. The fourth stage, return home, can be for seasonal work, social visits, or retirement, but usually reinforces the network and encourages more migration (Hamilton 1985:410-418).

It is important to keep both structural features of migration, as in Kearney's Articulatory Migrant Network, or Böhning's empirically-verified stages, and cultural and psychological features, as in Hamilton's approach, in view when studying particular cases of migration. A household level of analysis implies, I think realistically, that the timing, sequence, place and motive of migration is super-individual (Balán 1981:185). Another important insight is the two-way direction of both actual migration and its effects. As Goldsten notes: "We need especially to recognize that in discussing the relations between the total system and migration, cause and effect can operate in both directions with the system affecting types and levels of movements and these in turn having a significant impact on the system itself" (Goldsten 1981:338).[4]

Forced migration, or refugee flight, is a type of migration that is most pertinent here but that has only recently received attention, even though violent displacement of large population groups has been a constant in world history. The creation of international agencies which aid these refugee populations, such as the International Red Cross and the United Nations High Commissioner for Refugees, has perhaps encouraged studies of the phenomenon. According to Kunz' typology, the refugee is a distinct social type, because he moves against his will, although once settled, he is merged statistically with voluntary migrants. The basic difference is that the cause of migration (the push) is more important than the purpose (the pull). Acute refugee movements result in mass flight of family groups, often to camps set up by international agencies, from which a second wave becomes likely when conditions reach the intolerable level. The validity of a refugee's status is subjective and can never be tested: "It is the individual's interpretation of events and self-perceived danger or revulsion" which motivates the flight, but it can be partially verified by the date of departure and its correlation with events in the home country (Kunz 1973:128,130-133,136-138). The differences among the successive refugee wave populations, the so-called "fate-groups" or "event-conditioned categories" or "vintages" may be imperceptible to outsiders, especially if a move to a second asylum takes place, but the associative cohorts know that the date of departure is an indicator of the refugee's politics (Kunz 1973:137-138). In the case of the Mayas, the civil strife that occasioned the flight continues to affect relationships among refugees from different sides of the conflict.

In a study of Angolan refugees in Zambia, Hansen discovered that refugee flow was patterned on previous male labor migration; when people found themselves forced to choose between joining the revolutionaries, moving to the bush, staying in the crossfire, or flight, they chose flight, but used old and known patterns. Many preferred self-settlement to government camps, perhaps understanding that assistance programs often undercut the already eroded autonomy of forced migrants, but also motivated by fear of disease, forced repatriation, and restrictions on social and residence patterns (Hansen 1982:14-19, 21,31). Refugees are in many ways reduced to the status of children who must be resocialized: rights, material wealth and means of production, social networks, status, skills and language are all lost in the move. Women refugees lose even more, since they are often seen as simply extensions of the male refugees, and a force that preserves tradition and impedes "adaptation" (Spring 1982:38). Hansen and Oliver-Smith find that the "forced migrant is more oriented toward the retention or re-establishment of past conditions than the voluntary migrant" (Hansen and Oliver-Smith 1982:3,4). These findings are all corroborated, as will be seen, by the case of the Maya refugees in Indiantown: the use of previous knowledge gained through labor migration, the avoidance of or escape from United Nations camps, the "vintage" group rivalry, and the orientation toward the reestablishment of past conditions.

Refugee policies of national states lie at the intersection of domestic and international politics, and can be used as tools to manipulate foreign policy, as well as the domestic economy.[5] Historic patterns of economic migration from Mexico and Central America to the United States have had a substantial effect on the nature of the politically-motivated refugee flow. Pre-existing hostile relationships between the several nations make refugee issues questions of national security (Ferris 1987:6,8-10). Ferris concluded that Central America, Mexico, and the United States are all part of a single system in which tensions in one part of the system are transferred to another through refugee flows, much as has been hypothesized for economic migration (Ferris 1987:144). In politically-induced migration of indigenous peasant peoples, it has been found that adult men and women make up half of the configuration, while children make up the other half. This was certainly the case of the Mayas who fled from Guatemala to Mexico, and characterized the early years of Maya flight to the United States as well. These refugees have a difficult time proving a "well-founded fear of persecution," but they are victims of events that damage the public order, or "cross-fire refugees" (Aguayo 1986:103,109,119). The actual act of migrating has been neglected. There are few studies of routes and trails, and no agreement on how to define home or residence, in order to fix the starting point (Robinson 1990:6-7). Two exceptions are Conover (1987) and Aguayo (1986). The former is an anecdotal first person account of several northward migrations and reversals thereof, including clandestine border crossings. The latter finds that Central American refugees tend to travel in stages: that is, for economic reasons they stop to earn more funds to continue to travel, and to pay bribes, as well as to absorb local Mexican customs in order to disguise themselves as Mexicans. The migrants are very knowledgeable about routes, final destinations, red tape, and difficulties and are brought into this network of knowledge by family members and friends (Aguayo 1986:110-114, 133,152).

If studies about the physical act of migrating are scarce, the same is not true of incorporation into the receiving communities. This seems to fit better into the anthropological framework of local level research. Although most studies of incorporation or acculturation of migrants deal with the urbanization of rural peasants, they shed some light on the situation of the Mayas, who are found chiefly in semi-rural areas of the United States rather than in large cities. "Personal relationships are the essential means of organizing their environment and of making it secure"; getting essential information about employment, services, loans, etc. (Roberts 1973:153-335). Migrants survive by using the resources of kinship and friendship to create a "network of reciprocal exchange." Economic contributions from successful migrants channel new resources into the community of origin (Lomnitz 1977:40,54,67). This feedback effect of money sent home by migrants can also encourage more migration and increase inequality in the sending society (Goldsten 1982:338; King 1986:27).

Return migration and its effect on the community of origin has also been a topic of research in recent years. The greatest influence on the home community is probably—since returnees tend to depict themselves as successful—to encourage the young to migrate (Gmelch 1980: 147,

150, 151,153). Important links are forged between the capital city and the provinces by return migration, in which associations of migrants from the same origin contribute to village projects, send delegations (Roberts 1981:36-38), or maintain the agricultural base of the village (Arizpe 1981:189). Circular labor migration, or what Arizpe calls relay migration, enables peasant families to bring back to the household some of the wealth that the metropole extracts through unequal development (Arizpe 1981:201-204, 206-209).

Migration and ethnicity are intimately linked. If one's ethnicity is only noticed or defined in relation to (different) others, this implies some crossing of boundaries to provide the needed contact and contrast. If national borders are political constructs, and have little to do with ethnic groups, then movement across borders will result in questions and issues that involve differentiating national and ethnic identities.

In attempting to reach an adequate definition of ethnicity, it becomes apparent that the main problem is deciding whether to opt for objective or subjective unit boundaries. Most of the literature follows Barth's lead in viewing ethnicity as a subjective process of group identification. The concept can be applied to a wide range of phenomena (Cohen 1978: 381,383,386; Yinger 1985:157) from small kin groups to a large category such as "Hispanics"; it may even be conflated with nationality or country of origin. It is based on a belief in shared identity among members, often grounded in "descent-based cultural identifiers"(Cohen 1978:387) which are like a series of nested distinctions that increase in exclusiveness. The subjective image of the collective identity of the group is based on a common understanding of a set of symbols which arise from unique historical experience (Spicer 1980:347 as cited in Castile 1981b: xviii) and on segmentary processes of opposition to others (Castile 1981b: xix; Yinger 1985:158). An ethnic group, then, is a segment of a larger society whose members identify a common origin and culture and who share practices which use this shared origin and culture as symbols (Yinger 1985:159). The symbols used revolve around kinship, property, and political rights, and language, history and religion. These symbolize the existence of the group and at the same time constitute the group (Nash 1989:11; B. Williams 1989:431-432).[6]

Ethnic distinctions arise as a parallel to the political process of the formation of nation states or colonial intrusion. Ethnicity is situational, then: it has no existence apart from interethnic relations, and in this sense it is "segmentary" (Cohen 1978:388). The modern state makes it possible for ethnic mobilization to take place by increasing competition for rewards and enabling the emergency of trusted leaders who define the conflict, raise hopes, and articulate frustration. "Ethnicity is (potentially) more, not less, salient in modern nation-states because there is increased competition for scarce rewards" (Cohen 1978:396-397).

That ethnic groups form in response to pressures from the outside and the availability of resources to them if they mobilize together is shown by ethnographic evidence. Under pressure from politicians, and with promises of opportunities and resources to be made available if they presented themselves as an ethnic group, immigrant Haitians who had never shared a common culture in the homeland formed a citizens' council in New York City to represent their interests. Cultural symbols were elaborated that were a kind of common denominator, even though they may not have been part of the original, back home ethnic culture (Glick 1977:25-26,35). The "ethnogenesis" of the Garifuna of Central America, a black group with Amerindian culture, is also instructive. "Their story sheds light on how even a pre-literate society may use symbols of ethnicity to further its members' own interests and survive the onslaught of a stronger, technologically superior civilization." Ethnicity is a haven of intimacy and meaning which mobilizes energy and counteracts anomie, as well as providing a political identity (Gonzalez 1988:6,8,21,59,75).

A sense of peoplehood and membership is an antidote to the alienation and anomie of modern society (Cohen 1978:401; Yinger 1985:161). As Manning Nash, in his revealing reflection on ethnicity, puts it: "In the modern world of rootlessness, deracination, alienation, and the twin search for meaning and a usable past, the idea of a discoverable, fixed, comfortable, and historically continuous identity is highly charged with psychic rewards and appeal" (M. Nash 1989:4).

Similarly, long distance migrant workers from the Mixteca region of Oaxaca, Mexico, seem to be in the process of creating a new identity for themselves in their temporary labor camps in Mexico's northern border region. Their "traditional" allegiance is to their villages, but in the North, the oppression they clearly perceive in the new situation cannot be displaced onto rival villages. Those who at first live as satellite communities of their home villages soon discover their common bonds as exploited Mixtec and form new associations to press for their rights. These organizations are thus the result of a new creation, a pan-Mixtec identity, which is subsequently transferred back to Oaxaca. A latent identity is objectified under overt repression, bringing about a reversal of the "traditional" negative self-image (Nagengast and Kearney 1990:69,72,78,80-81,83,87). These findings mirror in many ways what is occurring among the Mayas of South Florida.

Ethnic persistence, revitalization, and reinvention within the recent past is probably best explained by the features of the modern nation-state which creates, sustains, and encourages this mobilization. Almost all the literature agrees that modern ethnic vitality is a product of modernization related to and legitimated by the nationalism that structures the world system today (Olzak 1983:355,356). Because world systems emphasize the nation-state as players, subnational and regional ethnic movements gain legitimacy in the competition for resources. Nationalism begets subnationalism, since the same ideology applies: only through statehood can a people make a claim in the international forum. Internally, ethnic regions and groups mobilize against the state center with claims of discrimination, internal colonialism, etc., in order to compete with other regions for education, housing, and welfare (Olzak 1983:362, 364,366,368). This model can explain both the selectivity of people when choosing the ethnic attributes which support their claims—"situational ethnicity" (Nagata 1974:331; Hicks and Leis 1977:17; Gonzalez 1989:4)—and the reinvention of ethnicity in the second or third post-migration generation, even when most of the cultural attributes have been left behind (Hicks and Leis 1977:8; Trueblood 1977:155).[7]

The mechanisms of ethnic identity maintenance, which preserve minimal structure and membership, even though actual persons move into and out of the group boundaries, seem to be connected to ritual and symbol, often religious and sometimes political. For many peoples, ritual serves as the mechanism for maintaining opposition and thus becomes their focus for identity (Barth 1969:34; Castile 1981b:xx; Yinger

1985:168; Gonzalez 1988:180-184). "The minimal action aspect of ethnicity. . . is the formal celebration of difference"(M. Nash 1989:15). Signs, symbols and their underlying values seem to be necessary for the conservation of a viable identity, but these signs and symbols themselves are situational, the "products of interaction with other groups" (Royce 1982:7,9). Change is thus constant even as a strategy of maintenance.

Another mechanism that may be operating in the maintenance of ethnicity among migrants is the resistance to "supertribalization"—the tendency of the hosts to lump all newcomers together. In this situation, ethnic markers become more rather than less relevant, and groups tend to develop more complex identities (Olzak 1983:367). This complexity includes the societies formed among immigrants to send aid to their home communities, which can lead to the creation of a transnational ethnic group which sustains its sense of unity and achieves political power with the aid of modern communication and transportation tools (Gonzalez 1988:11,181,183). Again, it becomes clear that conflict can enhance and even generate a close identification of self and group in ethnic terms. Migration may aid in the retention of ethnic traditions in the place of origin as well, through remittances (Arizpe 1978:104, 229; Gonzalez 1989:2,4) or through the adoption of a new pan-ethnic identity in opposition to former village dichotomization (Nagengast and Kearney 1990).

In applying these theoretical and empirical findings to a specific case, that of Maya refugees in the United States, most relevant are the theories of migration which stress a continuum of economic and political origins. The Maya refugee flow began with a political crisis but subsequent migration is more related to the long-term consequences of those events. Theories of ethnic persistence which stress strategic shifting of boundaries to define identity are the most pertinent to the present case. Ethnicity as a symbol system which can be maintained, created, or revived is an important survival tool for immigrant populations, and its importance is intensified in the case of refugees, for whom loss is the most salient feature of their new life. Especially applicable are the suggestions of Cohen and Glick that there is strategic political advantage for pressure groups based on ethnicity. In the present climate of mobilization of indigenous peoples, the Indiantown Mayas have found a

way to subvert the traditional subordinate meaning of their Indian
identity and turn it to their advantage. But beyond its uses as a political
lever, ethnicity as an end in itself, as the psychological grounding of
personal and group identity, pointed out by Gonzalez and Nash, is
important to the exiled Mayas. Their struggle to use elements of their
tradition to maintain their sense of peoplehood is evident in their praxis
described in Chapter IV.

The pattern outlined above which shows that development and, to
some extent, relative deprivation trigger migration is only part of the
historical picture in Guatemala. The ethnic lines there, as old as the
conquest, have always been sharply drawn between the *ladinos*, or
Hispanicized population, and the less Hispanicized indigenous people.
Both the government and the *ladino* populace have used many strategies
for keeping the Indians subordinate, including rhetoric which painted
them as dangerous, lazy, childlike, or mulish (Brintnall 1983:14; Adams
1990:147-148; C. Smith 1990:5). The Indian defense was avoidance and
humility, until the beginning of the emergence of conscious Indian
identity in the 1950s. During the Arévalo and Arbenz governments of
1944-1954, the freedom to elect Indian local officials, the growth of labor
and peasant unions and agrarian reform gave impulse to this identity.
The other great influence was the Catholic Action movement which was
introduced to the indigenous communities in 1948. It became a means of
resistance for young Indians educated by the missionaries and a support
for the cooperative movement (Davis 1983a:7,8; Booth 1991:51).
Literacy campaigns, pan-Indian associations, and church seminars
during the 1970s led to rising hopes that were dashed by the recession of
1973. Indian movements became radicalized and government repression
began (Arias 1990:239-240; Booth 1991:46). The Guatemalan military
initiated a policy of terror in 1978 in which death squads assassinated key
community leaders, including at least twenty members of the clergy.
Indian areas were bombed, burned, and over ten percent of the population
massacred (Davis 1983a:10; Carmack 1988:50; Arias 1990:252-255). In
many cases, division within the Indian *municipios* aided this repression,
as practitioners of the Maya *costumbre*, or traditional religion, accused
the Catholic Action members of being "communists" to the army
(Carmack 1988:50; Moore 1989:41; Arias 1990:247). Development, both

economic and human, created conflict at the local level which was used by the state apparatus for its own program of repression. "The Kanjobal Maya of Guatemala were on the brink of development until their ideas were labeled communist and radical and they were driven from their homelands altogether" (Gonzalez 1987:97). The cause of the explosion of violence was that the economic strategies of the Indians came into conflict with the development plans of the wealthy and powerful (Brintnall 1983:16).

There are many accounts of the brutal, even genocidal character of the repression, especially during 1980 to 1983 (Ferris 1987:27). [8] "During this period of conflict most normal routines have been altered. Such traditional activities as freely and openly working in the fields, going to the market, attending church, having fiestas, or migrating to lowland plantations are no longer taken for granted" (Manz 1983:42). Huehuetenango was especially hard hit: in July of 1982, forty-seven people were killed in San Mateo Ixtatán. Over two hundred were massacred in San Miguel Acatán on July 20 of that year, and three hundred fifty at Finca San Francisco (Davis 1983a:4; Manz 1983:38-42). Thousands were displaced internally within Guatemala, others fleeing to Mexico and the United States (Hamilton and Stoltz-Chinchilla 1991:96,99).

Various means are used by the government to control those Indians who did not flee: Vietnam-style model villages, in which "beans and bullets" kept the population terrorized (Ferris 1987: 27; C. Smith 1988:226; Manz 1988:44), and forced duty in civilian patrols which sapped both time and energy and constituted a permanent counterinsurgency (Anderson and Simon 1987:15,16,30,32; Carmack 1988:63). The civil patrol incorporated over a million men in Guatemala and caused those young men who used to work in temporary migrant labor to leave and never return, since they were suspect for being gone. The patrol also caused the destruction of trust within the community (C. Smith 1988:227-229). The terror is not over: bombing of villages in Indian areas has continued throughout 1992 and 1993, and army-led massacres in returnee villages in 1996 and 1997.

Many of the Guatemalan Mayas coming to the United States in the early 1980s had direct experience of violence, including torture or the killing of relatives, and/or were targets. Those not directly targeted were often "cross-fire refugees." In later years, the push factor was more likely to be the ravages of civil war on the economy. Economic conditions interact with violence, as both cause and effect. Those who are unemployed may be suspected of being subversive. A young man who is not in the army and does not have discharge papers from previous service is subject to monthly sweeps of forced draft, even at the age of thirteen or fourteen. Conditions of civil violence make usual economic activity impossible, and this breaks down the distinction between political and economic migration (Ferris 1987:5).

The history of the Hispanic minority in the United States also affects the situation of Guatemalan refugees. There is no natural barrier between the United States and the lands to the South: people have moved northward throughout historical time. During the colonial and Mexican national periods, this was an internal migration, not going to a "foreign" country. Hispanics only became a minority in 1848, when the United States annexed a third of Mexican territory by conquest.

"Hispanics," an umbrella term imposed by Euroamericans on a diverse group of people who have in common a heritage influenced by Spain, may now number ten percent of the total United States population (*Newsweek* 9 April 1990:18-20) and were seen from the beginning as a cheap labor source, especially for United States agribusiness, mining and railroads. From 1918 to 1964, workers from south of the border were imported for agricultural labor but were deported en masse during every economic depression, in the 1930s, the 1950s and in the 1980s. The United States Border Patrol was created in 1924 to enable surplus labor to be quickly deported. Immigration legislation is being continually adjusted to economic and political conditions in the dominant society.

Public reaction to immigrants in general, and of Hispanic undocumented immigrants in particular, has been increasingly hostile in the economically unstable 1990s. Headlines like "Fourteen Percent Don't Speak English at Home" (Green 1993:A-7) or "Asylum System Cannot Cope with Crowds of People at the Nation's Gate" (*Arizona Republic* 25 April 1993:A-26) set the tone. Debates between proponents of English-only laws and backers of bilingual education spar in the popular media. *Time* magazine, in a special issue devoted to immigration, reports that "Americans [are] increasingly concerned that their country is under siege, and, in the popular phraseology, 'has lost control of its own borders'" (*Time*, Fall 1993:10). Immigration backlash is particularly strong in Florida and California, states where large numbers of immigrants settle. Yet others reject the xenophopia: "They are hard-working migrants," says a police detective, describing the Guatemalan refugees in Homestead, Florida. "They deserve a chance" (O'Connor 1989:30). The least threatened would agree with writer Al Martinez: "At best, borders are false barriers to human progress, and the day will come when we will learn to live without them" (Martinez 1993:15A).

Immigration law is another factor which creates both opportunities and crises to which the Guatemalan refugees must react. The Immigration Reform and Control Act of 1986 (IRCA) allowed for the regularization of status for anyone who had been in the United States since 1982 or who had worked in agriculture ninety days during 1985. This legislation permitted many Guatemalan refugees to obtain resident status and to begin to think about making a new life in the United States. At the same time, the cut-off date and the sanctions levied against employers hiring non-documented persons made it impossible for any refugees arriving since 1988 to work. There is one alternative: to apply for political asylum. The odds are stacked against receiving a favorable judgment, since State Department concerns override humanitarian considerations. However, the asylum process is lengthy, and a person who has an asylum case pending may not be deported and can obtain work authorization. This liminal state characterizes perhaps two-thirds of the Guatemalans now in the United States. IRCA legislation included employer sanctions and increased border enforcement and detention space. One result of this is that many employers discriminate against racial minorities and the foreign born. More seriously, the law criminalizes workers without papers. Street corner labor, in which immigrants are hired by the day, is now common across the United States. Among other consequences, although undocumented workers pay taxes, they are ineligible for many benefits.

Guatemalans did not benefit from a 1990 program granting "Temporary Protected Status" to Salvadoran refugees for twenty months, but they did gain the right to have their political asylum cases re-adjudicated if they had been denied before 1990. The "American Baptist Church" (ABC) settlement was based on a decision that foreign-policy bias had caused ninety-seven percent of Guatemalan claims to be denied (Tactaquin, 1992:25-28).

Unable to get work permits any other way, Guatemalans arriving since 1990 usually file for political asylum. But the ABC provision, together with new applications, leaves thousands of cases waiting to be heard by a few asylum officers, and in an interim legal limbo. As Allan Burns notes, not all of these cases will meet the stringent criteria: "The Indians fleeing the political violence may have paved the way for a new wave of Guatemalan immigrants—this time fleeing poverty rather than politics. Once immigration patterns get started, they're hard to stop. It has an exponential effect. The first wave established networks for housing and jobs. The political violence and the breakdown of the economy are linked" (cited in O'Connor 1989:29).

IRCA and subsequent anti-immigrant legislation also seems to have encouraged the Border Patrol and others to step up abuses against undocumented immigrants, especially along the United States-Mexico border. Harassment and physical violence have increased dramatically (Tactaquin, 1992: 28). America's Watch claims that United States immigration agents routinely abuse migrants and sometimes shoot, torture or sexually abuse them (Palm Beach *Post*, 1 June 1992:A2).

In response to the lack of welcome that Guatemalan refugees find in the United States, many activist groups have founded projects to offer them support. The first and best known was the national Sanctuary Movement, in which a loose coalition of over three hundred churches defied United States law in order to provide humanitarian and legal protection to undocumented refugees (MacEoin 1985). Shelters opened up all along the border. Legal services were offered by hastily organized agencies like El Rescate in Los Angeles, Guadalupe Center in Immokalee, Florida, the American Friends Service Committee in Miami, and Centro Santa Cruz in Indiantown, Florida. Documentation support and research was provided by the Central American Resource Center at the University of Texas at Austin. Public information about human rights violations in Guatemala is disseminated by groups such as Policy

Alternatives for the Caribbean and Central America (PACCA), Guatemala Human Rights Commission/USA, Network in Solidarity with the People of Guatemala (NISGUA), Witness for Peace, and the Hemispheric Migration Project at Georgetown University. These projects became magnets for Guatemalan refugees; the legal services particularly attracted those who wanted help to prepare asylum petitions and soon became the centers of Guatemalan population concentrations within the United States. It is also within this field of support that Guatemalan Maya people began to find the conditions to organize themselves and make their voices heard in exile.

RITUAL, CARGOS AND MODERN CATHOLICISM

The other body of anthropological literature which helps to explain the context of Maya refugees in the United States is that which analyzes Mesoamerican popular religious traditions. Popular religion is that religion which is extra-ecclesiastical, transmitted outside the channels of official church communication, and characterized by a preoccupation with concrete manifestations of the supernatural in the midst of everyday experience. Popular religion does not exist in homogeneous, undifferentiated or "primitive" societies; it is only present when the contact and conflict of complex societies open up options, when the "official" religion proves inadequate (P. Williams 1989:9,10).

Anthropology's abiding interest in the religion of tribal people and peasants is based on the underlying assumption that religious beliefs, observable to some extent in religious practices, are a clue to understanding social structure (Morris 1987). In the same way that kinship beliefs, classification systems and languages have been examined to get at why people arrange their lives the way they do, religion is seen as a key to culture. This premise of the correlation between symbolic expression and social experience has generated countless studies. Popular religion has also been seen as a gauge of economic or social change. Religion can legitimize the prevailing institutional order and thus be an agent of alienation but also can be the seedbed of revolution and popular resistance (Berger and Luckmann 1967:59,85) If the church and the ruling classes can impose popular religion as a way of maintaining conditions of exploitation (Gramsci's view: see Sánchez-Arjona

1981:20), then popular religion can also provide a symbolic language through which the poor and oppressed can critique their condition and organize for rebellion (Ingham 1986:2).[9] Far from always being an anachronism or obstacle to development, popular religion can be an agent for change (Van Kessel and Droogers 1988:54), or a rallying point for resistance (Velasco-Rivero 1983:354).

Important in this regard is Kertzer's *Ritual, Politics and Power* (1988), which looks at the ways ritual is consciously used for political ends, usually to unify a group in the face of opposition or threats from without. Ritual essentially makes power, an abstraction, visible, but can also be used to constitute or create power. This involves legitimation and mystification, as well as meaning and identity, carried in ritual by memory, which links past, present and future, and gives humans confidence in a sense of self as continuous (Kertzer 1988:10). The conscious intentionality of the use of ritual is an important part of the argument of this book.

There are four main categories of Mesoamerican popular religion: the fiesta, ritual drama, life-cycle practices, and witchcraft, curing, and divining. The metacategories of time and place cut across these, arranging ritual events around the agricultural cycle and around traditional shrines or pilgrimage centers.

The religious fiesta is a ritual celebration which usually centers on a Catholic saint or an event in the life of Christ. The patron saint fiesta is the most publicly visible manifestation of religious ritual in Indiantown, although dance drama, birth and death rituals, and divining were all observed to be parts of the Maya religious practice in Florida. Nevertheless, the literature of most direct interest in analyzing Indiantown ritual is that dealing with the fiesta/cargo systems.[10] The fiesta system involves the sponsorship of the town's patron saint celebration either by an individual, a household, or by the community as a whole. The individual sponsor or administrator of the community sponsorship is called a *mayordomo*, which can be translated as overseer, foreman, or steward. Thus the complex is sometimes referred to as the *mayordomía* system.

The "classic" system supposedly is a hierarchy of ranked offices (cargos or burdens) that organize both civic and religious public life in a given locality, usually a *municipio* (county) in Mexico or Guatemala.

The civil offices articulate the community with regional and national political systems, while religious cargos are associated with the worship of local saints (and normally are only tenuously linked to the external church hierarchy). Individuals or couples representing different households ascend the ladder of service during their lifetimes, alternating back and forth between civil and religious posts (Chance 1990:27).

Those who successfully serve the top cargos become elders or *principales*. Although cargo and fiesta systems are often intertwined, they are not necessarily so, and are not synonymous. Chance (1990:28) suggests separating the civil hierarchy, the religious hierarchy, and fiesta sponsorship as the component parts of the system. This is useful in the present instance since the Indiantown Maya do not hold any civil offices, and fiesta sponsorship is one of the contested fields there.

A set of characteristics common to the Mesoamerican cargo/religious fiesta system can be derived from the literature. The system involves public, communal rituals (DeWalt 1975, Warren 1978, Farriss 1984) done for the "good of the community," usually to perpetuate, maintain or circumscribe it (Cámara 1952, Reina 1966, Vogt 1967, Collier 1975, Annis 1987, Earle 1990a). The ritual is Roman Catholic in form (Carmack 1981, Orellana 1984), focusing on the physical image of a saint, which, it is generally clear, serves as a symbol of the community (Foster 1953, Farriss 1984, Earle 1990a). The ritual is calendrical and cyclical (Bricker 1981, B. Tedlock 1982, Annis 1987). It is largely male-directed (DeWalt 1975, Brintnall 1979), although the household is usually the actual unit of service, which is unpaid, rotating, and semi-voluntary (DeWalt 1975, Foster 1979, Carmack 1981, Hill and Monaghan 1987). Especially suggestive are studies which show that local leaders control the ritual in relative autonomy from the national civic and church officials (DeWalt 1975, W. Smith 1977, Warren 1978, Stephen 1990).

My brief period of research in Huehuetenango leads me to conclude that the essence of the system as it is currently practiced there is sponsorship of a public religious fiesta to honor a patron saint which is an icon of the community's identity. The sponsors, who are male but supported by their households, offer their service as a sacrifice for the good of the community. Their donation may involve money, but certainly involves time and energy. Those who are in charge of organizing the public events do so within the context of local civil and ecclesiastical authorities, but in the case of the religious parts of the ceremonies, it is the lay leaders who inform the priest as to the schedule and arrangements. The ritual is performed yearly and is a marker for the renewal of commitment to community solidarity, as well as an opportunity for families and individuals to express gratitude for life and health to the supernatural patron and to petition for the same for the coming year. There is one principal patron saint for the *municipio /* parish/head town, but each neighborhood and *aldea* may also have a patron for whom a minor ritual is performed. An important aspect of the principal patronal fiesta is the inclusion of these lesser divisions symbolized by visits of all the minor patron images to the major patron. Solidarity with neighboring municipalities is expressed through mutual visits of the respective images and their clients in the form of processions which are received at the boundary markers of the host towns.

In Indiantown, no Mayas hold civil posts. There is no mention of cargos and no sense of permanent hierarchy of past fiesta sponsors. Yet a system which shares many of the characteristics which I take to be essential is in the process of being elaborated. As will be apparent in the ethnographic material which follows, there is disagreement about many issues, including the identity of the saint who represents the town as principal patron, but there is an emerging male leadership which donates time and energy to organize a yearly round of major and minor public ritual. The stated intentions of the organizers indicate that the rituals are performed for the good of the community. And the organizing is done autonomously by the Mayas, as it is in Guatemala.

Other commonly accepted characteristics of the classic system are less applicable: those which contend that the operation of the system in its traditional form results in a gerontocracy (Reina 1966, J. Nash 1970, Warren 1978, Brintnall 1979, Carmack 1981, Annis 1987) which correlates with prestige (Cancian 1965, Foster 1979); that there is an expenditure of individual or group funds (Cancian 1965) in order to re-distribute goods, especially food (Dow 1977, Greenberg 1981, Earle 1990a) and alcoholic drink (LaFarge 1947, Hillenbrand 1976) to the community, which action makes visible an ethic of reciprocity (Greenberg 1981). In Indiantown, the refugee community is overwhelmingly young; the formation of a gerontocracy may develop over time but at present, men in their early thirties are the leaders. Several older men have organized fiestas, but have not been able to recruit collaborators as the younger men have. Prestige is not the reward for the organizers, but political power and authority to speak legitimately for the community are linked to the donation or sacrifice of time and energy involved in organizing a fiesta. Group funds are expended in order to re-distribute goods, in this case entertainment and education, to the community. The reciprocity of the fiesta is between the supernatural patron and the community; life and protection are exchanged for the celebration of a proper fiesta. There is also reciprocity and solidarity among several Maya groups in south Florida. All of this is, after only a decade, still in the formative stage. Yet it is clear that there has been a successful re-establishment of at least the beginnings of a recognizable fiesta system in Indiantown.

Three ethnographies of Mesoamerican fiesta systems have particular relevance to this study of displaced highland Mayas. For Earle, such religious systems "have always played a central role in the political dynamics of the community, both internally and in relation to the larger sociopolitical system, regardless of their formal relationship to civil authorities People continue to fight for cultural and community survival by marshalling familiar institutions and symbols of community and ethnic identity" (Earle 1990a: 116). The saint's fiesta has a political-symbolic impact in that the saint is the symbolic embodiment of the social group. "Periodic ritualized reiteration of ethnic identity helped to socially unify and define the group, something of especially great value when a group is under acculturative and exploitative pressures." The system served also to sanctify and reward those who overcame kin interests for the sake of the larger group (Earle 1990a: 120-121). Earle's emphasis on ethnic identity enhanced through the fiesta and the legitimation of leadership through sacrifice are corroborated by my findings.

Watanabe advances a unique view of syncretism, which he sees as a feature of local identity rather than either a seamless fusion of native and Christian elements or a cover for persistent pre-conquest Maya culture. The patron saint becomes a "native" of the locality, who participates actively in the ceremonies which maintain the moral, physical and ethnic boundaries of the community. "The syncretism of Maya saint, ancestor and earth lord involves an emergent symbolic reassortment that continually alters the very cultural structure in which it occurs" (Watanabe 1990a:143). From Watanabe I have taken the idea of continual reassortment of symbols which not only reflect change in the social situation but also effect what they signify. However, the close identification of the saint with place, physical town boundaries and intense local loyalty is found to be expandable, in the sense that a saint's fiesta can migrate, along with its practitioners, to another country and the saint's power can be extended to include new places.

Greenberg's study in Oaxaca proposes that the religious system attempts to mediate the contradictions between the opposed modes of production in the metropole and the satellites. The individualism and class structure of the first is set up against the reciprocal and redistributional mode of the Indian community. The civil-religious hierarchy mediates between the state and the Indian community, preventing complete control by external authority and maintaining its ideology (Greenberg 1981:72,149,153,174-5, 190, 211). In Indiantown, the fiesta system attempts to preserve the reciprocal and redistributional ethic of the Indian community while it marks off a space that is not controlled by external authorities.

With these insights safely tucked away in my notebooks, I journeyed to Guatemala, to learn more about the physical context and more importantly, the *ambiente* (atmosphere, surrounding pervasive mood) of the highland communities which had been home to the refugees. The beauty of the Cuchumatán area is startling, but I was more surprised by two aspects of life there for which the literature had not prepared me: the insertion of people in a very remote area into international life through the media, travel, and communication with emigrants, and the vitality of modern Catholic church organization, both of which have been described in a preliminary way in Chapter I. Here I want only to circle back on these points briefly in order to set up my argument: that many indigenous Maya refugees in the United States have brought with them a great deal of political sophistication that has been gained through both widespread regional, national and international contacts and through experience in the organizational aspects of the Catholic church promotion of lay people.

The presence of satellite dishes in the electrified areas of the mountain department of Huehuetenango provides access not only to Guatemalan broadcasts but to Mexican television stations and to *Univisión*, the Florida-based Spanish-language channel for the United States. In the homes I visited, this channel was frequently tuned to the nightly world news. Video cassette recorders were also often available to play taped messages from relatives and former neighbors now in the United States. Video cameras were not an uncommon sight, and tapes were being made to send to those same relatives and friends. I have mentioned the frequent in-country travel; the constantly full buses provide inexpensive if rough transport between highland municipalities and connect easily with other departments and the national capital. Very revealing of the commonplace that travel is for the residents of the highlands, almost everyone with whom I spoke in Huehuetenango, men, women and teenagers, knew the twenty- four hour schedules of each of the more than twenty bus lines, and was able to tell me how to make connections.

In addition to the energetic participation of lay people in local Catholic church organization which I observed in San Miguel and Santa Eulalia, I was also able to obtain some of the training manuals, department-level plans and national policies of the Guatemalan Catholic church. These helped to shed light on the background of those Maya Catholics I would later meet in Indiantown, and on the religious organizational milieu from which they had come. In particular, there were two themes in the church's program which may have influenced the thinking of the exiles. One was a stress on the importance of training lay persons as agents of the church's work; the other was a constant reiteration of the value of Maya culture. On the national level, the most striking example of this thinking is the 1992 collective letter of the

Bishops of Guatemala, called *500 Years Sowing the Gospel*. It lauds the over fifty thousand lay church workers who are committed to working as religious representatives in their communities and the multiplication of training centers for these lay ministers all over the country. "The insertion of committed lay persons in the pastoral activity of the church is without a doubt the most characteristic note of the Guatemalan church . . . and constitutes the backbone of the Catholic Church in Guatemala" (Conferencia Episcopal de Guatemala 1992:20). The letter also astonishingly asks pardon of the Maya people for five hundred years of suffering imposed upon them by the church:

> They are five centuries of sowing, watered with laments, tears, and the blood of the Indian martyrs. This painful experience is for us the voice of God which demands of us conversion, honesty, respect and love for his chosen ones, his indigenous people of Guatemala. . . .We who are presently the pastors of the church, beg their pardon. We rejoice in the flourishing of the Maya spirit. . . .We want to construct an autochthonous church, with a Maya face, heart, and thoughts, pastoral agents and appropriate organization (Conferencia Episcopal de Guatemala 1992:54-55).

The document also contains a ten-page section written by the forty indigenous Catholic priests (of a total of 674) in the country, in which they say they want a church which can recognize the gospel values in the heart of the Mayas (Conferencia Episcopal de Guatemala 1992:48).[11]

In the department of Huehuetenango, church programs showed evidence of this same thinking and made the national church's program more explicit and practical. The local level Catholic entity, the parish (also a municipality), constantly sends lay people to other parishes or to the diocesan center in the departmental capital for meetings or training courses. Those who go have their expenses paid by the community which sends them, but in return take on the obligation of sharing the new information with their sponsoring group. This sense of representing a group to whom one has a commitment remained strong in the Mayas of Indiantown.

Problems the local church faces were named as: the destruction of the ecosystem, the unjust distribution of goods, family disintegration, gender inequality, alcoholism, the integration of returning refugees, the violation of human rights, and the national division into ladino and indigenous factions. The priorities of action for the local church, listed in their five-year plan, were the formation of lay agents, promotion of unity in the region, encouragment of a spirit of service, and investigation of the values of the several Maya ethnies (Diocese of Huehuetenango 1986 *Anexo* 2: 3-9,17). To achieve the last objective, the diocese began, in 1985, a grass roots research program called "Evangelization From Within the Cultures."[12] Preliminary results published in 1987 centered on the theme of land and inter-ethnic conflicts over land. A second report in 1990 outlined the responses of each ethnie on the topics of beliefs, myths, time, life cycles, community, prayers, blessings, offerings, and fiestas (Diocese of Huehuetenango 1987, 1990). The aim of the investigation is to discover Christian values within Maya philosophy in order to base the preaching and teaching of the church on these. Both reports have covers printed with the glyphs of the four Maya calendar year-bearers. This consciousness-raising effort has had a widespread effect in the area; talk of the Maya culture and pride in it was common in conversations with residents of San Miguel Acatán, San Rafael la Independencia, San Sebastián Coatán and Santa Eulalia. On one occasion, a group of lay persons were reflecting on the approaching five hundred year anniversary of the arrival of the Spanish. They commented: "What Gospel did the Spaniards bring? What Bible? It says: do not steal, do not lie; but that is all they did." On another occasion, I was asked to critique a questionnaire prepared by the local cultural committee, which they hoped to use in interviews with village elders.

Some of the findings of these grass-roots cultural committees will help to place the Indiantown fiestas in the context of what a fiesta "means" in the highlands of Guatemala. The common denominators among the nine different ethnic groups reporting on their titular fiestas are: new clothing, special food, firecrackers, music of the marimba, dances, and the offering of candles and incense. Other characteristics mentioned more than once are prayers for harvest, health and livestock, reconciliations with relatives by mutual confession, and pre-fiesta abstention from alcohol. The decoration of homes and streets with flowers and pine needles, fairs and commerce, games, races and of course the procession and mass to honor the saint were also mentioned. There are three types of dance, all accompanied by the marimba: the traditional religio-dramatic costumed dances; the *Convite*, a comic dance using animal costumes; and the social dance. In most towns, the Catholic church committees, choir members or catechists are the organizers of these activities; in several others, the *alcalde rezador* (prayer leader), the *mayordomos* (overseers) and *principales* (elders) take charge. The "sense" of the fiesta that permeates these reports is that of a world-renewing, year-beginning ritual in which supernatural patrons are invoked through the noise of the rockets, the music, dancing, special attire and feasting, as well as through explicit prayers (Diocese of Huehuetenango 1990:75-82). I personally observed most of these activities in San Miguel Acatán in the 1991 titular fiesta; however, because of a cholera epidemic, no masked dances were performed that year.

A search through descriptions of highland Maya fiestas in published ethnography finds these same elements described for other Huehuetenango municipalities. Brintnall (1979), and earlier MacArthur (1977), mention a procession with the saint statue, music, fireworks, candles, ritual dancing, and prayer for long life, good crops, healthy families and animals in Aguacatán. MacArthur mentions that the dancing is done to invoke and appease the ancestors, who are thought to live in the dancers' costumes (MacArthur 1977:12).

La Farge, who studied Santa Eulalia in the 1930s, describes the dance, incense, and candles. He, like other ethnographers, notes that Catholicism in general and the fiestas in particular were organized and led by lay leaders in the absence of clergy and finds that the social and agricultural year was defined for the inhabitants by the fiesta cycle (La Farge 1947:166). All of the fiesta elements I have listed are corroborated in Mérida Vásquez (1984). Watanabe, writing about Santiago Chimaltenango, describes the dressing and care of the saint statue, processions, incense, flowers, candles, flowers, and ceremonial meals (Watanabe 1990a:134,137). He, like Wagley, who studied the same municipality in 1949, found that the local ritual system was organized and led by sacristans and *mayordomos* connected with modern Catholicism who are the enduring core of the reconstructed Catholic church in Santiago Chimaltenango (Wagley 1949:50,79; Watanabe 1990a:136; 1990b:198; 1992:109,196).

In concluding this section on the fiesta system and modern Catholicism in highland Guatemala, it is clear first of all that historically introduced ritual originally intended to convert the Maya population is now used to affirm Maya control of the local religious system as well as ethnic identity. Earle notes: "The appropriation of early instruments of spiritual conquest for collective resistance to cultural and political decline over the centuries demonstrates a sophisticated indigenous understanding of what religion means in political terms. The dialectic of conquest and resistance continues (Earle 1990a:136). Second, the patron saint fiesta is intimately linked with the identity of each Maya language group, which corresponds closely with municipality, dress style, and Catholic parish. In Watanabe's view, the saint is an emblem of the community and is seen as the embodiment of the ideal member of that community. This close identification of patron saint with culture and language group will be seen to stand in the way of a communal agreement regarding the saints' fiestas in multi-ethnic Maya Indiantown.[13] Third, although it is not entirely clear in the literature, the highland Mayas now spend more time and energy resources on the rituals and practices of modern Catholicism than they do on traditional *costumbre*, the Maya-Christian syncretic practices. Nevertheless, there is a strong revival of pride in the Maya identity as such, and a movement of valorizing those traditions which are parallel to a Christian ethic. Concurrent with both the modern Catholic loyalties and the Maya revival is the strong emphasis on lay leadership by those who have been chosen by their local communities, trained by the diocesan Catholic organization and supported in their almost autonomous control of their local churches by the official church structure. Many of those so trained, committed, and with practice in organizational leadership, can now be found living in the Mayan diaspora.

THE MAYAN DIASPORA

The Mayan Diaspora is the name some have given to the forced dispersal of the Maya population from their ancestral homes in Western Guatemala (Earle 1989, 1990b; Camposeco 1991:1; Loucky 1991, Burns 1992b:41). It refers to the fact that people who identify themselves as Mayas are now to be found in Mexico, the United States, and Canada, and in internal exile within Guatemala, in significant numbers and often in organized groups. During the time of what the people call *la violencia* (the violence), in late 1981 through 1983, from 45,000 to 60,000 adults were killed and 80 percent of the remaining population of the primarily Maya departments of Huehuetenango, El Quiché, Chimaltenango and Alta Verapaz were displaced; that is 1.3 million persons (Moors 1992:3; Groupe de Surveillance 1992:11). The internally displaced population, in the slums of the capital city, on coastal farms, and in the northern jungles is still estimated at over a million(Aguayo 1985:26). The Communities of Population in Resistance (CPR) is the name given to the forty-five organized nomadic communities (25,000 persons) living in the areas known as the Sierra, Ixcán and El Petén. "The nomadic communities are desperately poor but organized, making up in communal efforts what they lack in material goods. 'We have achieved what we have through collective work,' said schoolteacher Domingo López Sajic. 'If we worked individually, we would not survive'" (Johnson 1993).

In 1994 there were 43,600 officially recognized refugees in the camps administered by the United Nations High Commissioner for Refugees (UNHCR) in the Mexican states of Chiapas, Campeche, and Quintana Roo and another estimated 150,000 undocumented Guatemalans living interspersed with the Mexican Mayas along the Mexico-Guatemala border. Not included in these figures are over 9000 undocumented children born in exile in the camps alone (NCOORD 1993:7). Both the recognized and unrecognized refugees in Mexico have formed organizations, called the Permanent Commissions of Guatemalan Refugees in Mexico (CCPP) to negotiate their safe return, accompanied by international observers and with human rights guarantees (Groupe de Surveillance 1992:11). Many of the residents of the camps "had been members of the cooperative movement in Guatemala; their experience of cooperative living helped to create strong community-based organizations at camp level" (Moors 1992:6).

The numbers of Maya people in the United States is unknown. The 1990 United States census did not have a category for native Americans other than the recognized North American tribes. The Palm Beach *Post* reports: "Many people who work with Guatemalans estimate that between 12,000 and 15,000 Guatemalans live in Palm Beach County"(Douthat 1992a). Indiantown observers estimate 5000 to 7000 there (Camposeco, Burns, personal communication). The Naples *Express* quotes a social worker as estimating 10,000 Maya in South Florida (Kidd 1991). These figures, if even close to reality, would mean there are at least 30,000 Maya people in Florida alone. James Loucky estimates up to 9000 Maya in the Los Angeles area (personal communication 1991), and there are known to be organized groups of Maya in San Francisco, Chicago, San Diego, Phoenix, Austin, and Houston. Allowing for the fact that fund-seeking agencies tend to inflate numbers, it still seems possible that there may be well over 100,000 Maya people in the United States in the mid-1990s, with hundreds arriving each week. When Attorney General Reno denied temporary protection for Guatemalans in March 1994, the media reported that 200,000 cases were affected by the decision (Univisión *Noticiero Nocturno* 10 March, 1994). This number would include non-Mayan Guatemalans as well as those who have returned to their country without withdrawing their asylum petitions.

Such a large group of refugees, although dispersed over the states, has attracted the attention of a small group of Mayanists, who have begun to document the history in exile of the Mayas. In the period of just over a decade since the diaspora began, publication has been sparse but generative, and the present study seeks to add to this small corpus. When eight Q'anjob'al Mayas were arrested on January 25, 1983, in Indiantown, one of the first on the scene was Shelton Davis, of the Anthropology Resource Center, who published an early account, "Guatemala's Uprooted Indians"(Davis 1983b:3-8). Also called in to help translate and prepare political asylum testimonies were Jerónimo Camposeco, a Jakaltek Maya who had fled in 1980, and Allan Burns, a professor at the University of Florida. Both scholars began a sustained effort to document the lives of the Mayas in Indiantown. Burns produced, with Alan Saperstein, two ethnographic films, *Maya in Exile* (1985) and *Maya Fiesta* (1988). Articles in *Cultural Survival* (Burns 1988a:41-45) and *Migration World* (Burns 1988b:20-26) explain both the conditions which prompted flight as well as the growing importance of Indiantown as a ceremonial center and document emerging leadership of the fiesta organization which he attributes to their experience in the religious cargo

systems in Guatemala. Burns was also able to encourage several of his
students to undertake research in Indiantown. This resulted in
publication of a study on immigration, ethnicity and work there (Burns
1989a) and an article on food habits of Guatemalan refugees (Miralles
1989). In a chapter in the book *Conflict, Migration and the Expression
of Ethnicity*, Burns (1989b:46-60) develops his thesis that the Indiantown
Maya have begun to stake out their internal and external identity in the
arenas of residence, work, leadership, religion, and communication. For
Burns, ethnicity is both a "shield" that protects people from outside
danger and an "emblem that provides self-awareness and confidence for
individuals and groups" (Burns 1989b:50-51). Several other articles
testify to Burns' continued contact with the Indiantown Mayas (1992a,
1992b), culminating in his book-length study *Maya in Exile* (1993b).
Camposeco collaborated with Burns on articles in 1990, 1991, and 1992,
often giving personal accounts of the same events recounted by Burns,
but also reflecting more of a political agenda, in terms of legal
recognition as refugees and as native Americans, for his Maya people.

Another anthropologist well known to the Indiantown Mayas who has
published his reflections is Duncan Earle. Earle cites the Maya's use of
cargo system experience as a springboard for organizing themselves in
exile, but he mentions, as Burns fails to, the much more recent
experience of the modern Catholic church that influences the
predominantly young refugees. His paper on rituals of resistance, as he
interprets the Ixcoy-Tz'uluma fiesta in Indiantown in 1989, has been
extremely helpful to my own interpretation, although I read this paper
only after I had been in my field site for several months. He suggests that
a renewed fiesta system is in the process of formation in Indiantown and
that symbols and discourse are an important part of the field of inquiry.
"The fiesta is viewed as a new creation speaking in familiar symbols and
forms, to depict and situate both dimensions of domination and avenues
of effective resistance to it, especially through the promotion of pan-Maya
identity and unity (Earle 1989:1). His paper also hints at the struggle
within the Maya community between assimilationists and indigenists
(Earle 1989:6). But his brief description of the fiesta only led me to want
to know more about the behind-the-scenes organizing that preceded it.[14]

This book is intended to complement the important beginnings made by Burns and Earle. Burns concentrates in his articles and book on the multi-ethnic relations within Indiantown and on the adjustments the Mayas have made to the world of work. He devotes only a few pages to an analysis of the San Miguel fiesta in Indiantown, and uses only his informants' descriptions of life in Guatemala. Earle's corpus relating to the United States Mayas consists almost entirely of papers presented at annual meetings. While these papers about ritual meaning and ethnic identity are generative and more analytical than Burns' work, they left many questions unanswered. I build on the work of these two colleagues by concentrating more specifically on the fiesta system in Indiantown and its surrounding political field than either has done. I am particularly interested in revealing the specifics of fiesta organizing and how power and legitimacy is achieved in the decisions that are made before and after public rituals. Another concern is to connect the Indiantown Maya more firmly to their Guatemalan roots, and to the context of the transnational Maya renaissance movement as well as to describe the nuts and bolts of the ways the Mayas themselves make these connections, and define their identity for themselves and for the United States host society. But first I will describe the smaller context in which the Indiantown Maya live: their town, their homes, their individual lives as women and men.

NOTES

1. "Mesoamerica" is a modern term used to denote both a geographical and a cultural reality. This has inevitably led to ambiguity and confusion. Kirchhoff (1952) uses a cultural delineation centered on the Aztec and Maya areas. Richard Adams (1956:894) confines Mesoamerican culture to Indian groups self-defined. Spicer (1969) and Helms (1975) widened the area to include Arizona and New Mexico. Salovesh (1983:178) argues that political borders are artifacts of conquest, and supranational cultural similarities make it difficult to define a culture area. In this light, the concept of the "imagined community" proposed by Anderson (1983) and Chavez (1991) is useful. Those who are seen and who see themselves as Mexicans, or Mayas, or Salvadorans would be so in any geographical setting. This would permit a study of Central American immigrants in the United States to be aligned with the tradition of Mesoamerican studies. But the analytical construct itself may have decreasing usefulness in an era of great population shifts and greater cultural exchange.

2. Decision-making models need to avoid romanticism and take into account the "internalized oppression" and "praxis of self-hatred" described by Tinker (1993:3). The results of such learned inferiority are evident in the question asked of Montejo in the vignette which opens this chapter.

3. Sassen (1992:14-19) elaborates on this paradigm: foreign investment in export-oriented agriculture encourages migration by displacing subsistence farmers. Moreover,"the linkages created by foreign investment also have a generalized ideological effect on a receiving country or region, making the culture of industrialized countries seem less foreign and the prospect of living there more attractive."

4. Empirical studies of migrations within and from Mesoamerica have been written by Gonzalez 1969, Dagodag 1975, Frisbie 1975, Butterworth 1975, Arizpe 1978, Diez-Canedo 1981, Portes 1985, and Diaz-Briquets 1989.

5. An example of such manipulation would be President Reagan's speech of June 20, 1983, in Jackson, Miss., in which he warned that a "string of anti-American Marxist dictatorships" in Central America could result in a "tidal wave of refugees, and this time they'll be 'feet people' and not 'boat people'" (Washington *Post* 21 June, 1983, cited in Aguayo 1986:96).

6. For a theory of symbols which sees them as mere markers which enable us to perceive the underlying cultural structure, see Hawkins 1984. I argue that symbolization, especially ritual, has the capability of effecting what it signifies. In complete contrast, the "primordialist" theory of ethnicity states that ethnicity is a deeply rooted affiliation based on common descent, real or putative, a preferential association with an extended kinship group. Phenotypical and language markers as well as conventional symbols, shared historical experience and shared territory are important elements of ethnic identity in this view (Van den Berghe 1981:11,16,17).

7. In the immediate post-migration period, the role of the broker becomes important. The culture broker aids in the initial adjustment and also in introducing later generations to their cultural heritage. In the first instance, this person mediates between the immigrant group and the host society, making direct communication between the two groups unnecessary and thereby maintaining the ethnic boundaries. But this same person often reappears as the intellectual, the myth-maker, the entrepreneur, or spokesperson when leadership is called for to change the status of the ethnic group (Trueblood 1977: 153,156-8; Brettell 1977:173, 175; Gonzalez 1988:184).

8. See Ashabranner 1986 for several eye-witness accounts. Also helpful is Rigoberta Menchú's personal witness, *I, Rigoberta Menchú* (1984) or Victor Montejo's *Testimony: Death of a GuatemalanVillage* (1987).

9. The history of interest in and positive evaluation of the "peasant ideologies" of millenarianism, nativism, and religious syncretism as creative efforts by indigenous and oppressed peoples to repair the torn social fabric is succinctly outlined by Kahn (1985).

10. Lynn Stephen notes that until recently, much anthropological work concerned with religious systems in Mesoamerica concentrated on the form, structure and meaning of civil-religious cargo systems. Indeed, she calls it a fixation (Stephen and Dow 1990:10-13). Chance concurs: "In sheer volume, more pages of ethnographic description and analysis probably have been devoted to cargo systems than to any other aspect of village life (Chance 1990:27).

11. The Diocese of El Quiché proposed that the Conference of Latin American Bishops meeting in Santo Domingo in October of 1992 recognize the authenticity of ten named martyrs, indigenous Christians who died because of their work with the church during 1981 and 1982 (Photocopied document 1992: *The Martyrs of the People of God in the Church of El Quiché*, in possession of author).

12. The word is plural because the diocese of Huehuetenango has within it Mam, Q'anjob'al, Chuj, Awakateko, Chalchiteko, Jakalteko, and ladino people.

13. A church official from Huehuetenango remarked to me, in this vein: "Each ethnie is a nation. They don't think they are part of Guatemala; their identity is in being Q'anjob'al or Jakaltek or K'iché. For that reason there are conflicts and there is not national identity. That is why we think inter-ethnic projects are good: that way people become aware of other worlds" (Field notes, July 1992).

14. Others who have worked with Maya refugees are Laura Martin, a Maya linguist who arranged both a field school in Indiantown and a week-long Maya seminar at Cleveland State University in 1992-1993; and James Loucky, who worked as an applied anthropologist with IXIM, the Maya organization in Los Angeles and is presently preparing a volume of articles on the Maya diaspora.

CHAPTER III

Mayan Men and Women in Indiantown

On this rainy July afternoon, the grounds maintenance crew at the electric plant has been let go early. Xunik (Juan) starts his bicycle trip home to Indiantown, two miles south. As he guides his bike along the highway past *Campo Azul* (Blue Camp), he sees dozens of landscape and agricultural workers standing around the doors of their apartments. Farther on, nearer to town, Xunik stops at the post office to check his box. His heart sinks as he finds it empty again. But the post office is crowded with people sending money orders home to Guatemala, and he greets several acquaintances. Across the street, his niece Angelina is attending clients at the Holy Cross Service Center, filling out Medicaid applications and nervously watching the chairs in her waiting room fill up as more and more people decide to take advantage of a forced day off work. The laundromat next door is nearly empty, but cars and vans splash through the puddles in the grocery parking lot. Xunik stops in to buy a candle for a healing ceremony he has been asked to perform, and talks briefly with Malín and Xusita, who have just come from their jobs at the sewing cooperative to buy food for supper. Xusita buys eggs; her husband Diego hasn't worked that many hours this week because of the rain and there isn't enough money for meat. Malín has her pot of beans ready at home but wants to get some KoolAid; her four children, husband and two boarders will be thirsty in the sticky heat. They are both in a

53

hurry to start their tortilla making. Xunik wheels past the basketball courts at Kiwanis Park, and waves to the small groups of men who are shooting baskets between rainshowers, encouraging each other in Q'anjob'al or K'iché. At the gas station, old school buses pull up to the tanks one after the other, filling up for tomorrow's trip to the tomato fields—hopeful that it won't rain again. The contractors who run the labor buses have to start picking up their work crews before 4 A.M. for the two-hour ride.

At the office of the Corn Maya agency, people drift in and out, seeking help with immigration papers. Xunik finds Alberto and Antonio busy answering questions and preparing forms, and heads for the back room where Julio and José are practicing the marimba.[1] He needs to arrange for them to play at an upcoming event. This taken care of, he rides his bicycle over to the Holy Cross church to light a candle in front of the statue of San Miguel. He finds a couple and their child praying there already. The church glows with the soft light of many candles. Out back, Palás and Elena are trying to plant their piece of *milpa* (cornfield) in the community garden before the rain, so frequent in the Florida summer months, gets too heavy. With all of his errands done, Xunik pedals down Southwest 150th Street to the room he rents, where he showers, eats, and waits for his patient.

Xunik's short bike ride on this typical day highlights some of the important public spaces in Indiantown life. This public arena, as well as some more private areas, will be examined in what follows.

The purpose of this chapter is to provide a context for the analysis of religious practice which begins in Chapter IV. The context is Indiantown, Florida, where some eight thousand Maya people live far from their highland Guatemala homes (Hahn 1990:5,25; Rohter 1991:A-18; Martin 1992:1). A descriptive overview of this rural town in south central Florida is followed by an introduction to the members of eight households, chosen because they represent, as a whole, the gamut of household types one finds in Indiantown. This is folowed by an exploration of the texture of life in exile in terms of the categories that are meaningful to Indiantown women and men.

INDIANTOWN CONTEXT

As noted in Chapter I and also in the description of Xunik's ride home, Indiantown has a variety of agencies and services. The United States Federal government provides a post office. The county government subsidizes a sheriff's station, health clinic, library, a large park, and elementary, middle, and adult education schools. High school students are bused 20 miles to Stuart. There are three social service agencies, all connected to the Catholic diocese of Palm Beach: Catholic Social Services, Holy Cross Service Center/ Thrift Shop, and Corn Maya, Inc. The white ranchers and retirees enjoy the marina, the equestrian arena, and the golf course at the mobile home park of Indianwood Estates. Seven gasoline stations attest to the fact that Indiantown is on a main inland truck route. Two groceries, a pizza parlor, several video-rental stores, a laundromat, a pharmacy, three hardware stores, three restaurants, and a feed and tack warehouse line busy Highway 710. Indiantown lacks a movie theater, a public swimming pool or any recreational facility other than the parks with their basketball and handball courts. It also lacks a supermarket and a resident doctor.

What is invisible to the casual visitor are the many entrepreneurial efforts which take place in the "unofficial" sector. A group of black cane-cutters sells watermelons every day at the Booker Park turn-off. Several of the video rental stores also sell Guatemalan traditional foodstuffs, like *pepitoria* (pumpkin seeds), *ajonjolí* (sesame seed), and *achiote* (annatto), and clothing, such as *cortes* (women's woven skirt-cloth), and *hiupiles* (embroidered blouses), as well as shoes imported from Guatemala. Several Maya women make bread and tamales to sell each weekend. One creative family owns an old school bus, painted the light blue of the Guatemalan flag and decorated with a large green quetzal bird, in which they take workers to the chile fields each day. At least seven women make *corte* skirts and *huipiles* to sell to their private clients. Almost everyone who rents an apartment or a house sub-rents rooms to others. Many Indiantown women cook for several *abonados* (boarders), single men who pay for a hot meal each evening.

The Guatemalan Mayas, although the majority, are not the only inhabitants of Indiantown. Mexican and Puerto Rican farm workers were there before them, encouraged to step out of the migrant stream by the availability of the New Hope housing project, Hope Rural School, and the Holy Cross Service Center. The white ranchers who own the bank, the grocery, the telephone and water, sewer and trash companies, and virtually all the small businesses, are a powerful minority (Shifrel 1993a). Haitians and African-Americans round out the multiethnic picture. The relationship among all these people was complicated enough; the influx of an overwhelming number of Maya speaking Guatemalans in the short period from 1982 to 1985 strained things further. Each ethnic group has carved out a residential enclave of sorts, based primarily on the fact that the Booker Park section of town was originally inhabited primarily by African-American people and the Maya people were afraid to live there. They only do so because of the severe housing shortage. Because of their small stature and their custom of carrying cash, they have been frequent victims of assaults and purse-snatchings. There are several known crack houses in Booker Park, and the Sheriff's Department admits that 80% of Indiantown crime is centered there (Hahn 1990:12-13).

One understandable reason for the notable lack of cross-cultural mixing is the language factor. English, Spanish, Haitian Creole and the Maya languages of Q'anjob'al, K'iché, Chuj, Jakalteko, and Awakateko are spoken by significant numbers of residents, but the very variety militates against the possibility of offering services in any one of them. The churches and their agencies are the only public places where the Maya languages are regularly used and honored. Even among the Maya people, Spanish has to be the common denominator, as it is in Guatemala, and this leaves many women without a voice.

The housing problem is acute all year long; it becomes impossible during the vegetable harvest months, and families can be found living in abandoned cars or camping in the pine woods. Blue Camp, an old motel now demolished, had sixty-four units with approximately 1300 residents (Hahn 1990:7). In many of these units up to twenty single men, perhaps from the same municipality in Guatemala, shared the rent of $220 per week.[2] Indiantown has one of the highest concentrations of substandard housing in Martin county. The duplexes and houses in the Indiantown Park area of town also have from six to thirty adults living in each unit.

Absentee landlords collect rent by the head each week (Hahn 1990:9,61,64; Burns 1989b:51; 1992a:2).

It is difficult to gauge the number of Maya people who live in Indiantown. Because of the fluctuations due to labor migration, census data is not useful but correlation of available data shows a clear pattern of increase.[3] Various published reports indicate that the years of greatest increment in the Maya population were from 1988 through 1990.(see Table 1). There at least three reasons to think that this is an accurate assessment and that the estimates have some validity. First, the initial violence against the indigenous communities in Guatemala, which triggered the emigration of the early 1980s was renewed in 1988 and 1989, accompanied by severe economic stress. Those highlanders who knew someone in *El Norte* would have had a more propitious opportunity and a greater motivation to leave Guatemala with the hope of finding a niche in the United States. Second, the Immigration Reform and Control Act (IRCA) of 1986 allowed many Maya agricultural workers to bypass the political asylum process and apply for residency as field hands. Word of this "amnesty" was quick to reach Guatemala and spurred emigration. Third, increasingly self-sufficient Maya began to move to other Florida cities in the 1990s as they outgrew the need for the "unofficial sanctuary" of Indiantown.

Other sources were helpful in arriving at an approximation of Maya population, especially the records of Corn Maya, Inc., a Maya-run social service agency, where renewals for work permits of those with pending political asylum cases are processed, and Holy Cross Catholic church baptism records. It is fairly simple to recognize most Maya names; Q'anjob'al names in particular consist of several first names.

Table 1. Maya Population of Indiantown from Various Sources

Estimates from Various Sources

	Low Estimate	High Estimate	Source
1983	50-400		Ballinger 1983:7; IPN 1983:3
		1000	Burns 1989b:46
1985	500		Miralles 1987:12
		700	Burns 1985 film
1986	800		Hiaasen 1986: Hahn 1990:5
		1000	
1988	2000-3000		Burns 1988a:41; Burns 1988b:41 Burns 1988 film; Santoli 1988:16
		5000	Burns 1993b:23
1989	3000		
		3500-6000	Hahn 1990:5,25; Florida HRS 1989
1990	4000		
		5000	Burns 1992b:41
1991			
		5000	Rohter 1991: A-18
1992	3000-5000		Erdmann 1992:44
		6000-8000	Martin 1992:1; Douthat 1992c; Auad 1992; Hahn 1990:26

It was thus possible to gather total numbers, and in some cases percentages, of Maya people served in these ways by these organizations. Counts based on data for clients with typical names like Miguel Juan Tomás, Pascual Andrés Juan, Juana Pedro, and Candelaria José only (and thus erring on the side of fewer rather than more) revealed that Corn Maya processed 61 Employment Authorization Documents (EAD's) in 1990, 107 in 1991 and 290 in 1992 (see Table 2). This of course does not include clients who went for this service to other agencies and those Indiantown Mayas who already have residency, but the figures show both a general increase and a pattern of dispersal to other Florida cities.

Baptism records at the Catholic church show peak years from 1987 to 1990, but what is more revealing is that in some years, Maya babies accounted for over half of all children baptized in Indiantown (see Table 3). These figures also show in a graphic way that women were a part of the early migration, as is typical for conflict and refugee situations but not for labor migration.

Sources of employment often require that the Maya worker travel from Indiantown daily for distances of from twenty-five to one hundred miles. Maya men and women have acquired a reputation for hard work, little complaining, and close attention to agricultural detail work. Thus they have found a welcome in Florida's plant and flower nurseries, in the landscaping required for the maintenance of golf-courses and exclusive residential areas, and in the delicate work of picking tomatoes, chiles and cucumbers. None of these employment opportunities exist within Indiantown; rather the people group together to pay for their rides to work. Many enterprising Mayas make extra money by filling their vans with workers going to Stuart, Hobe Sound, Jupiter, West Palm Beach or to the vegetable fields which border the Florida Turnpike. Several labor contractors provide buses for their workers; a typical day (including Saturday and Sunday) finds these buses and vans streaming out of town across the St. Lucie canal bridge before sunrise.

Table 2. EAD I-765 Documents Processed at Corn Maya Inc. 1990-1992

Employment Authorization Document (EAD I-765) Renewals Processed at Corn Maya, Inc., 1990-1992.

	Total Maya	Male	Female	Non-Indian-town Resident
1990	61	51	10	5
1991	107	85	22	14
1992	290	130	60	41

**Table 3. Maya Surnamed Children Baptized in Indiantown
Catholic Church, 1983-1992**

	Total Maya Baptisms	Male Baptisms	Female Baptisms	Total All	% Maya
1983	2	2	0	36	5
1984	0	0	0	45	0
1985	15	10	5	31	48
1986	19	13	6	55	35
1987	47	21	26	89	53
1988	39	21	18	75	52
1989	42	19	23	138	30
1990	86	46	40	157	55
1991	77	44	35	166	46
1992 (Jan.- Oct. only)	44	16	28	119	37

Other work is found in the citrus juice processing plant, right in Indiantown, or in maintenance at the electric plant or the schools. Maya people are not generally employed in picking citrus or in cutting sugar cane; their small size makes them unable to compete with the Mexicans and Haitians in these jobs.

One unique opportunity for women is found in the InDios Cooperative, a Catholic church sponsored sewing factory which employs around ten women, half of them Maya, in the production of clergy shirts which are shipped all over the United States. Other women earn money by caring for others' children, making or importing and reselling typical clothing, or cooking for boarders.

Several Mayas are employed in the service sector, working as teachers' aides in the schools, in the grocery, and as aides or translators for legal and health-care professionals. All of the employment available pays at least the minimum wage, but some jobs are year-round and offer health benefits, while others are seasonal and provide nothing beyond the base wage. Thus, most Indiantown Mayas who are working will bring home at least $150 per week or $600 per month. This compares favorably with plantation labor in Guatemala, where a day's work brings in the equivalent of about $2.

One of the ways in which the Indiantown Mayas attempt to Mayan-ize their new surroundings is through food, clothing, and leisure activities. All of the women make corn tortillas daily, not with dried corn kernels soaked in lime as in their home villages but with Maseca, a corn flour sold in five-pound bags. Some families use up to two bags per week. The corn powder is quickly mixed with water and kneaded into balls, which are pressed flat with a metal tortilla press. The flat cake is then cooked on a hot griddle a few minutes on each side. This process is very fast, and the women can have a pile of steaming fresh tortillas on the table in about ten minutes. The main dish at all of the three meals is usually a stew of chicken and vegetables. Beef is used sparingly. Tomatoes, onions, güisquiles (vegetable pears, called chayote in Mexico), yucca, zucchini, elote (corn on the cob) and potatoes are the favorite vegetables. This is usually accompanied by a fruit juice and water drink called fresco, or by soda, of which the favorite brand in all households is Mountain Dew. Both the name and the taste (fruity with little carbonation) appeal to the Mayas.[4] Black beans such as are raised and eaten in Guatemala are difficult to find and more expensive than pinto beans, so most Mayas have learned to eat the Mexican style beans. As noted above, specially imported typical spices and condiments are highly valued. Special occasions are celebrated with the Guatemalan tamale, a very large steamed corn meal cake with pork, turkey, or chicken meat in the center. In Guatemala, these are made with banana leaf wrappers, but in Indiantown, the leaves of the sea grape, among others, are used. Familes usually sit down together for supper between 6 and 7 P.M. Other meals are packed and taken to eat at work.[5]

One of the most striking aspects of Indiantown is the use by the women of their typical *traje* or clothing. This consists of a blouse, or *huipil*, and a *corte*, or long wrap-around skirt. The blouses are often heavy with embroidered flowers, and are made of cotton or satin. The *cortes* are an adaptation of the eight yard long cloth women use in the colder climate of highland Guatemala; Indiantown women reduce this to a two yard length held up with a *faja* or woven sash, or sew the cloth into a regular skirt with a back zipper. Sandals or closed black leather shoes are worn with no stockings. Women use no make-up or perfume and wear their hair in a single very long braid, usually entwined with ribbons or jeweled hair ornaments. Beads and earrings are almost always worn, even to work. The much-noted use of different colors and patterns of dress to distinguish different municipal origins in Guatemala holds true only somewhat in Indiantown: the most often seen dress corresponds roughly to the Q'anjob'al area. At ceremonial events, most women take care to identify their origin more exactly, if they have been able to procure their own typical clothing. A white *huipil* with a circular neck decoration of many rows of braid, rick-rack and lace, together with the green or blue vertical-striped *corte*, is the most common costume.

The Maya men also use typical clothing, but this goes unnoticed for the most part because it is similar to Western dress. Both in Guatemala and in Indiantown, the well-dressed highland male sports a yoked "cowboy" shirt, blue jeans or Western-cut slacks, riding boots, a leather belt with his name tooled into it, a large decorative belt buckle, and a high-crowned cowboy hat, usually of straw rather than of felt. More distinct and picturesque clothing is worn in some of the Mam-speaking towns of Huehuetenango, but there are almost no Mam Maya people in Indiantown. Some of the more politically conscious men have chosen to symbolize their indigenous identity with woven belts and *caites* or high-backed sandals, and bring out their black wool pullover jackets or *capixay* for ceremonial occasions.

Leisure time on week days is virtually non-existent. The two or three hours at the end of the long work day are spent watching television, especially the *Univision* channel which broadcasts news from Latin America in Spanish. Weekends allow more time for visiting, inviting friends for a special meal, renting movie videos, or attending a dance. Most of the men belong to a sports team or participate as spectators at the many soccer tournaments. During the period from June to September, 1992, over three hundred people gathered each Sunday to watch the day-long games of the Copa Quetzal tournament sponsored by the Corn Maya organization.

Problems with health are not frequent in the Indiantown Maya because the majority of this population consists of young to middle-aged men and women. Most trips to the clinic are for pre- and post-natal care, immunizations, WIC (Women and Infants Care, a Federal program which supplies food coupons to pregnant and lactating women), or work-related problems such as eye-strain or muscular aches. Although childbirth in highland Guatemala usually takes place at home with the help of the husband and the midwife, Indiantown Maya women have learned that regular clinic visits before the birth of their babies ensures a quick admission into the local hospitals when the time arrives. AIDS education and AA groups attempt to address prevention of the problems to which the single men are most subject.

Both United States immigration law and common sense indicate that visits to a country from which one has fled in fear are impossible. Nevertheless, most of the Maya men make regular visits to their families in Guatemala, sometimes yearly, but more often every two or three years.

The usual method is to fly to Guatemala City from Miami and return through Mexico by bus and on foot, crossing the Arizona border and connecting with "riteros" or coyotes at *La Huerta*. For men who have come to the United States without wife or children, the visit serves to keep the marriage viable. Many men sell their cars and liquidate other assets in order to make the trip and take a respectable amount of cash home. Upon their return, they begin again to acquire a vehicle, electronic appliances, and other gifts for the next visit. Some men gather the courage to bring their wives back with them; this is dangerous, arduous, and most often does not include small children, who are left with grandparents for years at a time.

Family reunification is one of the prime concerns of most Indiantown Maya people. Even apparently complete families often have one or more children left behind in Guatemala. Those who have residence papers may petition for visas for their wives, parents and children, and do so, but the long wait is not patiently borne, and some take matters into their own hands. During 1992, one family paid two thousand dollars each for their two pre-teen children to be brought to Florida by a couple who contract regularly to perform this service. Others who knew of this case tried to get the money to do the same. In the case of very small children left behind, parents agonize that the child will not remember or have any attachment to them. Wives in Guatemala worry that their husbands will begin living with other women in the United States and forget about them. The monthly money order that comes through the courier services KING Express and GIANT Express is eagerly awaited by these women at the local courier offices in each municipal capital. Several highland observers have expressed the worry that the remittances from the North have turned Huehuetenango into a welfare-dependent state.

In the time between visits, Indiantown Mayas communicate with their families in Guatemala with cassette recordings, since very few can read or write the Maya languages, and almost none of the wives or parents who receive the communications are literate in Spanish. In recent years, video tapes have become very common, as camcorders and VCR's proliferate both in the United States and in the Guatemalan highlands. Because of the great mobility of many Mayas, post office boxes are preferred to street addresses. Some use of the telephone to call Guatemala takes place, but it is extremely difficult, since there are only a few communal telephones in Huehuetenango, and none in most of the municipal centers. A radio-telephone can be used in emergencies to contact some highland towns, but for other phone communication, plans must be agreed upon well in advance. For this reason, very few Maya in Indiantown bother to establish home phone service. Most mail is sent through the above mentioned courier companies, since no one trusts the Guatemalan postal service.

The fear of deportation is a constant shadow over the lives of most Maya people in the United States. In Indiantown, thanks to early and constant education of the people as to their rights to request political asylum, and to the availability of legal services at no or low cost, almost all the Mayas who arrived in Indiantown before 1987 have legitimate work permits, and the Border Patrol learned that raids on Indiantown were singularly unproductive.[6] Many of those who have arrived since then have also filed asylum petitions and are able to obtain work permits within approximately six to eight months of arrival. The Border Patrol is not oppressively visible, as it is in Arizona and California. The processing of permits and work cards is done in Miami; the INS personnel are familiar with the Maya people and in general provide competent if not friendly service.[7] Many Indiantown Maya women do not have work permits, having come later after the free legal clinics for political asylum applications had ended; they are forced to find work in the hidden economy.

Money is usually kept as cash, on the person of the owner; this well-known fact has led to frequent assaults and robberies by members of other ethnic groups upon the Mayas. In 1992, the Indiantown Bank initiated a program to encourage the Maya to open savings or checking accounts and a Florida banking company advertised special consideration for mortgages to home buyers. But cash is still preferred, and payday means a steady line at the bank to have payroll checks cashed.

The new money system is learned quickly, but because of uncertainty about English skills, many Mayas pay any account with the largest bill they have, in order to avoid the embarrassment of having tendered insufficient cash or having to answer questions. They then ask the bank for coin wrappers to pack up the large number of coins they receive in change, and turn this in for bills. This system is particularly favored by the women, who must pay for groceries and postage, and whose Spanish is limited. They also need a large supply of quarters for the laundromat. In spite of this, the sight of a Maya woman in full traditional dress using an automatic teller machine is a good symbolic portrayal of the curious combination of traditional and modern cultural elements that this refugee population has managed to reconcile. To depict that combination has been the purpose of the foregoing description of the Indiantown context.

A more personal introduction into the lives of eight Indiantown Maya households follows. Brief household vignettes will introduce several of the individuals who play significant roles in the emerging fiesta system, but more importantly, will serve to emphasize for the reader the wide variety of experiences, motivations, and levels of engagement with the community that characterizes the refugees.

HOUSEHOLDS
Antonio and Margarita

Verbal invitations were issued a few days before the event, a December birthday party for five year-old Xahil, given by her parents Antonio and Margarita. The time is a Friday evening; it will be a fancy version of the casual get-togethers that Antonio likes to host on Saturday nights after the "Guatemalan Mass." The long back patio of the house has been decorated with a Christmas tree and a row of long tables covered with *corte* cloth. The tree glows with colored lights and numerous brightly colored cloth animals and bows made of typical Guatemalan weavings. Balloons are strung up on a clothesline overhead. The meal is served first, all of the friends and compadres of Antonio and Margarita taking turns to sit down in shifts, as is done in Guatemala. Cups of *caliente* (steaming hot pineapple punch) or hot mulled wine are placed before each guest. Tortillas are being cooked on one grill, meat on another. The plate of food each person receives is an aesthetic as well as culinary treat: *churrasco* (grilled steak) with *salsa*, colorful vegetable salad with mayonnaise dressing, rice with red chile bits. The taped marimba music fills the air. Mekel and Malín, Bartolo and Fabiana, Juan and Berta, Virves and Dolores, Gaspar and María Juana, Rosa and Roberto are all here with their children, as well as the usual crowd of single men with whom Antonio works at the Corn Maya office. Margarita's brother Nicho is videotaping the whole event so that Xahil's grandparents in Soloma and Santa Eulalia will be able to see how many friends her parents have and how proud they are to be able to host such a party. After Antonio helps his youngest daughter open her gifts, Julio serenades her with the guitar and all the balloons are burst in a fair simulation of the *bombas* (firecrackers) used to announce all happy events in Guatemala. Formal speeches by the parents and others are made for the camera. After the cake is cut and eaten, the marimba tapes are played again and dancing ensues.

Antonio and his wife are in their early 30s and have three daughters, the oldest of whom is paralyzed as a result of meningitis contracted shortly after she was born during the time of the worst *violencia*. [8] One of the principal reasons that the couple decided to emigrate was to look for better medical care for Gilda. Both Antonio and Margarita are health care professionals with certificates in rural health technology and nursing, respectively. They both have a restless drive to better their own situation but are also community organizers who are genuinely concerned about the well-being of the Indiantown Maya community. Each has siblings in other United States cities, but feel Indiantown is a more healthful environment for their children.

Their household includes, in addition to their children, three young women who are relatives of Antonio and three unrelated young men renters. Margarita prepares all the meals for these twelve people; she considers this part of her contribution to the family income but she also sews typical clothing to sell and gives medical consultations in Q'anjob'al to other women. Antonio works upholstering furniture and brings home around two hundred dollars per week.

The home of Antonio and Margarita is a gathering place for the members of the Corn Maya organization, of which Antonio was director from 1989 to the end of 1992, accepting only part time jobs so he could donate his time to the community. He is a complicated individual, who insists on his Maya identity, dressing in typical woven cloth shirts, belts, and *caites*, but who also perms his hair to avoid the Indian look. His wife and children consistently wear the *traje*. Antonio also believes that the Maya traditional religion is compatible with his Catholicism and observes the *dias de ora* (days of prayer to the Maya supernaturals).[9] In Guatemala, he was the leader of the choir in his parish and translated Bible readings from Spanish into Q'anjob'al. He traveled around to the *aldeas* as the coordinator of a retreat team, organizing the youth. He began the Catholic marimba choir in Indiantown and pushed for the Scripture to be read in Q'anjob'al during services. He is very conscious of the political credibility that he enjoys because of his involvement in the church; he says: "*Yo, por ejemplo, si no voy a Misa—si no me ven en Misa, no tengo buena fama aqui.*" (If I, for example, don't go to Mass—if I am not *seen* at Mass, I won't have a good reputation here). Margarita's connection to the church was also close in Guatemala; she still corresponds with the Maryknoll priests who were the pastors in her town. She graciously supports Antonio's activism on behalf of the community.

Antonio is also the connection between Corn Maya and several anthropologists who have worked in and written about Indiantown, and with field schools sponsored by the University of Florida and Cleveland State University. He has traveled to both campuses more than once in the company of other Corn Maya members to give presentations. At the time of Xahil's birthday party, Antonio was feeling burn-out over his years of unpaid work at Corn Maya and the dismal employment record that was the result. He despaired of being able to get a loan to purchase a home.

Corn Maya, Inc., is an entirely Maya-initiated cultural and service organization which operates from a rented building in central Indiantown. It has a board of directors, non-profit corporation status, and provides legal and social services for several hours nightly. It also serves as a recreational center and meeting place for many Indiantown Mayas. As a civic organization, it participates in clean-up campaigns, information fairs and other county events; as a cultural maintenance organization, the members sponsor several annual events for the Maya community. Funding comes from grants and foundations but only covers rent and supplies; all services are donated by a small core of eight to ten volunteers. Antonio was the elected director. A more detailed explanation of Corn Maya's importance in Indiantown will be found in Chapter V.

Antonio believes that Corn Maya must preserve its identity as an indigenous organization, in order for the public to understand that the Maya people are capable of organizing themselves. When asked if he and his co-organizers had ever thought of pressuring for a reservation like the Yaqui tribe of Arizona, he said: "We believe we have the right to live within this society and yet preserve our culture. A reservation makes it seem like we are cattle on display." Antonio is clearly one of the Maya leaders in Indianatown. As the chief organizer of the Copa Quetzal Festival of September 1992 and several prior fiestas, he is also important for this study.

Mekel and Malín

In early August, Malín (María) found it necessary to manage her household without her husband, Mekel. He had to make an unexpected trip to Guatemala when he received news of his mother's sudden death. Malín began wearing a black *huipil* and *corte* in deference to the Mexican women with whom she works at the co-op; the Mayas do not usually wear mourning but Malín knows the Mexicans think wearing bright colors when a relative has died signifies lack of grief. She asked

a friend to take her to the laundromat. No doubt this is a twice-weekly
chore for Mekel when he is home, since Malín doesn't drive. While
washing her four loads, using powdered detergent, softener and liquid
bleach, she explained what a wrinkle in their plans had been occasioned
by her mother-in-law's death. The couple had recently bought a
four-bedroom home, making it necessary for both of them, as well as
their eighteen year-old son, to work to make the payments. They had
planned that Mekel would return to San Miguel for the September 29
fiesta there and bring back their daughter, thirteen, and son, fifteen, who
would be finishing the school year at that time. Then the family would be
reunited, parents and six children. Malín could stop worrying that their
daughter would elope or that their son would have to join the army. But
Mekel's trip in July would have exhausted his vacation time at the golf
course where he works as well as his travel funds. The only other hope
would be to try to save the four thousand dollars that they would need to
have their children delivered to them in Indiantown, after school was out
in October.[10] Malín was also concerned because official-looking papers
arrived daily in their post box; she couldn't read them and feared that
they would lose their home over some technicality. Malín has never been
to school, although she did attend literacy classes in San Miguel as an
adult. Mekel, who only went to school for two years, is earning a good
salary, but Malín is lucky to make $150 a week for the piece work she
does at the sewing co-op. She sews well, but the pressure to produce
rapidly flusters her and she makes mistakes.

In the end, Mekel and Malín payed to have their children brought to
the United States and their house payments got made on time, but the
worries don't go away. Even successful families like theirs, which has
been described in the newspapers as an "American Dream Story" (Shifrel
1993b:1-A, 6-A) are subject to lightening-bolt reversals. Financially they
live on the edge. Nevertheless, the family struggles to have a tranquil life,
sitting down to dinner together each evening with their two boarders.
Their ranch-style home is a showplace, with the yard full of flowers and
typical Guatemalan plants like *chipilin* and coffee bushes and a row of
papaya trees. At Christmas, Lorenzo, who usually turns over his weekly
salary to his father, instead bought and installed enough colored lights to
outline the whole house as well as the Christmas tree. Mekel is
encouraging his *compadre* [11] Antonio to buy a house and Malín has
decided she needs to learn to read in Spanish. This family shows many
signs of settling permanently in the United States.

As a young man in San Miguel, Mekel was too poor to take on a cargo for the fiesta, but he remembers gathering palm branches and flowers to help decorate the church. He did help his father with a cargo for the feast of the Sacred Heart, a minor celebration. Now, however, he finds himself in the position of a respected elder among the young single men of Indiantown, and he has taken it upon himself to organize the decoration of the Catholic church for the San Miguel fiesta, and at Christmas. He likes things to be beautiful, *alegre* (joyful). He does this *por gusto* (because he likes doing it) and *por respeto a la casa de Dios* (out of respect for God's house).

Diego and Xusita

It is 2:30 on a fall afternoon. The six women in the English class at the sewing co-op have gathered around the cutting table. They are tired at the end of their work day which starts at 6A.M. Three of the women are barely literate but struggle to learn how to write their addresses, to compose notes to their children's teachers, and to make complaints to their landlords. Of the other three who have more schooling in their background, the brightest by far is Xusita. Only twenty-three, she came to join her husband just two years previously, but she already had a reputation in Indiantown for speaking out against anything she perceived as a slight to other Maya women. She finished her secondary education in Guatemala and married a man from a neighboring municipality who has a degree in marketing and accounting. Xusita hardly looks Guatemalan, much less indigenous: she has fair curly hair, freckles and blue eyes. Both her physical type and her educational achievement are fairly typical, however, of her hometown, Jacaltenango, from which several of the "culture brokers" in Indiantown also come. Although she and her husband Diego speak Jakalteko at home, Xusita speaks Q'anjob'al with the other Maya women at the co-op, to the great annoyance of the Mexicans. At the same time, the other Guatemalan women tease her about her Western dress, her decidedly stay-at-home husband, and her perceived heartlessness at leaving her baby daughter in Guatemala. So she finds herself in the middle, consciously Mayan and ready to defend her people, yet more accepted by the Mexicans because she is seen as less Indian.

Diego and Xusita are in the United States to raise enough capital to begin a small business in Guatemala. That is why they were willing to leave their little daughter behind. But it has been almost impossible to save money, what with having another little girl born here, paying for a car and rent, and sending money to both of their families. The time has passed by and they are no closer to their dream, yet consumed by anxiety for their child growing up without her parents. Their despair only increased after the arrival of Mekel and Malín's children in Indiantown.

Xusita is very connected to the church, although she and her husband have never sought a church marriage and rarely attend mass. Rather, her connections are personal. She has a first cousin who is a priest and several classmates who have also been ordained for the diocese of Huehuetenango. Both she and Diego attended Catholic schools. She feels at home with the clergy and often invites them for supper at her home. She also offered to host the visits, on two occasions, of Guatemalan priests to the Indiantown community. Diego, who is very reserved, is proud of his wife's intelligence and of her industry: she works all day, then prepares dinner for two renters and three boarders, as well as for himself and their child, Xeny. Partly because of his shyness, and partly because of their heavy workload and the problem of finding childcare, Diego and Xusita are not involved in any fiesta preparations, although they did attend at least one of the six events that took place during 1992. Diego was involved for some months with Corn Maya, volunteering help with the bookkeeping.

Gaspar and María Juana

Three days after the San Miguel fiesta, Gaspar and María Juana, who had been the chief movers and organizers of the secular part of the celebration, were busy with clean-up tasks. Gaspar was scouring the grills they had used to cook meat for the tacos they sold. María Juana was baking bread, as she does weekly. After spending the previous two days washing the large pots and pans used to prepare the food to sell at the two-day event in the park, she was exhausted from an almost continuous forty-eight hours on her feet. However, both she and Gaspar were happy that they had come out even and been able to send about five hundred dollars to their home parish of San Miguel Acatán for repairs to the church, not like other years when they worked as hard but came up short because of poor planning.

María Juana and Gaspar, who are in their fifties, have been in the United States since 1982 when the EGP guerrillas [12] came looking for them. They had coffee and cardamom land in the lowlands of northern Huehuetenango and a small store in San Miguel, and were perceived as rich and enemies of the revolution. Some of their nine children were away at school but they made their way together to Los Angeles, where the older ones finished high school. Arriving in Indiantown in 1986, they have done well, partly because of this advantage of their adult daughters. Now they own the home where they live with four of the children, María Juana's sister and brother-in-law, their three children, and two adopted nieces. The three oldest daughters are well-known in the area; two of them work as para-legals and social workers with the Guatemalan community; the third owns a small store together with her husband. The family has literally no one left in Guatemala. Their yearly visits are made to friends in the *Mayab Balam* refugee camp in Mexico.

Gaspar works as a custodian earning over seven dollars an hour, and María Juana sells bread and tamales door to door. Their plans for the future include buying a second house in Indiantown to rent out, and building a new house in San Miguel for their retirement.

Gaspar, María Juana, and their adult daughter Francisca work hard each year to organize ("produce" would be a better word, in the sense that one produces a rock concert) the cultural event-cum-dance in the park which is the secular side of the San Miguel fiesta. But they all complain constantly about how hard it is to get help or even cooperation from other Indiantown Mayas. As a matter of fact, many other people express considerable dissatisfaction with the sort of fiesta Gaspar's family has organized, a non-specific, non-Maya rowdy affair with Mexican music and no mention of the patron saint. But the family persists, citing their desire to please all the Hispanic people of the area by not foregrounding either ethnicity or religion. Perhaps they also feel a sense of responsibility for some continuity in their own practice: Gaspar was president of the parents' association and the improvement committee in San Miguel and María Juana always helped decorate the church for the fiesta and cooked the daily meal for the parish school. They worked on the San Miguel fiesta in Los Angeles when they were there; now Gaspar's brother is involved in that effort. But the family is the focus of many conflicts within the Maya community, only some of which have to do with the fiesta. Gaspar was and is solidly behind the Guatemalan military, and uses every opportunity to explain that the "subversives" are only getting what they deserve. In his view, the army bombing of the villages to which the refugees are returning is justified, since most of the Maya people who fled to Chiapas, Mexico are guerrillas. Given that most of the young men who are active in Corn Maya left Guatemala because of fear of the army, and the older men like Mekel left because the army massacred their neighbors, Gaspar is viewed with a mixture of respect, fear and dislike. But no one doubts that he and his family are important players in the Indiantown scene.

The four profiles in the preceding pages exemplify some of the ways in which family-centered households live their lives and involve themselves in local religio-politics. Indiantown is perhaps unique among Maya exile settlements in the United States because of the presence of so many women and children. But at least half of the households are non-families, people grouped by common immigration history, place of origin, or simple convenience in order to circumvent the high rents. The following pages show how they live.

Alberto, Julio, Gilberto, Efraín, Juan, Carlos, José, Miguel, Santos

Miguel and Gilberto made a trip to Stuart early on a Friday morning. They were to appear in court that day on DUI charges and expected to spend that and the next four weekends in jail. The good news was that Alberto, part-time member of their household and volunteer in the Corn Maya office, would be released early after serving more than a month of a six-week sentence for the same offense, and would return to Indiantown that day. Several single men in their early to mid-twenties live in the house; they are all K'iché speakers from Totonicapán or El Quiché departments. Alberto and Julio do not actually sleep in the house, but spend most of their time with the other seven. These last two are from Aguacatán, the Huehuetenango municipality closest to the K'iché speaking areas. The group is very close, although only Efraín, José and Santos are related (they are cousins), and Juan has just recently been joined by his brother Carlos. All have been touched by the violence which was acute in their area during the late 1980s. Most of them came to the United States between 1988 and 1991. The three cousins are fervent Seventh-Day Adventists, the others are Catholics. All are heavily involved in Corn Maya.

Average salaries are about $180 per week, and each man sends between $200 and $400 home each month to his parents. Several of the K'iché- speakers were artisans in Guatemala. Efraín was a leather crafter, making sandals and harnesses. José knows how to machine-embroider blouses and weave baskets, and Gilberto was a printer. Now, however, they work in landscaping or finishing furniture, although they have done some craft demonstrations for museums. Julio is the leader of the Indiantown marimba team and one of its two constant members, since labor migration takes the other marimba players to North Carolina for several months each year. He also plays the drums and sings.

The involvement of several of these men with alcohol has caused some serious disruption in their lives, particularly in terms of suspended driving licenses, fines, and jail time. It is well known that alcoholism is a severe and wide-spread malady among the highland Maya. Witness Siegel's descriptions in 1941, La Farge's in 1947, and Watanabe's in 1992. But the consequences of getting falling-down-drunk are not nearly as serious in a society where very few drive, there is little motor traffic on town streets, and both public law and public opinion are more tolerant. It is a great surprise to the Maya people to find the United States has statutes in every state regarding alcohol consumption, especially when combined with driving. The inability to drive to work, or, even after the license is reinstated, the inability to purchase the required auto insurance, is a big problem. On the personal level, the effects are usually a short-lived embarrassment, but sometimes there are fights. In this group of co-residents, however, there is genuine concern for each other and the desire to help each other over the bad times.

The Adventists belong to a small local congregation which includes about thirty Q'anjob'al speakers from San Rafael and San Miguel. Catholic members of the household are all involved in the marimba choir, except Alberto, who has formed a second choir for the second Spanish language mass at Holy Cross church. He plays the guitar and organ and chooses the music, leading a small group of young Mexican men and women.

Julio was a member of the youth choir and the youth group in Aguacatán; his father is an *animador*, or church leader, there. An energetic, funny, generous young man, he is well liked in Indiantown, and has been at the forefront of many of the sports events sponsored by Corn Maya. Alberto was a student at the Christian Brothers high school in Huehuetenango and a member of the Order for several years. His skills are secretarial as well as musical, and he donates four to five hours daily to helping other Indiantown Mayas with legal forms. He is also part of the planning committee of Corn Maya and deeply involved in all its public events. More reflective than most, he notes that since single youths are not involved in organizing the fiestas in Guatemala, but become so after marriage, it is difficult to plan an event that will appeal to the young men of Indiantown, who are, after all, not so much interested in preserving past tradition as in making a future for themselves. He was successful, however, in planning and carrying out a memorial service for eight of his townsmen who were killed in 1991 in a tragic irrigation canal accident (Rohter 1991, Shifrel and Shuchman 1992a).

Almost any evening finds the majority of these nine men hanging out at the Corn Maya office or at the home of Antonio and Margarita. The marimba, the ping-pong table, and "survival" English classes give them a way to spend their after-work hours. Together with three or four others, including Antonio, they make up the core of activist Mayas in Indiantown. Although they vary in their commitment to indigenism as a philosophy, they are all concerned about their identity inasmuch as it affects their future life, which they all believe will be in Guatemala.

Xepel and Eul

The papayas hung heavy on the little tree by the door on a late afternoon in early January, 1993. Inside, the three bedroom house Eul (Eulalia) rents together with her aunt Xepel (Isabel) is spotless. Eul is busy at the stove preparing supper and Xepel is in her room at her sewing machine, making a *huipil*. At the same time, she is listening to a tape recording in Q'anjob'al. She received that tape from her parents and her daughter, who live in Guatemala City, in time for Christmas and she is getting ready to record a reply and send it, together with money, as soon as possible. Xepel is forty-five, divorced, and came to the United States alone in 1985. Her niece Eul, who is now nineteen, joined her in 1987. They both work in a flower nursery, earning around $150 per week and suffering equally from painful sinus conditions and runny eyes as a result of the insecticides they use daily. Both are from an *aldea* of San Miguel, speak Q'anjob'al better than Spanish, and neither has ever been to school. Both claim to be Catholic but they attend church services only rarely. However, Xepel's communication with her family in Guatemala is timed by the fiesta cycle, she says, and Eul was a flower-bearer in the procession to honor San Miguel in Indiantown in 1992. They both wear typical Migueleño dress except at work.

Xepel worked for some years in Guatemala City as a food vendor, but wanted an opportunity to earn more money and to avoid being under her father's authority again after her divorce. Eul worked in her family's cornfield and in the home, mostly collecting firewood, and came to the United States to help her parents financially. She has two brothers somewhere in *El Norte* (unspecified northern states).

Both of these women are found frequently in the offices of Corn Maya, and have traveled with the marimba team to demonstrate how to dance the *son*,[13] and to serve as living exhibits of Maya women's dress. Because they are unmarried and unfettered by children, they are free to go on trips with the marimba team. It would be impossible for any of the married women to even think of getting permission from their husbands to do such a thing. Also, because of their inability to read and write, or even understand very much Spanish, Xepel and Eul are in frequent need of the translation services at Corn Maya.

Domingo, Antonio, Lucas, Miguel, Santiago

Rain thunders down during the Saturday night service at Holy Cross church. The mass is supposed to begin at seven but Padre Juan is not terribly concerned; he knows that the church will be full of his Guatemalan Maya parishioners no matter what time he starts, since they all come early to hear the marimba choir practicing. Those who come in are welcomed and shown to their seats by the ushers, among whom are Domingo, Antonio and Lucas. These three men in their forties are not related, but they share an apartment, a *renta,* in Blue Camp. Domingo's two nephews, Miguel, twenty-eight, and Santiago, thirty-two, also live there. All arrived in Indiantown in 1989 after spending about a year in California, doing the same work they do here, picking vegetables for about $200 a week. All of them were corn farmers, working either their own little steep mountainside plots, or for their fathers. Some of them are from Soloma, the others from the neighboring town of San Juan Ixcoy, and all speak Q'anjob'al.

These men lead a sober life in both senses of the word. Several of them have renounced liquor after joining AA in Guatemala. One of the reasons they stay together is to present a united front to temptation. And since all five men are married, with wives and children in Guatemala, their only social life revolves around the Saturday evening mass, the Thursday evening Bible study group at the church, AA, letters from home, and their longing and saving for their next visit.[14]

Their schooling levels go from zero to three years; nevertheless, all of them had leadership roles in the church in Guatemala. They were *catequistas,* teachers of doctrine, who had to attend a monthly preparation session in the municipal center and then hold a day-long lesson for their villages. This modern "cargo" also involved training courses in Huehuetenango several times a year. When they arrived in

Indiantown, they were delighted to find that the pastor there understood and appreciated their culture and allowed them to begin acting as ushers. They found a liturgical celebration not unlike the ones they were used to in Guatemala, with at least some of the Bible readings proclaimed in Q'anjob'al, many personal petitions read before the start of the service, and of course, the marimba choir. Although none of these five men is involved in Corn Maya except as a client, they assisted with the church celebration of San Miguel and again for San Rafael. Lucas, Antonio, Domingo, Santiago and Miguel are examples of the commited corps of lay Catholics who are active in the modern version of Catholicism that is being promoted in Huehuetenango. They have found a small niche within which to continue with their dedication in Indiantown.

Xunik Tumáx

Juan Tomás (Xunik Tumáx in Q'anjob'al) was introduced in the opening vignette of this chapter. He is very visible in Indiantown, where he can be found daily lighting his candles before the statue of San Miguel in the church. Xunik is a true elder, a fifty-seven year old man who spends a lot of time teaching the younger Maya men of Indiantown how to perform the old ceremonies. He performs his curing ceremonies in his small rented room, which has a cot and two wooden chairs and a large wooden table that he uses as an altar. Two images grace the plain walls: Jesus and St. Michael the archangel. On the table is a bottle of oil, several brands of deep heat rub, and a jar full of coins, plus several packages of herbs which his wife sends to him from Guatemala. There are also some votive candles of the type the grocery sells for $1.50, with saints' pictures on the glass containers. Xunik treats joint pain, fallen uteruses, bones out of place, and assisted at childbirth in Guatemala, tying off the umbilical cord, and wrapping the placenta in newspaper and placing it in a tree so the child will grow straight and tall. But before any cure, he addresses each of six saints (God, represented by the Sacred Heart of Jesus, St. Michael, St. Peter, St. Martin, St. Felipe de Jesús and Hermano Pedro) with a candle and a bow from a kneeling position. He begins his circle of address *donde sale el sol* (where the sun rises). A cure requires two candles each day for nine days; one candle for the church and one for Xunik's altar. The candles are provided by the patient; Xunik claims he charges only what his medicine costs, but accepts food and money donations.

Xunik also knows how to make pine ropes to decorate the church and the carrying platform where the San Miguel statue is placed for the fiesta procession. On the days before the events, he gathers a crew of eight or nine men with their little sons at the church grounds. While some of the men climb up the pine trees to cut and throw down branches, others chop the needles into uniform eight-inch lengths with machetes. Xunik, meanwhile, rigs up his wheel and twine, and then feeds handfuls of pine needles into the space between two lengths of twine while an assistant turns the wheel. The result is beautifully fragrant fresh green pine garlands, which are then festooned around the inside and outside of the church.

It is widely believed in Indiantown that Xunik also *hace costumbre*, that is, he practices the Maya religion. He claims he knows how to do secret ceremonies in the cemetery, and that his father does *oráculo* (divination) with *maizitos* (little corn grains), casting them on a board and counting them out, then checking the number in a book. In spite of his reputation as an occult practitioner, no one in Indiantown fears Xunik; they know he is a good friend and confidant of Father Juan, and that his traditional religion is not employed to harm anyone.

Xunik has a wife and five children in San Miguel; his only relative in the United States is his niece, María Juana, wife of Gaspar. He left San Miguel, he says, because God warned him in a dream that his calumniators wanted to kill him. That was in 1983, and he hated to leave his productive orange grove in hot country. In spite of having never gone to school, and his great difficulty in speaking Spanish, he has a good job *sembrando paipe* ("planting" irrigation pipe, at $280 a week. He has worked all over the United States, and visits San Miguel every other year.

Xunik considers himself a true Catholic, in spite of his traditional practices. He was a member of the parish council, and helped count the collection in his parish in Guatemala; he also says he donated one day a week to the church. He played the *tun* or wooden drum in the cemetery on the Day of the Dead, and also had a marimba band. Xunik is one of the most interesting members of the Maya community, a well-known participant in the preparations for all the church fiestas, and probably has more power, through suggestion and through his close association with the priest, than his humble demeanor would reveal.

WOMENS' LIVES

The section above attempts to show that although all the Indiantown
Mayas were corn farmers in Guatemala, their identity was, and is, in no
way confined to that aspect of their lives. As individuals interacting with
one another, each with a personal history and point of view, they together
configure the refugee community. As noted, one of the unique features of
that community is the presence of a large number of women. In order to
contextualize their lives further, and precisely because their voices are
not often heard, the following section is a dialogue about some of the
topics that are important to them. In this conversation, the changes in
their lives occasioned by wage labor schedules, Western fashion and
health care systems, and family separations are the main themes.[15]

Work and Money

Xusita: I would say that it's almost the same here as in Guatemala. In
               Guatemala, one has to get up before the man, mop, clean the
               house, whatever. The only difference is, here, the woman gets up
               and goes to work; in Guatemala, she gets up, sends the children
               to school, and then begins her housework or goes to the market.
               Here or there, you have to get up, give breakfast to your husband.
               But in Guatemala we don't have money. The men keep the
               money.

Catal: [Here] one has money, see; on the other hand, there you have to
               ask for it.

Xusita: Here we have gotten used to having money, every weekend, to
               buy what we want. In Guatemala, if the husband is a farmer he
               earns 6.50 quetzales [about $1.20] per day. But sometimes they
               only work two or three days a week, and if the man doesn't work,
               how will the children live? Here, however, we women, if we work
               or don't work, the government helps us with milk, and a lot of
               people have that custom, they have children every year, since it
               doesn't cost them anything, but in Guatemala it does.

Catal: On the other hand, here we have "El Pamper."

Xusita: We don't use cloth diapers any more, but when we return to
               Guatemala it's going to be very difficult. The same thing, a lot of
               people I have seen say "Oh, no, I live too far to go to the store, I
               can't walk, I will die!" Before, when I first came here, I walked
               from my job home every day. I'm used to it, there we go by foot
               everywhere, one doesn't go by car in our country. But since here
               there are many cars, they no longer can walk. But when we return,
               we'll have to adapt.

Maria Diega: There we were at home all day, we took care of the house, but here, we work, we arrive home tired, right? Back in Guatemala, one doesn't get so tired, so thirsty, but here we work really hard.

Dress and Language

Xepel: Indiantown is pretty.

Xusita: It's pretty because there are a lot of people from Guatemala, and if one lives in West Palm Beach maybe they are there, but separated, but here, one sees people like at home, it's almost the same. We go to the store, we see people who speak our language.

Maria Juana: Here we can go out, greet each other on the street. I lived five years in California. O God, there one cannot walk around at ease. Here it is better than in a city.

Catal: In Los Angeles, the girls who live there do not wear their *corte*, no one puts it on because they make fun of you. But here, who is going to make fun? We are all from Guatemala.

Maria Juana: Here what happens is that we don't work [outside the home]. There in California all the women work in the factory and then they change and use make-up.

Catal: It's true, they even dye their hair.

Maria Diega: The first time one wears a dress or skirts, one feels bad, because we are used to the *corte*. One feels that one has no clothes on.

Catal: That's how it was for me, when I put on a skirt the first time. Ay! I was very ashamed, very embarrassed. And slacks or pants too. In Los Angeles we were using just, what do you call them?, skirts or dresses.

Maria Diega: And if the cloth is thin, one doesn't feel anything; you can't tell if you have anything on.

Micaela: When I first changed, I felt undressed, but I got used to skirts, and now when I use my *corte*, I feel it is too tight; I feel like fainting.

Fabiana: It was very hard to stop using the *corte* ; I changed for the first time in Huehuetenango. I felt my legs were cold. Now it feels too hot, and bulky around the waist.

Rosa: I used to wear the *corte* when I was teaching, but that was only three or four months. I got used to Western dress in boarding school where we wore shorts for sports. Now I wear only skirts.

Xepel: When one has to put aside the *traje* for the first time, ah, one feels bad, like one doesn't have any clothes on, like one isn't well covered, because our clothing is thick. I compromised by using jeans, that's the only way I feel a little better.[16]

Maria Diega: When I went back to using the *corte* again, I tried to walk quickly, but I felt like I would slip.

Elena: The first time I put on pants I felt very ugly, because I wasn't used to that clothing. Now, I'm used to it, and skirts too. When I put on the *corte* now, it's a little difficult, it seems like it weighs a lot and hurts my waist. But I still like the *traje* best. We never used Western dress at home.[17]

Childbirth and Children

Catal: I left my children in Guatemala, I have to return. I wonder all day how my children are.

Maria Diega: Here, when women give birth, it's not like over there in Guatemala; [there] they give you something hot to drink.

Catal: Here they put ice in your drink. And there they don't let us wash clothes until two months go by; we can only wash diapers. We can't work. And the same day, we go into the *chuj*. Ay, what a pleasure, and we do it often.

Maria Diega: The same day that one gives birth, because I have seen my mother when she gave birth, my grandmother goes too and takes her into the *chuj* (sweat bath-house) and they wash the baby. First the baby, then the mother.

Catal: Then they tie her stomach very tightly. The women who have a baby here say they feel real bad, sick, They don't want to eat, and their body hurts.

Maria Diega: My sister-in-law gave birth here, it was her first time, and she said they put ice in her soda, real cold, and they put her into a cold water bath. That's why she's sick, she said, Now she is real thin, because she has two children born here, and she had to drink real cold water, not like in Guatemala, a hot coffee, a hot drink and hot food, with chile. There, they put chile in their food so they warm up more.

Catal: So a lot of milk will come out.

Maria Diega: And here, the women don't give their breasts to the babies, just canned milk.

Catal: There they taught us with a health promoter; well, for those who have money the bottle is OK, but for the poor, for us, I mean, women who don't have a job, who are in the house, and the men looking for money, no way is that money going to be enough for the milk.

Maria Diega: And the babies get sick. Not like those that take the breast.

Catal: Figure it out. There a can of milk costs eight or nine quetzales. It could be 350 quetzales a year!

Maria Diega: There, when children are five or six, and walking well, they let them walk, but before that they are carried. I like to carry them when they are small.[18] I had a little sister, very small; she was

three, but she didn't grow. I carried her until I came here, and
then I left her and she became very sad.

Catal: My baby girl, I was carrying her up until I came; now my mother
is carrying her. She is almost four. The other girl will be seven in
July. She is already big. I sent her to school in our *aldea* but there
is a river there. They tell me my little girl almost got carried away
by the river so I sent word to my mother, better not send her
anymore. Because there is no one to watch her. I'm going to allow
her to get a little bigger, maybe when she's nine or ten, I'll send
her to school. Although I am poor, I have to *luchar* (struggle) for
my children, so they turn out well. That is, not a lot of study, but
perhaps so they can read or get a little Spanish, and get ahead.

Maria Diega: I don't know Spanish well, I don't know how to talk very well. I
went to school but only to my second grade. Because when my
father died, my mother took me out of school. But now I regret it.
I wish I could do it again.

Men, Women and Alcohol

Maria Juana: Well, you have to pay attention to the man. Because he is bringing
the money. All men are the same; it is unusual for a man to allow
his woman to live her life. Women here have no one to support
them; [in Guatemala] she has her mother and her father. A lot of
men come here and give their money to another woman, and they
are married men.

Xusita: Sometimes, for example, a single girl here starts going with a
man, and they live together, but he has his wife in Guatemala, and
has to send her money each month. Sometimes you think he's just
a kid, probably not married, but there he has his wife and
children.

Maria Juana: Not only that but they have two or three women. Also, when one
is a girl, one takes care of herself, but when she has kids, she
doesn't take care of herself like before; she doesn't think about
what she will wear, about fixing her hair, like when she had a
boyfriend. When she has a baby, she can't be changing clothes
often. The man loses interest.

Xusita: Here we're talking about them, right, but also they talk about us;
it's the same. But when the man is jealous, when he's not sure of
you, you have to talk with him.

Maria Juana: You have to have patience. It's like we're saying, because they
earn money, they spend money. It's easier here, they earn and
they spend. And if he gets his check on Saturday and goes to
drink, well. In Guatemala, some of them drink frequently, usually
those who come into town from the far away *aldeas*, they come to

	sell their corn, their firewood, their beans, and they buy beer and drink.
Xusita:	Then they go stumbling out on the road. And if he has a table on his head (laughs). [19] Here it's not a table, but a car (imitates a car weaving.)
Catal:	They earn money, at times fifty or sixty dollars a day. But there, where we live, the most they earn is ten quetzales a day. That's why they don't drink every day, they drink just once a week, those little jugs that they sell for a quetzal, the poorest. But here, money for beer is plentiful.
Xusita:	I think there is a bigger problem here, more vice.
María Juana:	The vice of liquor, the vice of women, . . . and of cars.
Catal:	It's hard when the men come alone, I mean, they come alone here; the wife stays there, it's hard there for the wives too. If he doesn't send money to his wife, what will she do with her children? And worse, as we said, if he looks for another [woman] here. And there the wife waits. She has to return to her father. And here we have renters. There in Guatemala we don't live among so many people. Each family is alone.
Xusita:	For my part, the reason I came to this country was for my husband, to be where he is. In Guatemala, the man has to give his wife a little money, but not here, because they both came to do something here, so they won't go back quite as poor.

MEN'S LIVES

These conversations serve to highlight some of the perceptions, feelings, attitudes and concerns of the Maya women of Indiantown. Through them, one glimpses as well the concerns and categories that mean the most to the men. When María Juana says: "The vice of liquor, the vice of women, and of cars" she has named the most serious problems men face, save one, AIDS. As noted above in the vignette of Alberto, Julio, Gilberto and friends, the legal connection between alcohol and driving in the United States is the source of the majority of the setbacks the young single men face.

The extreme gender imbalance, the almost absolute unavailability of young single Maya women, prohibits anything like courtship and marriage in the United States for all but a very few, at least in the present generation. The vanloads of prostitutes who visited Blue Camp each Friday and Saturday night, when they knew the men had their week's wages, were the vectors of the spread of AIDS to the most remote

Guatemalan villages, when the men return to their wives or girlfriends there.

Eating well is another concern of the men who live without their families. Those who *abonar* (board) at the home of a married couple are assured of a healthy hot meal each evening; for the others, fast food or canned food is the less-than-ideal solution. Most men know how to fry eggs, or meat, and reheat beans and tortillas, but only a few can really cook, so there is some dietary inadequacy. One man confessed: "It is only when we are here that we appreciate women's work. Here we have to do everything just like when we go to work on the fincas."

Most of the Indiantown Maya men live truly exiled lives, away from their homes, wives, children, and parents, the center of their existence. A tape or letter from home, a photo, the hope of a visit once every two years or so, are the only rays of joy in their lives of work. It is perhaps for this reason that families like Antonio's or Mekel's tend to collect a satellite of young men friends who become pro-tem extended family around these households. That is where they spend their leisure time. However, the capitalist work schedule doesn't allow for nearly the amount of leisure time that the Mayas enjoy in highland Guatemala, and so it is especially revealing of what is important to them to know how they invest their precious free time and energy. The most extraordinary investment is made in the emerging fiesta system. That will be the subject of the next chapter.

NOTES

1. The marimba is a wooden instrument similar to a xylophone, played by up to eight men at a time, each with two *vaquetas*, wood sticks with rubber-wrapped heads, in each hand. The keys are made of *hormiga* wood, which has a special resonance. The sound is produced by a sound box, also wood, suspended under each key. As the marimba is a key symbol of the Maya renaissance, it will be discussed in more detail later.

2. This information as well as other details about Indiantown life were shared by Sister Teresa Auad, director of InDios Cooperative.

3. The 1990 census for Indiantown population shows a total of 12,007, of whom seven thousand are male, five thousand female. The Hispanic population is listed as 25%, with Blacks also at 25%. This is not helpful in assessing the Guatemalan population, some of which is hidden in the Hispanic figures but most of which is not reported at all due to its undocumented status. Informants told William McKinney, a researcher from Cleveland State University, that there were about three thousand Guatemalans and one hundred Haitians in Indiantown (McKinney 1992).

4. This predilection for Mountain Dew is strikingly similar in all the Mayan communities throughout the United States in which I have been a guest. This includes groups in Homestead, Immokalee, Palm Beach and Lake Worth in Florida, Los Angeles, California, and Mesa, Arizona.

5. See Miralles (1987) for a detailed description of her findings in regard to food habits of Indiantown Maya. In several cases I believe her data to be incorrect due to translation problems.

6. The presence in Indiantown of Holy Cross Service Center, set up in 1980 to help Mexican farmworkers, was part of the reason for the Mayas to congregate there. Father Frank O'Laughlin, pastor of Indiantown from 1977 to 1986, is reported to have instructed his congregation during church services thus: *"No diga nada, no firme nada, hable con un abogado."* (Don't say anything, don't sign anything, talk to a lawyer). This conscientization of the Maya people about their rights is what made Indiantown an unofficial "sanctuary" in the sense of being part of the Sanctuary Movement, giving shelter and aid to Central Americans fleeing civil war.

7. Personal communication with the chief officer of the Riviera Beach immigration office confirmed for me the fact that the Border Patrol and the Immigration Service are two branches of the same entity with radically opposite missions, training, and attitudes. The first concentrates on deporting as many people as possible, the second is established to facilitate legal documentation of immigrants' rights to be here.

8. *La violencia* (the violence) is what most Maya people call the time from 1981 to 1983 when so many villages were razed, so many people massacred, so many refugees forced to leave their country.

9. According to the much-studied Mayan calendar system, each 20-day month has 4 year-bearer days on which special prayers and candles are offered. These year-bearer days correspond to the names of the gods which are the only ones with which a new year can begin. In Q'anjob'al they are Watan, Lambat, Ben and Chinax, and occur every fifth day.

10. The Guatemalan school year goes from January to the end of September. The two thousand dollar cost for each child was what could be called a smuggling fee; there are people who contract to bring children to the United States with false visas.

11. The system of ritual co-parenthood through the sponsorship of baptism of another couple's child is used in Guatemala much the same way as in Mexico, where it has been thoroughly studied. See Nutini and Bell 1980.

12. The *Ejército Guerrillero de los Pobres*, one of the four or five guerrilla groups operating in the western border areas of Guatemala during the early 1980's. The name means the Guerrilla Army of the Poor.

13. The *son* is also the word in many Maya languages for marimba, and denotes the slow waltz that is done to the most typical marimba music. The marimba can be used for any musical genre, but the slow three-count tunes are the most favored.

14. Each of these men has gone to Guatemala almost every year.

15. The conversations took place during a meeting where six women were present, other parts were recorded during a trip to Homestead to visit the Maya community there. The dialogue was tape recorded with the participants' permission, then transcribed and translated. The translations are all the author's.

16. In fact most of the women who use skirts use the ones made of bluejean cloth; its thickness compared to other cloth seems to suit them better.

17. A *corte* costs from $60 to $150, and many women have two or three. According to Burns (personal communication) the women did not wear *traje* in Indiantown before 1987. It is obvious that some men pride themselves on the richness with which they are able to clothe their wives; this includes gold chains, bracelets, and earrings as well as the *corte* and *huipil*.

18. What María Diega means is that they are carried by their mothers or sisters in the *peraje*, or shawl. Even heavy two or three year olds are hoisted up on the mother's back in the folds of the shawl, or swung around the front to nurse.

19. She means if he came to sell in the market plaza, he probably tied a small table to his back or carried it on his head, and the table is what is seen weaving and stumbling.

CHAPTER IV

Fiestas, Cargos and Identity

Fiesta! The word brings to mind a whirl of color, music, dance, food and spectacle. At least six public religio-cultural events are celebrated in Indiantown during the months between June and January. To understand the transfer of Mayan identity, let us move backstage, so to speak, to describe and analyze not only the event visible to the public, but the planning, organizing and negotiating that went on behind the scenes before and after the fiestas. The contestation among leaders, the rise of new leadership, and the formulation of new symbols all take place in the wings, and are essential to an understanding of the processes through which Mayan ethnic identity is defined in ritual.[1]

HISTORY OF FIESTAS IN INDIANTOWN

There is some confusion of memory about the origins of the oldest fiesta in Indiantown, that of the patron saint of San Miguel Acatán, St. Michael. Anthropologists (Earle 1989:9; Burns 1988b:25) and several Indiantown informants give the first year of the fiesta as 1984, but a printed program of the *Festividad de San Miguel Arcangel de la Comunidad Guatemalteca Kanjobal en Florida* (Festivity of St. Michael Archangel of the Guatemalan Kanjobal Community in Florida) is clearly dated October 1st, 1983. The event was organized by the Catholic pastor with members of one large family from San Miguel. This family also seems to have taken almost all of the public roles. The fiesta took place at the Catholic church, beginning with a religious service, followed by a socio-cultural ceremony in the school hall. The ritual pattern established at that time contained the same elements that were repeated in subsequent years: singing of the national anthem of Guatemala, a procession with the flag, a ceremonial entrance with a man and a woman dressed as elders or ancestors carrying incense, and the coronation of a queen. This was followed by poems, folklore dances and a closing with speeches meant to educate the public as well as honor the "helping community" of activist North Americans. The 1983 date is amazingly soon after the arrival of the first Mayas in Indiantown in late 1982 (Burns 1989b:49).

Similar material or oral memories from 1984 or 1985 were not available. Burns (1989b:53) says the Fiesta of San Miguel was held in 1986, 1987 and 1988, timed to correspond with the return of migrant workers from the North. Of course, the dates of saints' fiestas have been set by the official Catholic calendar since the Middle Ages; St. Michael's day has always been September 29.[2] In this case the fiesta timing has the advantage of fitting into the migrant labor cycle, as it fits the agricultural cycle in Guatemala. Burns described the 1986 fiesta (Burns 1989b:53ff) and filmed parts of it as well (Burns and Saperstien 1988).[3]

The program for the 1988 Festival de San Miguel announced an outdoor dance and sale of "all kinds of typical Latin American food" for Friday, September 30, with music provided by a unnamed marimba group and a Salvadoran disk jockey. Saturday's events included the coronation of the "Kanjobal queen" and her court, followed by "special recognition for persons who have collaborated with the Kanjobal community" and a dance. Sunday, October 2, saw, according to the program, a parade, a soccer game, a procession with the image of St. Michael, a solemn Catholic mass, and the awarding of trophies. The general organizer was Antonio, with Gaspar as president and Mekel as treasurer, and Xunik as responsible for decor. The entire organizing committee included thirty-seven people, most of whom were still active in some aspect of fiesta organization during the early 1990s.

The differences between the 1983 program and the 1988 one are remarkable: the latter event shows all the signs of being far more autonomously planned and executed by the Maya, with significant evidence pointing to both a shift from a strictly San Miguel Acatán focus toward a pan-Maya one, and a self-conscious valorization of Maya culture. An exhibition of typical women's dress was followed by a poetic evocation of each of ten municipal cultures, homes of Indiantown residents, and ended with this lament: "This is the message for the son absent from his beloved fatherland, with the notes of our beloved autochthonous instrument, the marimba, the sound of the *hormigo* wood which still weeps for the blood of the hero Tecún Umán."

The 1989 event had the title "*Maya Fiesta San Miguel Acatán de Guatemala en Indiantown Florida*" and took place September 29 to October 1. In that year the activities were held for the first time at the Big Mound Park rather than on the Catholic church grounds. The order of events was similar to the previous year, but now the local marimba had a name: *La Marimba Maya Sonora Tikal*. The printed program of four pages also had an elaborate drawing of Guatemala covered with symbols of indigenous pride, a page in English, and a last page dedicated to a tri-lingual explanation of the Corn Maya project, with its new logo and slogan, *Yamanon y co Cawilal yul K'exan Conob* (Seeking the unity, the dignity and the cultural survival of the Maize People.) The organizing committee was again headed by Antonio but absent Gaspar. Many of the same names appear on the list, but the total number is smaller. This reflects growing control of the event by Antonio and the Corn Maya members and their continued efforts to widen the focus beyond San Miguel. But even more revealing of this was the organization of a second fiesta, in honor of St. John (June 24), patron of San Juan Ixcoy and St. Peter (June 29), patron of San Pedro Soloma, two Q'anjob'al *municipios* near San Miguel in Huehuetenango. The *Festival Ixcoy Tz'uluma de Guatemala en Indiantown, Florida* was entirely sponsored by Corn Maya, had a tri-lingual three page program and even used the Maya enumeration and day names in the Q'anjob'al version. The cover shows a drawing of the archaeological site of Tikal with a border of Maya glyphs, reflecting the growing indigenism movement among at least the leaders of Corn Maya. Again, the fiesta offered a combination of a cultural festival, social dance, and soccer tourney, with masses in honor of the saints. The first night's activities took place at the Indiantown Civic Center, signalling a new sense of the rights of the Mayas to use public spaces in Indiantown.

Part of this event has been ably described by Earle (1989) who unpacks the symbolism to show how the fiesta, although a pastiche of secular ladino customs, costumes and traditions from widely disparate Maya areas, and historical and geographical inaccuracies, is at the same time a communication strategy for revitalization of Maya identity, an internal conversation with the Indiantown community about their exile situation:

> The Fiesta of Ixcoy-Tz'uluma provides a social text authored by those community members seeking to express in public ritual the current crises of the Guatemalan Mayas of South Florida and, through the appropriation

and transformation of indigenous and non-indigenous elements derived
from common, shared experience, to express a vision of how to encounter
and begin to resolve it. As leaders and supporters of the only Maya
community cultural organization in South Florida, they are rewriting
history as a myth which speaks forward from the present, a charter for a
cultural formation still in flux. (Earle 1989:17)

Photographs on the walls of the Corn Maya office were the only
evidence of the two fiestas of 1990: the *Velada Socio-Cultural Guatemex
90, 15 Septiembre* (Socio-cultural Soiree Guatemala-Mexico 1990),
which informants said was an attempt to unite the Guatemalan and
Mexican communities on the date of their countries' independence, and
the *Misa en Honor a San Miguel, Septiembre 29, 1990* (Mass in Honor
of St. Michael, September 29, 1990). For 1991, there is only the word of
informants that Gaspar was not involved with any of the events at the
church. This perhaps marks the beginning of the more obvious separation
between the Maya-oriented, religious events and the generalized Latino
secular festival.

All of this history came to bear on the organization and the execution
of the public festivals of 1992. In the study of ritual, departures from the
formulaic are quite as significant, perhaps even more so, than the
prescribed order of events. Each actualization of a ritual is a distinct
historical moment, even as it strives to recreate a mythical past, so that
history accumulates with each new "re-presentation." This is why it is
essential to know as much as possible about previous years' celebrations
in order to understand any annual ritual, since changes from past
procedure are signals of more than indiosyncrasy. As Earle notes, several
dynamics had created tension already by 1989, and the continued
presence of rival leadership, goals, interpretations, and symbol sets
continued into, and affected, the events of 1992. One of these tensions
had and has to do with an assimilationist stance versus an increasingly
polarized indigenism and the perceptions of the leaders about who in the
"gringo" world could be counted upon to support either position. Another
related tension involved the search for themes promoting unity rather
than the divisions present in Indiantown (and in Guatemala) between
Catholics and Evangelical Protestants, ladinos and Indians, and
advocates of a pan-Maya entity versus those focused on loyalty to their
own *municipio* and language-group. Furthermore, there was always
present among all the observers and participants of the events a deep
distrust regarding the financial accountability of the leadership. It is

against this background that we now turn to a description and analysis of the 1992 fiesta cycle in Indiantown.

FIESTA CYCLE 1992

In mid-May, 1992, a full five months before the Fiesta of San Miguel, the cycle began with the elaborate organization for the Copa Quetzal soccer tournament, which lasted thirteen weeks, leading into the Festival Maya Quetzal in mid-September. St. Michael's day was indeed observed at the end of September, with secular and religious commemorations in the neighboring town of Lake Worth as well as in Indiantown. Dissatisfaction with the non-Mayanness of these fiestas led to a spur-of-the-moment organization of the Fiesta de San Rafael in October. Two other minor events could also be considered a part of the cycle: a memorial to mark the first anniversary of the deaths of seven Maya cane-cutters in a tragic accident, and an end of the year dance on December 31. Thus, if one were writing a tourist guide for folk fiestas in the Indiantown area during 1992, the list would look like this:

June 21 through September 6:	Copa Quetzal Soccer Tournament
September 13:	Festival Maya Quetzal
September 19, 27:	Lake Worth San Miguel Festival
September 26, 27:	Indiantown Fiesta de San Miguel
October 22:	Memorial Awakateko
October 24:	Fiesta de San Rafael
December 31:	New Year Fiesta

Since this order of events affected the dynamics of the cycle as a whole, the following treatment will be chronological.

Copa Quetzal/Festival Maya Quetzal

June 21 dawned hot and sunny. By eight-thirty the sports field behind the Indiantown Middle School had been transformed into a micrcosm of Maya life in the United States. Over two hundred athletes, officials and organizers, as well as over three hundred spectators, had gathered for the inauguration ceremonies of the Copa Quetzal soccer tournament. On the preceding Sundays the field had also seen action as eight soccer teams practiced for the thirteen weeks of play, the umpires attended training classes, and Maya entrepreneurs set up their food sale booths. Other preparations took place at the offices of Corn Maya, the sponsoring organization, as players came in to purchase their photo ID cards, team captains paid their $175 entry fee, vendors solicited permits ($10) to sell food on the grounds, and officials studied the handbook of rules sent from Guatemala.

On inauguration day, the eight teams paraded onto the field, resplendent in uniforms displaying their team names. Each team of twenty-two players was accompanied by a *madrina*, a young woman in Maya dress. Loudspeakers blared the national anthems as the flags of Guatemala and the United States were placed next to the broadcast booth. Speeches were made by Corn Maya officials, Julio, Emilio and Antonio. The vendors, including Gaspar with his "San Miguel Dining Room" were starting to prepare the food and drinks they would sell. Admission of $.50 was collected at the gate; the Corn Maya organizers attempted to forestall critiques of their financial operations by assigning this task to church personnel. The announcers provided "color commentary" on the games, interspersed with taped marimba music.

Four games were played each Sunday from June 21 to September 6; this was a preparation for the ensuing Fiesta Maya Quetzal held on September 13. The dates are significant in several ways. The inauguration in late June corresponded not only to the summer solstice but also to the traditional Fiesta of San Juan-San Pedro, the patronal celebration of Antonio's home municipality. The summer-long tournament was meant to provide a healthy pastime for the stable Indiantown population, those who do not join the migrant stream from May to September.[4] At the same time, the September Fiesta was deliberately placed near the traditional Independence Day date [5] in order to meet the expectations that there would be some public event timed to reunite all the migrants and residents.

The sports teams were formed by young men from the same municipality/language group. Thus *Club Awakateco* had a majority of members from Aguacatán, *Deportivo Totonicapán* represented the K'iché speakers, *Deportivo Atlanta* and *Deportivo Indiantown* were made up of Indiantown Maya not from San Miguel, while *Juventud Migueleño* and *Club Amistad* were predominantly Migueleños. *Jupiter* and *Savana '92* were from the coast near Indiantown, and had a higher percentage of ladino players.

The course of the thirteen-week tournament was not entirely smooth. The rivalry between Corn Maya organizers and Gaspar's family, who had initiated the San Miguel fiesta preparations, broke out on several occasions, masked as protests about umpires' calls, disagreements about insurance for injured players, and questions about the vendor fees. However, in a replication of Maya community councils in Guatemala, the disputes were settled by talk circles held at night in the Corn Maya office. Frank and direct criticism of the organizers was accepted gracefully, and several men with a real talent for conciliation suggested positive solutions. On one occasion Julio told the critics: "Your word here is a step for us, a step forward, not backward, because it helps us to become better."

A huge green and white striped tent in the public space of Big Mound Park was the scene of the Festival Maya Quetzal. A stage at one end faced chairs arranged as in a theater. Although it was raining, it was dry under the tent, and the *corte* cloth covering the front of the stage and the stairs up to the queen's throne lent a colorful touch. The marimba was in place as well as a large canvas mural representing the mountain homeland.[6] A printed program was available; it had also been distributed the evening before at the Catholic "Guatemalan" mass. There Antonio had made a speech thanking God for ten years of Maya presence in Indiantown and inviting everyone to the Festival, and the priest had publicly recognized the young women who were to be queens at the event. The program was a hodgepodge of photos, symbols, and bilingual messages promoting unity and celebrating the years of peaceful life in the United States.

The actual order of events followed the established pattern. Emilio, dressed in a suit and tie, welcomed the representatives of Martin County, Florida Atlantic University, the University of Florida, and then led the singing of the interminable Guatemalan anthem. The blue and white flag was honored not as a symbol of the Guatemalan nation, but for the quetzal bird in its center, a bird, according to the announcer, which cannot live in captivity. The microphone was passed from Emilio to Carlos, a visitor from Guatemala, who had brought the rented costumes for the Conquest Dance. Carlos: (over a marimba crescendo) "Thus the marimba identifies Guatemala. When we speak of custom, we speak of the Maya people." Antonio: "Corn Maya takes satisfaction and pleasure that for the first time all Guatemalans celebrate under this roof without any distinction of races or languages."

The soccer team godmothers then spoke. Sonia: "We all unite, one Guatemalan people. We are here in this foreign country becoming more fraternal, walking together." She quoted from the *Pop Vuh*[7] and added, "We want to share our culture with you. When we as Mayas were enslaved by the Spanish people, we had our hero; thanks to him we have our freedom, to share with you. We unite with every country that gives us a hand and makes us welcome." Note that Sonia conflates Guatemalan independence (1821) with the native uprising of Atanasio Tzul (1820), or perhaps with the original opposition to the conquest led by Tecún Umán in 1524. She also speaks, as do all the organizers, as if her principal audience is the non-Mayan public, when in fact the only white faces present belong to anthropologists, several University of Florida students, and the priest and nuns from the Catholic church. One of the stated purposes of the Festival, to share Mayan culture with other Indiantown residents, was frustrated by the lack of interest on the part of these "others," but the speeches had been prepared long in advance.

The formal entrance procession began with two small boys carrying a toy marimba. A tiny girl carrying the sash for the princess was followed by the young *Princesa K'iché*, an invited guest from Guatemala. She was accompanied by Santiago, dressed as a *zahorín* or native priest, carrying burning incense. As they reached the stage, the couple knelt to kiss the earth in the four cardinal directions. The princess spoke in Spanish and K'iché, then received her crown and sash, which read: *Mial Rikal Tinamit Mayab* (the daughter of the Maya people).

Trophies and diplomas were distributed to the participants of the soccer tournament. A Mexican dance troupe performed. Throughout all this nonstop programming, the crowd of perhaps a thousand was quiet, respectful and passive. Everyone perked up and began to crowd around the stage, however, when the next part of the program began. For the first time in ten years of exile, the masked dancers of the *Baile de la Conquista* (Dance of the Conquest) appeared before the astonished eyes of the Indiantown Mayas. Fifteen masked dancers, [8] eleven representing Spanish conquistadores, two in black face representing the Mayas, including Tecún Umán, and two who represented missionaries, danced for almost an hour, with small intricate steps, stifled in heavy costumes covered by mirrors and ribbons. One marimba player accompanied them. This was quite a coup for Corn Maya, and had only become possible because of Antonio's trip to Guatemala, the support of the Guatemalan ministry of tourism INGUAT, and the Cleveland State University Maya Studies Program. There was keen interest in this part of the program but what followed brought laughter and applause. The *Conquista* dancers were all Awakatekos, but the men from Totonicapán had also organized a dance, which they called *Convite Totonicapán*. *Convite* could perhaps best be translated by the word "amusement"; the intent was farcical, since the dancers wore halloween costumes representing animals and clowns, but mimicked the steps of the Conquest Dance. These dancers were recalled by audience demand, and performed several times. The *Convite* dance is not unknown in Guatemala but the element of surprise was an added attraction.[9]

The crowd was gone by 5:30P.M., apparently well satisfied with the combination of civic event and Maya patronal fiesta. The entertainment had included food booths, the sale of typical Maya clothing, and of T-shirts bearing the legend *Fiesta Maya Quetzal, Indiantown Florida, 1992* and graced by a quetzal bird flying over Lake Atitlán. These symbols had been combined with the marimba music, Maya royalty, incense and traditional dancing to produce a celebration that had a definite Maya character, yet was deftly adapted to the exile situation.

The evaluation of the event—one of the chief duties of an organizing committee according to the modern Catholic training given in Guatemala—began during the clean-up that Sunday night, but continued each time a group of people gathered in the Corn Maya office over the next three weeks. Stated goals were to promote unity, educate the Maya people about their own culture, and present a showcase to the outside world. The financial outlay, which fell short of income more than three thousand dollars, was not a cause for chagrin; the Corn Maya leadership declared themselves proud to have proved to their detractors that they were able to organize a festival successful in the ways that counted for them—attendance, the apparent satisfaction of the audience, the opportunity to educate. If anything, the deficit was considered proof of the self-sacrificing nature of the Corn Maya organization. Although some attendees, among them Diego and Xusita, remarked that the Conquest Dance was hardly authentic since in Guatemala those chosen to dance dedicate themselves by religious vow to a year of preparation, and the significance of the dance is sacred and world-renewing rather than entertainment, they were pleased that the attempt to approximate the old customs had been made.

Antonio, director of Corn Maya, expressed satisfaction that the invented Maya cultural festival had been well received. Past celebrations of Independence Day had been met with complaints that it was "not ours—not indigenous." But he had not wished to leave the ladinos out completely—the word Quetzal in the festival title was meant as a signal to them of a unity of national origin.

At one point several months later, Julio offered the assessment that Corn Maya ought to forget about organizing sports events; as competitive activities, they divide rather than unite, and cause greater expense than income. Pablo, another leader, admitted that he had never seen the Conquest Dance or the *Convite* in his Huehuetenango town, saying: "The person who has two or three years of school and has worked with a machete his whole life is not that enthusiastic about cultural displays; we need to educate the people." As time went on, other negative assessments were voiced. Alberto and Genaro were both bitter about what they perceived as the autocratic way Antonio had set the schedule for the fiesta. With hindsight, there was also some disagreement about the intended audience and goals. As can be noted in the following statements, the goal of displaying Maya culture to non-Mayas took a back seat to the goal of unity for Guatemalans.

Antonio:	The fiesta was for Guatemalans, to conscienticize and teach them, to provide for an annual reunion.
Alberto:	The fiesta was to unify the Guatemalan community, but should have included more members and more women in the planning.
Julio:	The fiesta was for all the people, indigenous or not, to educate them, to help them forget the problems, the violence, to do something joyful, to strengthen us as Maya leaders. We didn't want to focus on September 15th and Independence; we don't have freedom in Guatemala, that's why we are here.
Pablo:	The fiesta was for Guatemalans, for us to appreciate our own culture, and to let Americans know there is a group of people interested in preserving our culture even here. It was to remember our country and to unite the people in the memory.
Genaro:	The fiesta was to find a space to show a little of what is ours; to unify the people more, to share with our neighbors the way we are.

When one considers the investment of time and energy of these same leaders, the centrality of the event in their own lives becomes obvious. The hours represent evenings after work, usually four or five days a week, plus a commitment to most of Saturday and Sunday, for a period from May through September. Approximate hours donated to the fiesta are listed here:

Antonio:	600 hours
Alberto:	128
Julio:	480
Emilio:	480

Pablo: 480
Genaro: 100

For several of these men, their contribution to the fiesta was between
eight and ten percent of their total waking hours in a year. For most of
them, the elation of having orchestrated an elaborate public event
successfully, the increased prestige gained for their organization, Corn
Maya, through the traditional path of self-sacrifice for the community,
the consequent growth of their own leadership capabilities, and the
camaraderie of the group was sufficient reward for their investment.

Fiesta San Miguel-Lake Worth

Two weeks after the Festival Maya Quetzal was the traditional date for
the celebration of San Miguel. An organization in Lake Worth, Florida,
Centro Guatemalteco, sponsored a cultural festival and social dance on
Saturday, September 19 in the Sons of Italy Lodge, followed by a mass
in honor of St. Michael at a local Catholic church on Sunday, September
27. Although this event did not take place in Indiantown, it is included
in the Indiantown fiesta cycle because the Maya population moves
frequently between the two towns; because most of the organizers of the
Indiantown fiestas, including Antonio and Gaspar, were present in Lake
Worth; and because an almost electric connection of expectations,
contestation, rivalry and mutual influence linked the sponsoring groups
and their largely overlapping constituencies.

   More analysis of the place of the Centro Guatemalteco in the South
Florida Maya power grid will be provided in Chapter V; for now, suffice
it to explain that this is a social and legal services agency serving
Guatemalans, founded by the former Catholic pastor of Indiantown with
a group of Cuban and Colombian supporters. The Cuban director and
Guatemalan staff were perceived by at least two other groups as sell-outs
to assimilation. The Guatemalan ladino population of North Palm Beach
and Jupiter claimed to have proposed the Centro, only to see its
ownership taken over by others. The more radical indigenists of Corn
Maya scorn what they call the Centro's patronizing of Maya clients.

   With this background in mind, the wording of the flyer announcing
the September 19 festival was no surprise. The conflicts were evident in
the text. "Great Guatemalan Fiesta" it said, "in honor of our patron St.
Michael the Archangel and our independence. The queen of the fiesta
Kanjobal and Miss Independence will be invested. Our autochthonous

instrument the marimba will entertain us. . . . Come to participate in our 'Chapin' fiesta "[10]

The stage in the corner of the Sons of Italy lodge was adorned with a painted mural of two large quetzal birds facing each other across a Maya pyramid. *Corte* cloth covered the risers to the stage. Antonio and his family were seated at a table in another corner, listening to the Indiantown marimba *Sonora Tikal*. Gaspar and his family were in the kitchen, preparing to sell tostadas and sodas. The early arrivers were mostly young men from Indiantown, looking for a dance; they cheered wildly when the second marimba group, of middle-aged ladinos from Miami, invited Julio, the Indiantown drummer, to play with them. The announcer, a ladino member of the Centro staff, took the stage and opened the ceremonies with the entrance of the Guatemalan flag and the singing of the anthem. He amplified: "It doesn't matter what our hometown may be, we are all Guatemalans." By this time, the seats were beginning to fill up. One of Gaspar's daughters, also a member of the Centro staff, continued with a long impassioned speech about the independence of Guatemala from the conquering Spanish, the way Guatemalans have preserved their customs, how they have suffered and continue to suffer in the refugee camps, as other Latin peoples, including Cubans, have suffered.[11] She repeated her exhortation in Q'anjob'al and then in English. The male staff member then spoke about unity: "It doesn't matter if you are from the West, the East or the North, [12] here we are all Guatemalan. We also want to remind you, this country has given opportunity to all, all who want to better themselves. We want to give thanks to this great country which protects us, gives us everything, without our even looking for it, if we work hard. All Guatemalans are men and women of work; this is why we want to demonstrate our qualities. We can better ourselves, education is open to all."

He returned the microphone to the Q'anjob'al woman, who began: "It gives me great pleasure to present our culture, although our country represents many cultures . . ." At this the court of the *Reina Indígena* (Indian Queen), pairs of children, entered dancing the *son*. The very young woman "queen" also approached her place on the stage with the steps of the *son*, played by the Indiantown marimba. After they took their places, the male announcer introduced the *Señorita Independencia* (or Miss Guatemala, as the program had it), and her two maids of honor, young women in formal gowns, escorted by young men in suits and ties. They entered the hall accompanied by the Miami marimba.

This blatant separation of ladino and indigenous symbols, including the two announcers, the two marimba bands, the different dress, music, steps, language, and even the age difference between the two honored young women was commented upon with sadness and shock by the Indiantown Mayas who were present. The confusion of messages was further scrambled when the priest-founder of the Centro introduced a visiting Huehuetenango priest to the audience, and they both proceeded to crown Miss Independence and invest with a ceremonial *huipil* the "Indian Queen." The Q'anjob'al mistress of ceremonies was at the same moment announcing that the Centro is for all, no matter what religion. The "Indian Queen" was allowed to speak and invoked the blessing of St. Michael and exhorted the audience not to forget Huehuetenango, Tikal, the quetzal, their mountains, and so on. It is likely that the loud applause which greeted her had more to do with her status as a single Maya woman and the anxiety of the young, largely male audience to get on with the dance than with her words. The dance began in due time, but the unequal number of men and women made for many unwilling wallflowers. The entire event was a display of mixed messages which, it must be noted, cannot be blamed on the organizers. The divisions apparent in the evening's activities run deep in Guatemalan society, where the two sides meet each other socially only in peripheral ways. But in the exile situation, attempts to assume or to force unity appear assimilationist or patronizing. On this occasion, the resentment at what appeared to the Mayas as condescension surfaced later in the fiesta cycle.

A week after the festival at the Sons of Italy Lodge, which location could be read as an attempt on the part of the non-Guatemalan organizers to showcase how immigrant groups are expected to assimilate yet retain a largely superficial ethnicity, the same Centro Guatemalteco leadership sponsored a special procession at a regular Sunday evening Spanish language mass in Saint Luke's church, Lake Worth. Only about a fourth of the congregation was Guatemalan, but it included all of the staff and families associated with the Centro. A small statue of the archangel was carried around the inside of the church by four of the Q'anjob'al dressed in their typical clothing. A brief reception in the church hall afterward was crowded with a general mix of Latin Americans who wanted to try Guatemalan tamales and see how the *son* is danced. This was the one event where the oft-stated purpose of showing/explaining Maya culture to non-Mayas actually was implemented and, even in this case, only for a few. The Indiantown Mayas were not present at this later event, because it conflicted in time with the last hours of the two-day San Miguel fiesta there. It is to that central celebration that we now turn.

Fiesta San Miguel-Indiantown

It is Friday evening, the day before the Fiesta de San Miguel, and preparations are underway all over Indiantown. At the store belonging to Gaspar's daughter Francisca, a crudely-lettered sign announces: "FOR ALL GUATEMALANS, GRAND FIESTA, at Indian Mound Park, Saturday 8P.M., Sunday 10-7, Music by Miguel Angel. Surprises for children." Indeed, at Big Mound Park, a large red and white striped tent has been set up, but there is no visible activity there. Farm labor buses are rolling into town, some from North Carolina. At the Catholic church grounds, several families arrive with seeds to plant their corn in the community garden. Xunik and his crew of men and boys have begun to chop pine needles and make the *pita*, the garlands with which they will adorn the carrying platform for the statue of St. Michael. Inside the church, Mekel and his friends are stringing up crepe paper chains in fall colors, sprays of feathers and silk flowers. The pillars are wrapped with blue and white ribbons, the color of Guatemala's flag. Mekel revealed that he and Xunik were the heads of the "church committee" for the fiesta and that he had made two trips to Stuart to buy the decorations. He had been on the "fiesta committee" with Gaspar in other years, but quit because decisions were made in his absence and because Gaspar was not involved in the religious portion of the celebration, and claimed to be too busy to attend the mass for the patron saint. The pastor, Fr. Juan, filled out the picture: he is happy to promote the religious side of the fiesta but has little sympathy for the social aspect. He has been concerned that no preparations were being made at the church, and was delighted when Mekel and Xunik came to him and offered to form a committee, saying: *Padre, vamos a hacer la fiesta como Dios manda* (Father, we are going to put on the fiesta the way God commands).

By five-thirty on Saturday afternoon, the marimba choir *Peregrinos de la Cruz* (Pilgrims of the Cross)[13] is practicing, the decor is all in place, including St. Michael sharing his platform with bright *corte* cloth and potted chrysanthemums. The altar as well is covered with a *corte*. The usual church bulletin has been replaced by a printed song sheet announcing "Solemn sung mass in honor of St. Michael Archangel in the Catholic Church of Holy Cross, 7P.M., concelebrated by Padre Juan and Padre Alfredo, a visiting Guatemalan priest. Procession with the image of the holy patron." A printed image of St. Michael driving a sword of justice into the back of the devil decorates one corner of the program, a scroll proclaiming "Mayas Present in Florida" another, and a map of Guatemala is surrounded by the words of the songs to be sung, including the traditional song to St. Michael:

> *Quién como Dios, nadie como Dios.*
> *San Miguel Arcangel, gran batallador,*
> *Defienda la Iglesia que Cristo fundó.*
> *San Miguel Arcangel, oye la oración*
> *De este pobre pueblo que implora perdón.*
> (Who is like God, No one is like God.
> St. Michael Archangel, Great warrior,
> Defend the church, which Christ founded.
> St. Michael Archangel, hear the prayer
> Of this poor people who begs pardon.) [14]

The choice of music and the printed program were the work of the choir, led by Antonio and made up of all the leadership of Corn Maya. Those activists who are K'iché speakers from Totonicapán are familiar with St. Michael who is also patron of their town, and they are enthusiastically supportive of this celebration which is ostensibly for the people of San Miguel Acatán, Huehuetenango, but which they read with an expanded meaning.

Antonio, who knows the power of the microphone, explains to the assembled congregation in both Spanish and Q'anjob'al the meaning of the fiesta and the order of the procession. However, he deftly avoids the criticism he has experienced previously for taking a leadership role. He explains that he has "been asked to announce this." Everyone has a candle in hand. The cross-bearer goes first, followed by all the women in a double line, resplendent in their new *huipiles* and *cortes*. [15] Then come Eul and Dolores carrying flowers and the elderly couple who represent the *Txutxmam* (ancestors) carrying incense, followed by the image of the saint carried by four men. The two priests and all the other men fall in behind the statue and the marimba players bring up the end of the procession,[16] which takes one turn around the church grounds, [17] and reenters the church. Holy Cross church holds about 250 people seated, but tonight it is more like 400 and there are not even places to stand. The incense and the smoke of the snuffed candles makes the air too opaque to take pictures and adds to the general feeling of similarity to the parallel event in Guatemala. Missing however, are the loud firecrackers, the crowded streets through which the procession winds, visiting saints' statues from neighborhoods of the town and from nearby municipalities, and the pine needles on the floor of the church. The Mayas espressed regret at not being able to do these things, but claim that United States law prohibits them.

Father Juan begins the service, just as is done in Guatemala, with a long list of petitions requested by individuals:

> We are celebrating this holy mass in thanksgiving for Antonio José Tomás, Isabel Francisco, Juan de Juan. We also ask for the health of María Pedro, who is in Guatemala, for Juana Martín Pedro, for the eternal rest of Felipe Aguilar and for his daughter Petrona Aguilar and also for blessings on Angel, the child of Gabriel, who is with us here.

The effect of this litany (it takes place at every Saturday night mass but is especially long tonight) is to surround the congregation with familiar sounding names, to unite families in thought, if not physically, and to signal the seriousness of the ritual when performed in exile.

When Antonio's wife Margarita begins to read the Scripture lesson, all hear the account of a heavenly battle (Apocalypsis 12:7-12) in which Michael and his angels entered into combat with the devil and cast him under the earth. This corresponds to the visual image of the angel clad in armor, sword in hand, standing on the neck of the fanged and winged black dragon, with flames licking around him. The choice between good and evil is made crystal clear and to have St. Michael on one's side is portrayed as a guarantee of spiritual victory.[18]

Padre Alfredo reads the Bible story of Jesus' meeting with Philip and Nathaniel, in which Jesus tells Nathaniel that he will see the heavens opened and the angels of God carrying messages up and down. This text (John I:43-51) establishes the connection between Christ and the angels as his messengers. The lengthy but forcefully delivered sermon is an appeal to reject the allure of the materialism of the United States, to remember the traditions of Guatemala, the language and music, but above all the faith. He exhorts the people to place themselves under the protection of St. Michael, who reminds us that there is no one and nothing to compare to God.

The mass continues through its regular sequence, and at the end there is a rush for a photo opportunity in front of the statue. However, there is no other activity at the church; everyone knows that the entire community is anxious to rush over to Big Mound Park to attend the secular part of the fiesta.

By 9 P.M. there is little space to park. The tone of the event is evident in the pushing and shoving at the entrance gate where Gaspar's family members are collecting a five dollar fee. The pre-teen girls who are designated as the court of the "queen of San Miguel" are already standing on the stage with their even younger escorts, dressed in white Q'anjob'al *huipiles*. A backdrop mural of St. Michael gives a symbolic representation of the reason for the fiesta. Gaspar's daughter Francisca tries to speak over the loud hoots, catcalls, and whistles of the large crowd of over two thousand. The contast with the tranquil crowd at the Fiesta Maya Quetzal could not be greater. The featured performer of the evening, a rock bandleader from El Salvador, stage-named Miguel Angel, invests the girls with sashes. The announcer has to plead with the rowdy audience six times to open a space so the pairs of children can leave the stage. Francisca tries to give a little speech. "We have the great presence of Miguel Angel, I hope you enjoy it because it is for you. This is exclusively for the people of Indiantown and its neighboring towns." She is shouted out by the increasingly restless crowd, who are mostly young, male, and eager to get their money's worth of dancing started. She hands over the mike to a male announcer, who needs to keep talking for about an hour and a half before the music begins, because there is a short in the sound system. He tries an off-color joke which is met with only subdued and embarrassed laughter. He tries *Viva Guatemala!, Viva Mexico! Viva El Salvador!, Viva los Estados Unidos!* Judging from the crowd reaction after each *viva*, the crowd is predominantly Mexican. It is late when the dancing starts, but, as at the Lake Worth event, there are so few young women present that the men resort to dancing without partners.

All during this time, the Maya men, women, and children, most of them dressed in their typical clothing, are seated on bleachers at the back of the tent. It is clear that they have no desire or intention to do more than listen to the Mexican salsa music. Anyone who had hoped to dance in the old way, to dance the *son* all night to celebrate the end of one year and to push the gods of time into granting another year, was left out of this generic Latino festival, which had tried hard to be for everyone. The comments of Mekel and Malín, Fabiana, Dolores, Antonio, Margarita, and others who had been at the church, and had arrived at the park too late for the short cultural program, are to the point, in a symbolic fashion: *No hay marimba* —There is no marimba. Gaspar is busy selling tacos and soda until well after midnight. There are a good number of inebriated men under the tent and in small groups clustered around ice chests in the parking lot. Sunday's crowd is much thinner, more like five hundred people. Today the entrance fee is three dollars. A soccer game, the last of a one week "lightning" tournament, is being played between *Aguacatán* and *Jupiter*, a team which is made up of Jakaltekos from the coastal Florida town of that name. Julio and his friends are videotaping the game to send back to Aguacatán. Under the red tent, the Maya families again crowd the bleachers, while the young men, some Mayas and some Mexican, mill around listening to the salsa. It is hot and soda sales are brisk. There are no more public announcements or ceremonies; the fiesta ends in the early evening.

Gaspar and his family were the sole organizers of this secular fiesta. Prior to that weekend, he had complained that no one wanted to be on his committee. He also complained about the criticism that had been directed at him in past years when he used to go house to house collecting start-up funds for the event. He had decided to raise the money through food sales at the Maya Quetzal soccer tournament; that way, no one could accuse him of using community money for his own profit. He had indeed raised over $3000 with his sales, but had over $8000 in fiesta expenses. Nevertheless, he and his wife were pleased that they had not lost money and had been able to send $500 to aid the reconstruction of the church in San Miguel Acatán.[19] It was never learned whether there was a profit for Gaspar, and there was never a public disclosure of the accounting. The whole affair was a private effort. He stated he had moved it from the church grounds so that non-Catholics would not think it was a church event. *Ahora no es de la iglesia, pero es Católica, porque es para el santo*, he said. "Now it is not a church affair, but it is Catholic, because it is for the saint." However, he and María Juana were very tired, and doubted they would "make" the fiesta again. They would avoid it by returning to Guatemala for San Miguel's day the next year. María Juana was the lone woman cooking, and was left with all the pots and pans to wash. In effect, Gaspar and María Juana probably each put in just a little under four hundred hours of work, mostly buying, preparing and selling food for the thirteen weeks prior to the fiesta. Their daughter Francisca, who was in charge of tent rental, insurance, security guards, musical entertainment, the cultural ceremony, and the "lightning" soccer tournament, worked around three hundred hours. On the church side of the event, Mekel and his small committee of two spent perhaps twenty hours each, while Xunik donated about ten hours to the effort. The marimba choir which played before and during the mass also required a time investment by its members, but this is a regular weekly commitment for them.

It is interesting to compare the answers given to the question of "For whom was this fiesta?" with those given in connection with the Fiesta Maya Quetzal. In general, the purpose of the San Miguel event had not been thought through at all by its organizers and the reasons enunciated were widely different, reflecting the much looser organization, *ad hoc* planning, and the non-ideological nature of Gaspar's leadership. It must be emphasized that both Mekel and Xunik, although they had been associated with Gaspar in organizing the event in former years, had little or no articulation with him and his family in the 1992 celebration.

Mekel: The fiesta is for all of us, to remember our culture. It isn't the same [as what we did in Guatemala] but it is similar. I do it [decorate the church] to remember, to respect God's house, to create joy. It is also for the Americans, to show who we are. Gaspar does it outside, not in the church.

Xunik: Those who don't make a fiesta are Protestants; they no longer believe. They don't even use candles. The saint doesn't eat, but he needs light. It is an obligation to give up the day and to give the saint his candles.

Gaspar: The fiesta is for the children, those who came as refugees in 1982 or 1983, those who don't remember the culture of Guatemala. We are real refugees; those who come later are immigrants. We, my family, wanted to make the fiesta as we do in Guatemala, so they learn about it, so they don't forget, and leave behind their heritage.[20]

Maria Juana: The committee members make the fiesta to give honor to the patron, in order to not forget the fiesta in our land.

Francisca: The fiesta is for entertainment. Gringos can't understand that. We also do it in honor of the patron of our town on the customary date. It is for Guatemalans, but we can't turn our back on others. It used to be at the church but it no longer is because there are too many people, and people from other religions are annoyed.

Around town in the weeks following September 27, there was one consistent comment: *No hubo marimba.* There was no marimba. This was a symbolic way, as noted earlier, of saying the fiesta was not typical, was not Mayan, was not Guatemalan. Perhaps there was also some nostalgia at not having been able to dance, and some discomfort with being lumped together with the general Latino population in terms of their perceived musical taste. The dissatisfaction signified by *No hubo marimba* surfaced soon enough in several iniatives taken by other groups to remedy the lack and to provide occasions for the Maya people to dance the *son*. A small group of Q'anjob'al people representing the *municipio* of San Rafael La Independencia began almost immediately to organize what they hoped would be a more typically Maya event for their saint's day on October 24, and the directors of Corn Maya began thinking about a possible social event featuring the marimba for November or December. Before either of these could take place, however, another public ritual was organized and carried out, this time through the unexpected initiative of one of the quieter residents of Indiantown, Alberto.

Memorial Awakateko

Seven large votive candles had been placed on the step in front of the altar at Holy Cross church. Each candle represented one of the Maya men killed in a farm accident that had repercussions from Tallahassee to Aguacatán, a Maya *municipio* near the departmental capital of Huehuetenango. On October 17, 1991, seven Awakateko sugar cane workers from Indiantown lost their lives when their contractor's car went into an unfenced irrigation canal in the early morning mist. The event was reported in a four-column story in the New York *Times* (Rohter 1991) together with a description of Maya life in Indiantown and the violence in Guatemala from which they fled.[21] A video made during the funeral service at the Palm Beach Catholic cathedral shows a solemn ceremony attended by many hundreds of Maya people and packed with the press, local and national. The bishop and ten priests officiated together; the music and Scripture readings were in the K'iché, Awakateko and Q'anjob'al Maya languages. Antonio and another Indiantown activist named Alejandro had organized the collection to send the bodies back home, and lined up interviews for the press, while the former Catholic pastor of Indiantown concentrated on seeking compensation from the Okeelanta Sugar Corporation, and working with the Florida Department of Labor to promote changes in farm labor transportation regulations. The Palm Beach *Post* sent a reporter to Aguacatán in October, 1992 to check on the workers' compensation checks being sent to the victims' families (Shifrel and Shuchman 1992a). The court cases were still undecided at that time.

But in Indiantown, the anniversary of the accident impelled Alberto to organize his fellow Awakatekos and other friends to hold a memorial service, beginning with the usual Thursday evening Catholic mass. After an opening hymn sung in Awakateko proclaimed "Today, brothers, we have faith and will to live; God has a place for us" he gave an inspiring talk from the altar. "We need to remember our brothers, and we all need to live as if we expect to die any day." He had brought the seven candles and had also arranged for a flower nursery worker to bring two large bouquets to put on the altar. Father Juan, a special friend of Alberto's, mentioned the names of the seven victims at least four times in his sermon. "They were killed," he said, "because they were doing their duty; they were going to work to help their families."

After the church service, Alberto invited all those attending to a *vigilio*, a vigil, to be held at the White Camp house where two of the victims had lived. He and his friends had set up rows of chairs outside the house, and about a hundred people gathered there to watch the video of the funeral. The young men had prepared, just as at a wake in Guatemala, hot chocolate and sweet rolls for the mourners. Several people bought copies of the video. The respectful silence continued until the video ended, when people talked quietly among themselves and then went home.

Alberto was justifiably proud of himself for the success of his efforts. The event also served for him as a farewell; it was the following day when he had to report to serve six weeks in jail for his DUI offense. Although at the time of the accident in 1991 Antonio and Alejandro had taken the leadership roles in organizing a way for Indiantown to respond, a year later Alberto's iniative and leadership came into play, and with assurance and quiet dignity he provided a satisfying ritual moment for the community. His friends expressed their admiration and gratitude.

Fiesta San Rafael

On a misty evening just two weeks after the San Miguel fiesta in the park, two Migueleños came to the Corn Maya office to consult with Antonio. Joaquín and Miguel were the spokespersons for the large number of Indiantown Maya who were unhappy and unsatisfied with the fiesta. Joaquín explained: "That fiesta was not about San Miguel. It was no good. [Before] everyone used to contribute something, tortillas, meat; then it was really nice. Then that Gaspar came and ruined everything." What the two men proposed was to organize a fiesta for the day of San

Rafael, October 24. Could they use the Corn Maya marimba and
marimba team? How much did Antonio think a mass would cost?
Antonio appeared pleased to be consulted by two men older than himself,
especially since the plan would bring into the public arena the
commonly-held poor opinion of Gaspar's effort. It would be even more
pointed because Joaquín and Miguel were not from San Rafael La
Independencia, a municipality that had legally separated itself from San
Miguel within living memory and whose sons and daughters could be
expected to try to rival anything the Migueleños did. No, these two men
were from San Miguel itself, but, as Joaquín explained, almost all the
thirty members of his work crew were from San Rafael and were willing
to cooperate. What was wanted was a celebration that would be more
typically Mayan, more familiar to the community, more a statement of
their identity. Antonio suggested a simple affair of refreshments and
marimba music after the regular Saturday mass, and encouraged the two
men to look for marimba players from their own town, who would be able
to provide familiar music. Agreeing to this, Joaquín and Miguel went off
to make their arrangements.

Later, it was discovered that the Corn Maya marimba and its players
had been previously engaged for a cultural festival in Cleveland, Ohio.
This forced Joaquín and Miguel to ask Gaspar to bring back to
Indiantown the community marimba which he had lent, without
consultation, to the Centro Guatemalteco in Lake Worth. Although they
had hoped to pull off their rival fiesta without any contact with Gaspar,
this circumstance forced the split among the Migueleños into the open.
Also, with Antonio and the Corn Maya marimba team gone to Cleveland,
Joaquín was forced to take the entire responsibility for the San Rafael
event.

When October 24 arrived, just twelve days after the idea was
originated, the fiesta took place and was successful in a way entirely
different from either the Maya Quetzal or the San Miguel celebrations.
Although the Catholic church has no image of the archangel St. Raphael,
the crepe paper garlands and fresh flower bouquets signaled something
special. As people arrived for the evening mass, they could appreciate the
enticing aroma of beef frying on the grills set up outside the parish hall.
The standing room was soon gone, and the din of babies only died down
when the marimba music started. Father Juan, obviously pleased with the
efforts of the hastily organized fiesta committee, thanked them by name.
It seems that Joaquín joined forces with Mekel and his decoration crew.
The mass was dedicated to the forty-seven men and one woman who had

died in a massacre in San Rafael la Independencia eleven years before, during the violence. The names of some of the victims were printed in the bulletin. At the end of the mass, Joaquín announced that each person present would receive a ticket upon leaving church; the ticket entitled the holder to a plate of tacos and a cup of *fresco*. As people lined up at the grill, the marimba team of seven moved the community double marimba out onto the grass and were immediately surrounded by hundreds of Maya straining to watch. Several couples danced the *sones* and at least two men danced alone for several hours.

Joaquín's wife, while serving styro cups of *fresco* as fast as she could, stressed that the custom in Guatemala is to *regalar* the fiesta—to provide it to the community as a gift. She and her husband and his friends had raised the money for this; they expected to have expenses of close to a thousand dollars. They had contracted with a Mexican family to make the tacos, for which they would be paid a dollar each, accounted for with the tickets. A donation of one hundred dollars was also given to the church, and the marimba team was paid for the playing which only ended after midnight. The fiesta is not to make money, Joaquín's wife reiterated, and said, "It is not our custom to charge an entrance fee." Clearly, she was referring to Gaspar's unacceptable—from the traditional Maya point of view—fiesta. Gaspar's family was not present at the San Rafael celebration; his daughter Francisca was sponsoring a dance in Stuart as an inaugural event for a new soccer tourney. So the rivalry became more open, and the split between the assimilationist position of Gaspar's family and his friends at the Centro Guatemalteco and the more traditional views of many of the Indiantown Maya became visible once more.

A later interview with Joaquín revealed that he had worked on the fiesta for a week of evenings plus two entire days, or about fifty hours, to honor San Rafael and the Rafaeleños. He was not concerned about the cost. Joaquín and his wife were labor contractors, who owned a bus to transport workers, and had recently bought an eighteen-wheel tractor and trailer to transport citrus fruit. Although they lived simply, they owned their house and were sending their children to college. Joaquín's anxiety and his chief motive was to *quitarle a don Gaspar su interés del dinero, quitarle la vergüenza* "to remove don Gaspar's interest in money, to take away the shame [caused by his money-making fiesta]." He also said,"I wanted the fiesta to be thoroughly Guatemalan."

Fiesta de Fin de Año

The last public ceremonial-social event of the 1992 cycle was the *Fiesta de Fin de Año*—End of the Year Party—organized by the Corn Maya leaders for December 31st. Although this was a pay-at-the-door event, Corn Maya ended up covering a two hundred dollar shortfall. But Antonio was pleased with his attempt on several counts. First, he had provided a way for the Maya community to "say goodbye to '92 and receive'93 in the Guatemalan style," as the hand-lettered flier announced. Second, a door was opened for increased cooperation between Corn Maya and other Mayan groups in Florida. Although the *Sonora Tikal* marimba team from Indiantown played that night, Antonio invited two other groups. In exchange for the loan of the Corn Maya marimba for their February titular fiesta, the Mayan community of Santa Eulalia in Homestead, Florida sent their musicians to play for the Indiantown party. And the young men from Cuilco, Huehuetenango had come from Jupiter with their disk jockey equipment to fill in the breaks.

The event was held in the Indiantown Civic Center, a small public hall, and although the attendance was not sufficient to meet expenses, it was *muy alegre* (very joyful) and almost everyone danced. The lack of women partners and the non-availibility of alcohol probably accounted for the low attendance. However, "authentic Guatemalan tamales" and *caliente* were served. It also seems that many families who did not attend the dance did stop at the Civic Center after midnight to share the traditional embrace to welcome the new year.

OTHER RELIGIOUS PRACTICE

The fiestas described above were the public religio-political or civic-secular events organized by the Mayas of Indiantown. These events, for all the controversy and hidden conflict they occasioned, were ritual, in the sense that they followed expected patterns of ceremonial action. They were religious, in the sense of being offered to the community, and sometimes to spiritual entities as well, by their organizers as world-renewing markers of time and history. They also provided proof of the organizers' commitment to the common good even to the point of self-sacrifice. However, these mass public moments certainly did not exhaust the repertoire of religious practice of the Indiantown Mayas. There were several other evidences of religious activity organized according to highland Maya custom, both modern popular Catholicism and traditional Maya religion in its syncretic form. Here we will discuss briefly two examples of the first, namely, the regular Saturday night "Guatemalan" mass and the weekly prayer group; and two examples of the second, the use of candles to accompany prayer, and the presence in the community of "born-again pagans" or practitioners of *costumbre* [22] among Indiantown young adults.

Candles

In the *pueblos* in northern Huehuetenango, there is widespread use of wax tapers by people praying in the churches. This practice is not mentioned in the literature except in connection with *costumbre*, where Maya people burn candles at outdoor shrines or before large crosses, together with offerings of incense, turkey blood and liquor. But every church has a constant stream of men and women, who enter, kneel on the floor, light a handful of tapers, and remain kneeling in prayer for periods of up to two hours. The traffic is greater on the *días de ora*, the year-bearer days of the Maya calendar, which occur every fifth day. The Catholic priests and catechists are entirely accepting of this. One priest is reputed to hold baptisms and marriages exclusively on *días de ora*.

The Catholic church in Indiantown has a statue about four feet high of St. Michael, and similar-size images of Jesus and Mary, each with a metal rack of glass-encased votive candles before it. Since most Catholic churches have similar devotional decor, there was no immediate connection with this so-typical Catholic devotional practice and highland Maya usage. The numbers of burning candles (out of a total of forty-four, set out on Saturday and sometimes renewed midweek), showed no consistently great numerical increase connected with the sacred days of *Lambat, Ben, Chinax* and *Watan* ; [23] nevertheless, there was great use of the candles to accompany prayer.

The candles were the sort that burn several days and cost around a dollar. Most afternoons Maya men and women could be found kneeling in front of the altar or of the San Miguel image, holding a lighted candle. On rainy days, when the agricultural and landscaping workers were sent home early, the church traffic was heavier. Almost every Monday, all forty-four candles were burning, with several having been removed from their stands and placed on the altar step.

One traditionally offers a candle on days of personal significance, a birthday, anniversary of death of a loved one, or when beginning a new job or a journey. Xunik lights a candle every day for nine days when he is involved in a cure, claiming that the *santo*, San Miguel, needs the gift of light. Often people mentioned offering a candle to God or a saint as a gift. Elena said that her mother taught her to pray every day for everyone; indeed one could hear her murmer as she prayed in Q'anjob'al the words *txutx* (mother), *mam* (father), *masanil* (everyone), *conob'* (town, people, community) and *Estados Unidos* (United States)! Jaime, a teacher in Guatemala but a farm laborer in Indiantown, visited the church on his daily run. Many other men stopped by the church to light a candle and pray; often couples would come together but not necessarily end their prayers at the same time.[24] Fr. Juan reported that people came in to light candles at all hours of the night.

When the statue of San Miguel was placed on the floor near the altar, decorated with pine garlands and flowers at the time of the fiesta, the candles were hard to keep stocked. The supply was depleted several times that week as people young and old paid special visits to the church.

This tradition of concentrated and frequent prayer, accompanied by the gift of a *candela* (candle), has been adapted to the Indiantown circumstances. The visits are not made in the morning, as they are in Guatemala, where a farmer's time is his own, and the supplicants do not stay in church until their candles burn out, or for several hours, as they do with the tapers they can buy for a penny or two in their hometown. But many have not forgotten this religious ritual and continue to practice it in exile.[25]

"Guatemalan" Mass

As has been mentioned several times, the Indiantown Catholic parish scheduled two masses in Spanish (and two in English) every weekend. But the 7:30 Saturday evening mass was considered by all to be the "Guatemalan" mass. The almost exclusively Maya attendance at that time can be attributed to the fact that many agricultural workers labor seven days a week; Saturday evening is their only time free to attend mass. But other factors contribute to the Maya "flavor" of the ritual. In the first place, there is the question of "critical mass." Just as in Indiantown as a whole, the concentrated presence of Maya people packed into the small church, most of the women dressed in their *traje*, creates an atmosphere of familiarity. The more people attend, the more want to attend. The music provided by the choir is another factor. The nine or ten young men with guitars and a small marimba, singing hymns copied from the hymnal published by the Diocese of Huehuetenango, occasionally offering a hymn in one of the Maya languages, attracts a crowd which usually fills the church by 6:30. Most of the musicians were involved in church choirs in Guatemala, and are delighted to have a forum in Indiantown. Their commitment involves about three hours a week. Antonio was the director during 1992, presiding over a core of regulars and some shifting membership because of labor migration. The hymns chosen frequently spoke to issues of peace, justice and unity; the selection was made by two or three choir members in the Corn Maya office on Friday. This same group donated an entire Saturday the week before Christmas, to decorate the church inside and out with colored lights, pine garlands, and a Christmas tree festooned with bows and other decor made from native cloth. Outside, they built a *jacal*, a thatch-roofed hut of bamboo stalks, their version of the stable at Bethlehem.

Another important factor in the "Guatemalan" mass was the genuine interest of Father Juan in providing a culturally appropriate ritual. A Spaniard who had worked almost thirty years with migrant farm workers in South Florida, he learned to appreciate the peculiar customs of the Huehuetenango Catholics. Before each mass, he read a long list of *intenciones* (petitions) as is done in the highlands parishes. A typical sample: "We ask blessings for the relatives of Diego Juan, also for the safe arrival from Guatemala of our friend Domingo Gaspar, and we also ask for his family and his children. We ask for the health of the brother of Francisco Xuncax. And I want also to pray for all the families here." He spoke slowly and gently, never failing to mention the saints important in Huehuetenango. He had chosen an elderly couple who were practitioners of *costumbre* in Guatemala as his assistants to distribute the communion bread and wine, and after mass gathered all the mothers and children around the altar for a blessing. Then he put marimba tapes on the public address system to enliven the clean-up.

The influence of official church personnel and their own beliefs and personalities on a community of worshippers is often overlooked in ethnographies. But Father Juan's openness to promote the Maya peoples' ownership of their weekly ritual is clearly important here. He recognized that many Mayan men had come from Guatemala with a thorough preparation in church work, but had lost their self confidence in the United States situation. He tried to remedy this by allowing free rein to Xuin, for example, to read the gospel in Q'anjob'al. He frequently asked Antonio or his wife to translate his Spanish sermon. He, in fact, allowed the Mayas to be "in charge" of the mass much as they do in the lay-centered Huehuetenango parishes. This was not the case, for example, at the other Spanish mass on Sunday, attended by the general

Latino population and by a handful of Mayan people interested in blending with this group. Nor was this freedom experienced by Mayan Catholics in Homestead, West Palm Beach, Los Angeles, or Mesa, Arizona; it contributed to the attraction Indiantown holds as a ceremonial center.[26] Father Juan also preached frequently on the need to remember and pray for wives and children left in Guatemala, and the importance of overcoming municipality-based rivalries in order to be united as one people in exile.

Prayer Group

This openness on the part of their pastor encouraged another religious expression among Mayan Catholics, a group formed expressly to pray together, study the Bible and promote devotional rituals. *El Grupo de Oración y Amistad* (Prayer and Friendship Group) was formed by the initiative of a pious Mexican migrant worker together with Domingo, who was profiled in Chapter III. Consisting of a regular core of twenty members, the group met each Thursday evening for two hours in the church. Mayan men, single or temporarily single while in the United States, made up four-fifths of the group, which also sponsored simple ritual celebrations of several saints' days. Most of the Maya members explained that they were interested in participating because their fathers had been catechists in Guatemala, and they were happy for an opportunity to prepare themselves to exercise this office when they returned.[27]

Traditional Religion

A fourth manifestation of religious practice influenced by Maya custom was the presence in Indiantown of several young people who claimed to have returned to the religion of their pre-conquest ancestors. These individuals, like Xunik, profiled in Chapter III, did not thereby reject modern Catholic practice entirely, but rather saw the two systems as mutually enriching and not necessarily incompatible. Genaro, the culture and education committee chairperson for Corn Maya, a twenty-nine year old K'iché with an impressive record of social work on local and departmental levels in Guatemala, professed to believe that it was strategically important to ally oneself with the priest if one hoped for success in any sort of health, town improvement or unionizing activity. But he stated that his religion is Maya, and he was only rarely seen in the Catholic church. His practice was entirely private except when he dressed as a Mayan daykeeper and gave a speech about the achievements of the classic Mayas during a leadership conference. He also participated in a weekly radio program sponsored by Corn Maya, in which he gave capsule explanations of Maya culture interspersed with marimba music. Antonio, the Corn Maya director, it has already been noted, kept the day count privately, and publically promoted resurgent Maya *costumbre*. An example of this was his trip to Guatemala to rent the costumes for the Conquest Dance. The third person who openly claimed to follow the ancestral religion was Francisca, who despite having been educated in a convent school and having worked closely with the Catholic refugee effort in Los Angeles for several years, claimed she is "only 5% Catholic" although she attended mass occasionally. There is no organized cult in Indiantown, no cargo hierarchy, no *principales*, and no *alcalde rezador* or *ajtxum*, [28] but Francisca claims that many Maya people are not Christians. These three neo-Maya believers are all around thirty years old and share an apparent desire to promote pride in the Maya past, but they are rivals in every other sense and do not meet with each other. Thus there is no public expression of Maya religion even though some young people seem to view it as a personal option and as an ideological basis for their activism on behalf of the Maya community of Indiantown.

OTHER MAYAN GROUPS

It should be noted that the public fiestas held in Indiantown in 1992 and other years are not the only such manifestations of Maya resurgence, organization to establish identity, and ethnic assertion. The placement of various Maya groups across the United States has been touched upon in Chapter II; this section expands upon the connections and communications that occur among them and the effect of these on a sense of place. Celebrations of saints' fiestas were held by Maya groups in Los Angeles and in Homestead, Florida, and many Indiantown Mayas have relatives who are part of those groups, and knew of the fiestas. This had at least three repercussions: a sense that Maya people all over the United States are united in their effort to preserve at least some elements of their tradition; a sense of empowerment for the organizers, who knew that such efforts could be successful because they had precedent; and an element of friendly competition.

It was well known by members of Corn Maya, by Gaspar's family, and by the directors of the Centro Guatemalteco, for example, that IXIM, the first Maya organization in Los Angeles, had been sponsoring a San

Miguel fiesta for years. The non-profit group, composed primarily of former residents of San Miguel Acatán, had its official start in 1986, and has participated in several California cultural festivals. The September 29, 1990 celebration of San Miguel was described in the IXIM bulletin as having been attended by over nine hundred persons who came to see the Deer Dance, performed with costumes rented in Guatemala. IXIM also secured a grant from the City of Los Angeles, purchased a new marimba, and began to publish music tapes and folklore stories in Q'anjob'al. Some donations were sent to the town of San Miguel Acatán for improvements to the community and the Catholic parish church (Peñalosa, personal communication). The sociologist-advisor of IXIM has a close and supportive connection with Antonio and visited him in Indiantown in November 1992.

A second large Los Angeles organization is composed of over eight hundred former residents of Santa Eulalia, Huehuetenango. This association, *Fraternidad Eulense Maya Q'anjob'al* or FEMAQ, has a more religiously oriented purpose, helding a weekly prayer session led by a faith-animator trained in Guatemala, organizing basketball and soccer tournaments, celebrating the annual *Fiesta de Santa Eulalia*, and other cultural events. It also has a construction and health committee, dedicated to supporting their home Catholic church's projects of a health clinic, a rural health insurance program, and a fifteen-bed hospital. In past years they have contributed to the reconstruction of their church [29] and the salary of a resident doctor. They also have several marimbas and seek to increase their income through public appearances.

The February 13, 1993, fiesta in honor of Santa Eulalia in Los Angeles followed the predictable pattern of civic ceremony, sports trophy awards, investiture of queens, and exhortations to preserve Maya culture. Over a thousand Mayas attended. In Los Angeles, there are more single Maya women than in Florida, due to the availability of sewing jobs for them; the social dance was a great success. Representatives from IXIM and from a smaller group in San Diego were also present. A religious service to honor the patron saint had taken place several weeks previously.

A third group whose practice was similar was the unnamed Q'anjob'al prayer group in Homestead, Florida, also composed primarily of Santa Eulalia Maya Catholics. This group of about one hundred members met weekly at the local Catholic church and had a marimba team but no marimba. When they decided to sponsor the fiesta for their saint in February of 1993, chiefly in order to regroup after the devastation of

Hurricane Andrew, they worked out a deal with Corn Maya, sending their musicians to play at the New Year party and in return getting the use of the Corn Maya marimba for February.

Both the Santa Eulalia groups cooperated with Mayas from San Sebastián Coatán, who have religiously-organized groups in Los Angeles, Immokalee, Florida, and Mesa, Arizona, to bring their pastor from Guatemala for annual spiritual visits. This involved a great deal of coordination, in terms of communication, scheduling and financing. Across the United States, there is common knowledge about all these events among the Mayas, who are connected chiefly by kinship ties. The knowledge serves to spur each group on to more effective organization and public display.

One way in which these various outposts of the Maya Diaspora communicate with each other is by video tape. This will be discussed in Chapter VI; suffice it to say here that any recently received video from Guatemala is likely to be copied and re-copied and sent all over the United States. Video tapes are also made of Maya events in *el Norte* and are widely seen in Huehuetenango, as the example of Julio's taping of the Aguacatán soccer game shows. On both ends of the migration route, people gather to see if a loved one's face will appear in the latest video, bringing an assurance that an audio cassette cannot quite match.

An interesting effect of this growing network among organized Maya groups is the sense of control of geography that Maya people are beginning to acquire. Within Guatemala, the Maya people are, on the whole, well-traveled; in the United States the distances are far greater, but the knowledge that a group of ethnically related people lives in some sense as a face-to-face community in some other part of the United States makes travel less risky, makes available instant updates on conditions of employment and immigration restrictions, and contributes to a feeling of place for the exiled Maya.

KEY SYMBOLS

Ritual is a type of communication that uses visual, audio and kinetic display as its language (Rappaport 1968:192). Many of the "words" of this ritual language have been mentioned in the preceding description of the ritual cycle in the Maya Diaspora; here several of them are highlighted in a more analytic way. Nevertheless, the reader will understand that analysis is an operation of dissection and that what gets cut are the linkages each "word" has with other "words" in the ritual language. Although the focus here is on the patron saint, the physical adornment of the participants together with their speech, the marimba, and the time and space markers that are noted in the settings for and the discourse surrounding the events, it is clear that much of the semantic load carried by each symbol seeps over into other symbols to form a related whole. It is also to be noted that the symbols spoken of here are not "natural" (Douglas 1970) but are highly manipulable because of their conventional nature.

Santo/a

The most important fiesta symbol, in the United States as well as in Guatemala, is the saint. Three of the celebrations in Indiantown used at least the name of the saint and the date in the church calendar as a grounding point: San Miguel and San Rafael. The Festival Maya Quetzal began near the dates of San Juan/San Pedro and was offered as an alternative to San Miguel.

This saint-centered practice is extremely ambiguous. The saint represents not only himself/herself, a person believed to have lived in heroic virtue and to be in the presence of God, but also a *municipio* which usually has the same name, an ethnic and language group which is largely co-terminous with the *municipio*, a Catholic church affiliation, and a traditional or modern religious or sacred orientation. But in another sense, the saint symbol is not multivocal enough: there is no saint which is commonly accepted as standing for the nation-state of Guatemala in the way Our Lady of Guadalupe does for Mexico. The saint is also unable to speak to the large number of evangelical Protestant Mayas or those who prefer to observe a strictly secular fiesta, and has no ability to unite Maya people as a class or ethnic group. This is the very reason the Corn Maya board decided to sponsor a cultural festival, the Festival Maya Quetzal, that overcame these limitations. Therefore, the choice to organize a fiesta around a saint's day implies other options which are inherently political.

When the ladino and North American leadership of the Centro Guatemalteco decided to use San Miguel as a way to showcase their newly opened service center, they counted on attracting the large number of Migueleño refugees in South Florida who think of San Miguel as their guarantor of refugee status as well as a spiritual protector. Their identification as Migueleños gives them a better chance at legal recognition as refugees, since it is well documented that San Miguel

Acatán was the scene of brutal massacres in the early 1980s. But since the Centro staff was interested in serving non-indigenous Guatemalans as well, their fiesta was a striking contrast of juxtaposed syles, the national Guatemalan cultural markers taking precedence over the indigenous ones, which were relegated to the status of folklore. The saint himself and the municipality he stands for were referred to only in passing by the announcers at that fiesta.

The organizers of the Indiantown San Miguel fiesta were, in contrast, almost exclusively indigenous, but in that case the Gaspar family wanted to downplay the sacred and Catholic aspects of the celebration, as well as its identification with one municipality, and used the date only as the occasion for a secular event. The group headed by Mekel and Xunik were not aiming to create a secular or pan-Latino appeal in the fiesta but wanted rather to ensure the protection of the saint, as a supernatural personage, for their *pueblo* and their people in the United States.

The *municipio* rivalry aspect of saints came to the surface quite blatantly with the organization of the San Rafael fiesta. As Migueleños, Joaquín and his wife wanted to make "right" the damage done to their saint's reputation, their *municipio*, and their supernatural protection by sponsoring the ritual for another archangel, patron of a neighboring municipality that had once belonged to San Miguel. The San Miguel and Santa Eulalia fiestas in Homestead and in Los Angeles only underline the municipal rivalries that undercut all attempts at a pan-Maya organization.[30] Nevertheless, the invitations extended to "rival" groups, the recognition of their representatives in the rituals themselves, and the communications links and incipient cooperative gestures (loan of a marimba or a marimba team, sharing the expenses for a visit from their pastor) show the possibilities of cooperation in the future. It will be revealing to note whether the number of named saints' fiestas proliferates or declines.

Candela

The only use of the *candela* in all these public rituals was in the procession with the Saint Michael statue at the Indiantown Catholic church. Even though there is some evidence that wax candles were a part of pre-conquest Maya rites (LaFarge 1947:73), they have perhaps at this point in history become too identified with the church to be a good symbol of Maya religion. Incense, however, retains enough ambiguity that it was chosen to be used in several of these rites, carried in procession by persons representing the Maya elders, ancestors or *alcalde rezador*. Thus incense becomes a key marker of the choice to preserve, honor, and promote pre-conquest Maya traditions. It also lent an air of the sacred to the secular fiestas where it was used.

Traje, Trenzas and Lengua

In Guatemala, it is customary in the Maya towns for all members of the family to receive a complete set of new clothing at fiesta time if finances permit. One reason for this is the increased availability and competitive prices offered by the vendors who travel from one fiesta to another. But in a more profound sense, new clothes are a sign of a new year, a dying and birthing, a new round of ritual and secular activities, and a new pact with the supernatural patrons to guard the people for another year. The appearance of widespread daily use of women's *traje* in Indiantown sometime around 1987 marked several things: an increased sense of "critical mass" of Maya population which led women to feel that they would not appear out of place if they did wear their typical skirts and blouses, a growing number of Maya people with the necessary documents to allow them to move without fear in public spaces, and an increased financial ability to send for the expensive clothing items. In Los Angeles, the Maya population is too dispersed to meet the condition of critical mass, although the women often wear *traje* at home. In Indiantown, only Francisca and some of her sisters who are ardent assimilationists, and several semi-ladinoized Mayas like Xusita wear Western clothing. The women who work in the fields usually change into *traje* from their bluejeans when they return home. Many find it more practical to wear pullover T-shirts instead of the lacy *huipiles* at least some of the time. But most prefer to wear the *corte* skirts and feel more physically protected by them, welcoming the opportunity to use them without fear of being arrested by the Border Patrol or being the target of ridicule. The fiesta is an opportunity to show off the very best of their typical wardrobe. The Maya women's use of *traje* does not signify a conscious strategy of ethnic identification in the political sense.

Men's dress does not change drastically in the exile situation. Men, however, use the dress of their women as a way to proclaim their financial success. The *traje* is very expensive and is usually complemented with gold bracelets, earrings and rings as well, so the elegance with which the women are arrayed is an indicator of the men's monetary surplus. Some men also have begun to try out some kinds of symbolic clothing to communicate ethnic pride. Shirts of multi-colored *jaspé* cloth [31] and multicolored woven belts are the most commonly seen items, but some men also affect *caites*, the high-backed sandals seen in pre-conquest frescoes. At the present this use is confined to a minority of Maya activists. For them, their own dress and that of their wives and children is indeed a political statement, meant to assert not only their right to live legally in the United States but also their right to maintain their cultural traditions.

Hairstyle is another aspect of dress that has not yet been mentioned, but which is also used as a communication device. In the Huehuetenango villages, young women wear a single long braid or *trenza* while older women wrap the braid or ponytail around their head like a crown, or pull it forward into a knot. In most cases the hair is braided with colored scarves, ribbons or woven sashes, and clasped with a fancy pearl barrette. The older people there criticize the young women who wear their hair simply pulled back and fastened, without the braid, as being morally careless. However, in the United States, this fashion has become much more acceptable, as the women adapt to majority style. No women, however, have short hair; in Guatemala short hair is a sign of either ladino identity or advanced studies; the same view is retained in the United States. At the fiesta, women use their most festive hair ornaments, but do not use the elaborate crowns and knots. Men's hair is usually kept short, in contrast to Native American usage in the United States. One reason is linked to the perception held by the Guatemalan military during the armed conflict that long hair on a male denoted guerrilla ties; most Maya men do not want to risk suspicion. Some Maya men get permanent waves. The motive is usually to escape detection by the Border Patrol, to more easily pass as a Mexican and avoid the typical profile of a Guatemalan Indian. But in some cases, such as Antonio's, a different sort of political statement is being made: an attempt to reconcile the ladino-Indian separation by being a personal bridge between his friends and co-workers from both sides of the divide.

Choice of language is another arena that carries a symbolic load. In all the fiestas, the queens and other spotlighted persons were required to give their speeches in at least two languages and if possible, three: Spanish, Maya and English. The use of Q'anjob'al in the rituals of several Indiantown churches, the pressure brought to bear on the Florida health services to provide translators for Maya clients, and the continued use of Maya names is an indicator of ardent defense of Maya identity on the part of the men. [32] But on the other hand, the only language that Maya people from different municipalities have in common is Spanish, and it is necessarily the main communication tool. This fact automatically sidelines or marginalizes many Indiantown women, effectively preventing them from participating in public meetings, for while most of them understand Spanish, the majority claim they cannot speak well. At the women's sewing cooperative, the workers are directed not to use the Maya languages. This is an attempt to promote unity between Maya and Mexican women, but the rule is resented by the Mayas.

Printed material in Maya languages has been prepared for the fiestas in Indiantown for the past several years. This is a clear sign of growing comfort with a Maya identity. It also has connections to the growing amount of published material in Maya appearing in Guatemala, a result of laws legitimizing the Academy of Maya Languages and the activism of the League of Maya Writers, among other groups.[33]

Marimba

The marimba, to many Maya people, embodies the soul of their culture. The sonorous boom of the *hormigo* wood keys forcing air through the wooden sound boxes seldom fails to elicit a feeling of sheer joy mixed with nostalgia in the hearts of the exiles. In recent years, there have been attempts to prove an autochthonous origin for the instrument, arising from the discovery of a codex picturing the *marinmaya de brazo*, a string of keys fastened to an outstretched arm. (Gómez 1993:8-9).[34] Many songs speak of the *son*, a Spanish word which refers to the instrument, the waltz rhythm music that is most identified with Maya dancing, and the dance steps themselves. Although the marimba is capable of lending itself to any musical style, and indeed is frequently used by ladino musicians for salsa and other Latin rhythms, it is the *son*, the slow and plaintive melody of the highlands, that helps the exiled Maya to both chase away their sorrow and yet remember it. The marimba is also played cooperatively, usually by seven musicians, and this is sometimes refered to as a symbol of the cooperative rather than competitive nature of the indigenous community life and organization. As was noted in the descriptions of the fiestas, the marimba is considered their essential element, and a shorthand way to express dissatisfaction about a fiesta where it was not present is *No hubo marimba*—"There was no marimba." The negotiating that went on between Corn Maya and the Homestead group, the San Rafael promotors and the Centro Guatemalteco and Gaspar, and the blatant use of two marimba teams, indigenous and ladino, to accompany the two queens at the Lake Worth fiesta were all political uses of the marimba as symbol of ethnic identity.

One aspect of marimba music is intriguing: women are seldom seen playing the instrument, either in Guatemala or in the United States. Jerónimo Camposeco, a recognized expert who has given lectures about the marimba, claims that this is because the marimba is associated with occasions where there are men who drink to excess. He knows of no formal taboo; it is simply that parents do not wish their daughters to be associated with the evening events where the marimba is played. The sacred dances, the Conquest and the Deer Dance, may have very young girls as dancers, but not women, according to Camposeco.

In 1973, the Mohawk tribe sent representatives to Jacaltenango, Camposeco's home, and saw how important the marimba was to the indigenous identity. In 1974, he made his first tour of the United States at their invitation, and was involved in presentations in the United States and Canada each year thereafter, bringing a marimba to stay on one of those trips. He thinks this helped create the association between the Maya and the marimba in public perception, especially after 1984, when he played at a festival of nations in Washington, D.C. The Mexico pavillion at Disney World has a marimba team, and many Miami restaurants do as well. The Los Angeles groups IXIM and FEMAQ have imported marimbas from Santa Eulalia, one of the recognized centers of marimba craft, at great expense.[35]

The marimba gathers the community. The first notes bring smiles of recognition and pleasure, then sadness at the lament hidden in the sound. Cassette tapes are used frequently in car tape players and in Maya households; marimba sounds on a video tape or newscast bring folks running, and some Mayas have confided that only hearing the sound of the wooden keys alleviates the pain in their hearts for what they have lost, their families, their homes, their cornfields, their animals. The marimba is without doubt a key symbol, both internally, for the Maya themselves, and externally, for the public.[36]

Time and Space Markers

One of the recognized effects of ritual is to create both sacred time and sacred space, a moment of time-out-of-time and a place apart, nearer to the supernatural, to the center of the universe, than the streets and plazas of everyday. Ritual renews the world by offering an opportunity for the participants to step outside of it; it renews time by bringing the past, the present and the future together. All of this "work" of ritual is done through symbols: objects, actions and words which induce intellectual, emotional and even physical states. In the Maya fiestas of Indiantown, a thicket of symbols trapped the attention of the audience. The organizers in each case carefully planned for the desired effects and consciously attempted to bring together memories of other places and times past with reminders of the present moment of exile in Florida.

The decor for the Fiesta Maya Quetzal included a stage set with *corte* cloth, a painted canvas backdrop representing the Cuchumatán mountains of Huehuetenango, and T-shirts with a quetzal bird hovering over Lake Atitlán, all evocative of "there"; the United States flag, the video cameras, the presence of representatives of Martin County but above all the discourse, spoke to "here." "With this Festival we thank our God and the State of Florida in giving us the opportunity to live in peace for this first Decade—sharing our hard work and our cultural values with the citizens of this County and the United States," proclaimed the printed program. The presence of the costumed dancers and the K'iché princess were ways to trick the senses into thinking one was still in Guatemala, but the speeches about the importance of preserving Maya traditions in exile, the talk about the hope of a return to the beloved home, and the telegrams and messages from persons in Guatemala brought the audience into the reality of their location.

The stage settings for the San Miguel fiesta at the park, the Lake Worth event, and the New Year party were all similar, using a stage, *corte* cloth, the flag of Guatemala, and painted backdrops to allude to another place. In the church-centered events, the pine garlands, the saint image, the familiar words of the Catholic ritual provided the contact with memories of home. The disjunctures brought the present time and place into view. The Mayas commented on the inability to process through public streets; the absence of firecrackers, pine needle carpets, drum and flute. The petitions for relatives so far away, and the discourse relating to the importance of avoiding contamination by United States materialism and individualism were further reality checks. The Memorial Awakateko was planned not only to remember the seven victims of the accident, but to provide an opportunity for mourning all those who died while their sons and daughters were so far from home and unable to comply with traditional last rites.

The timing of the fiesta cycle itself, with the main events clustered around the end and the beginning of the secular year, from September to February, corresponds to the deep sense of responsibility for time that has been noted in the Maya culture by students of both historical and contemporary evidence (D. Tedlock 1985:62; B. Tedlock 1983:243). A people that goes to the trouble of calculating the Venus cycle is, to say the least, concerned about the part humans play in making sure the rounds do not end. This culturally taught sense of responsibility led to the self-sacrifice implied in the organizing of each of the Indiantown fiestas. This, joined with the experience of community organizing learned from the modern Catholic church, the availability of a full treasury of symbols and the conscious concern to establish their distinctive identity in the United States, led to the semantically rich cultural celebrations of Indiantown.

Those who took on the responsibility of organizing the fiestas were recognized as being powerful leaders in their context: the following chapter examines the development of leadership in Indiantown.

NOTES

1. From June, 1992 to January 1993, I was fortunate to observe the fiestas in Indiantown This chapter includes assessments based on my observations.

2. There is evidence that often the Spanish missionaries named a new mission for the day on which it was founded; see Van Oss 1986 for the case of highland Guatemala. But the question remains: why did some saints and their dates become more popular than others? I speculate that the proximity to the autumnal equinox may hold part of the answer in the case of St. Michael. It is also near the date of the corn harvest and marks the end of the rainy season. St. Michael may have been identified during the early conquest period with *Q'anil/Lambat*, the day-god who represents lightning, perhaps because of the cosmic clash in which he participated, according to Apocalypse 12:7-9.

3. In the film, two Jakalteko culture brokers in Indiantown claim to have originated the fiesta at the request of the community.

4. A well-known slogan, often repeated during the tournament, stated this goal in succinct form: *Un deportista más, un delincuente menos* (One more athlete, one less delinquent). Another publically unstated goal: to encourage sobriety. The athletes had to stay sober until Sunday evening, and then would not be likely to drink to excess before the work day Monday.

5. The countries of Central America celebrate their independence from Spain in 1821 on September 15-16, as does Mexico.

6. This backdrop is described in Earle 1989:8,15, where he misidentifies it as Coxpin mountain, which stands between the two towns of San Juan Ixcoy and San Pedro Soloma. The mountain is Capcín, and is located between San Juan Ixcoy and Huehuetenango, as was pointed out to me during my travels in the region.

7. The *Pop Vuh*, or *Popol Vuh*, is the post-conquest document which is believed to be a copy of a K'iché codex now lost. It is a creation story, but continues into and beyond the time of the conquest in 1524. See D. Tedlock, 1985.

8. Thirty costumes had been rented, but only fifteen were large enough to fit the Indiantown men who wanted to dance. Improved protein intake in the United States may be partially responsible.

9. The *Convite* was a part of the January 1994 celebration of the patronal fiesta of San Sebastián Coatán, Huehuetenango, appearing on a video tape circulated widely among the Coatán community of Mesa, Arizona and seen by the author. The dancers wore full body costumes representing mice, raccoons, ducks, toucans and clowns. It is unknown if this is an adaptation of Carnival or a way to circumvent the high cost of renting the costumes for the more traditional dances.

10. "Chapín" is a slang word used by Guatemalans to identify themselves among other Latin Americans. The flyer was of course printed in Spanish.

11. Her parents had recently visited Migueleño friends in a camp in Mexico; the mention of Cubans was to include her supervisor, the director of the Centro.

12. In Guatemala, these cardinal points are used as subtle racial indicators; people from the West or North are predominantly indigenous, whereas people from the East are generally ladinos. For historical reasons for this divide in residence patterns, see Van Oss, 1986.

13. The name resonates with the name of the parish, Holy Cross, but also with the Maya tradition of praying before large crosses, and with the self-identification of the members as pilgrims or people on the move, in exile, away from home.

14. The hymn was sung at the San Miguel fiesta in San Miguel Acatán when I was there in 1991; the words of the first line are painted on the roof beam of the church. They are taken from the Hebrew meaning of Michael (like unto God). The hymn was also familiar to the K'iché people of San Miguel Totonicapán, several of whom were in the choir.

15. New clothes are an important part of the world-renewing aspect of the patronal fiesta in Maya Guatemala; the vendors travel from one town to another for what they know are sure sales, since everyone who can possibly afford to buys a new set of clothing for every member of the family. In Indiantown, the recent turn to typical dress for the women gives the men a way to show their success.

16. The marimba is portable, at least in some of its forms, and is traditionally carried in the saints' processions.

17. Counter-clockwise, for readers of Evon Vogt.

18. One can speculate that the armor reminded early Mayas of the successful conquest by Spanish soldiers, and that the dragon had been depicted by the early friars as a representation of the "pagan" religious practices of the Mayas. Like the dance of the conquest, the St. Michael image is not without ambiguity for the indigenous people.

19. Gaspar had told me he had a video tape from the reconstruction committee in Guatemala, asking for help. I later learned that the video camera was a gift to the parish of San Miguel Acatán from the Los Angeles organization IXIM.

20. Kunz (1973:137-138) points out that "fate-groups" or "event-conditioned categories" or "vintages" may be imperceptible to outsiders, but these associative cohorts know that the date of departure is an indicator of the refugee's politics. In this statement, Gaspar seeks to establish his authenticity as a refugee as against what the United States Immigration law classifies as ineligible "economic refugees." It is important to note that this distinction is not accepted by many refugee aid agencies.

21. A. Silvestre, an Indiantown Maya resident was quoted: "The indigenous peoples of Guatemala have always been exploited, marginalized, and killed, so something like this merely enhances a feeling of solidarity in suffering." (Rohter 1991).

22. *Costumbre* (custom) is the name given to all the actions of Maya priests, daykeepers, and others who use their services. The people themselves are referred to as *costumbristas*. These people, in general, adhere to universal Catholicism only insofar as they accept baptism and prayer to saints.

23. These are the Q'anjob'al names, which correspond to the more often noted K'iché names of *Aq'b'al, Kanil, Aj and Tijax*. See B. Tedlock (1982) and Diocese of Huehuetenango (1990:20-24). I did note that when the traditional days fell on weekends, there was a run on the candle supply, but since most of the visits by people to light the candles took place late at night (the chapel was left open twenty-four hours), I was not able to rule out other motives for their use on those days.

24. I do not know if any Indiantown couples practiced the custom, common in Huehuetenango, of mutual confession. This is usually done by the couple sitting together on the steps in front of the church.

25. The Chuj Maya community of Mesa, Arizona, holds a weekly prayer ritual at which a candle is burned before a saint's image on a temporary altar set up in the host's home. When I was unsure of the address of the host, I often was able to find the home by the candle flame seen through the curtains.

26. One Indiantown Maya observer remarked on the need for United States priests to visit Guatemala in order to understand the style of church practice there: *Por más buena voluntad que tengan, no pueden comprender, y hacen errores* (No matter how good their intentions, they cannot understand, and they make mistakes).

27. In the Guatemala context, catechist refers to men prepared to teach the adult Catholic community about the Bible and prepare them for marriage, confirmation and the baptism of their children. As with most North American Catholic parishes, in Indiantown, catechists are women who teach Christian doctrine to children. There they were all Mexican or Anglo women.

28. *Principales* are the power behind the scene in Maya towns, those elders who choose the ritual hierarchy each year. The *alcalde rezador* is a man (and usually his wife as well) who is selected to dedicate a year to praying for the town. The *Aj txum* are the shamans and diviners who operate in the outlying villages (Diocese of Huehuetenango 1990:61-66). My Guatemalan informants all assure me that there are very few people in most municipalities who practice *only* the traditional religion.

29. The church of Santa Eulalia, built around 1750, was burned in 1984 by unknown persons. The common talk in that town is that it had to do with rivalry between Catholics and adherants of other sects, who were trying to kill the Padre. The façade remained intact, and the reconstruction of the rest of the church was completed in 1993, at enormous cost.

30. There is some evidence that it is not just a question of rivalries or home-town loyalties at play in Guatemala, but that there may have existed a sort of hierarchy of municipalities in which some were subject ceremonially to others. See La Farge 1947: 131. The history of ecclesiastical jurisdiction also enters here: see Van Oss 1986.

31. Tie-dyed woven cloth.

32. As the reader will have noticed above, each Christian name has a Maya equivalent, such as Malín for María, Xun for Juan, Palás for Francisco, Mekel for Miguel, or Catal for Catalina. The Maya use these names among themselves; see Camposeco 1992:48.

33. The Academy was established by Legislative Decree 65-90, November 15, 1990. See Academia de las Lenguas Mayas de Guatemala.

34. Speculation is that the instrument had an independent origin in three different culture areas: in Africa, in Asia and in southern Mesoamerica. Its use in Mesoamerica is still centered on Veracruz, other southern Mexican states and Guatemala.

35. The IXIM marimba cost $600 plus another $1700 to import (El Vocero de Ixim, No. 5, Jan. 1991). The FEMAQ group took years to pay off their marimba, brought to the United States in 1992. They also have purchased a van with which to transport it and rent a room in which to house it.

36. Allan Burns has written about the external and internal identity of the Indiantown Maya, see Burns 1988,1989a,1989b.

CHAPTER V

Power, Leadership and Sacrifice in Indiantown

Miles of sandy road overarched with tropical foliage lead to Dunklin Memorial Camp, a Baptist church-sponsored retreat deep in the pine woods of South Florida. The damp green tunnel could have been one of the back roads near Guatemala's south coast coffee plantations or *fincas*. Here there were no coffee trees in sight; the fields on either side belong to Florida cattle growers. But the whine of the mosquitos and the croaking of the bullfrogs were an even stronger reminder of the finca area; the participants traveling to the Maya Leadership Training Program were reminded of their own coffee-picking seasons.

The camp was to be the setting for a three-day meeting of Mayan leaders, sponsored by the Martin County Board of Commissioners.[1] The gathering had brought together Maya people of many language groups and from all across South Florida, who were able to speak to each other only in Spanish, as they learn to do on the plantations. Among the invited "leaders" were several Indiantown residents the reader has already met; they introduced themselves as they do in Guatemala, by their municipality of origin: Alberto and Julio from Aguacatán; Efraín, Santos, José and Juan from Totonicapán; Angelina, Eul and Mekel from San Miguel Acatán; and Emilio from Cuilco. They are joined by the organizers and facilitators, Antonio and Genaro of Corn Maya organization and the Martin County district representative, a former Peace Corps worker in Guatemala.

The live-in leadership course brought together for three days almost all of the Maya power holders in Indiantown who had organized fiestas. Although the planning committee had originated within Corn Maya, the

group of thirteen men and two women who took their places for the
opening session included members of Gaspar's family, several officers of
the West Palm Beach Maya Quetzal organization, the Migueleños who
worked on the San Miguel and San Rafael fiestas at the Catholic church,
and many members of the marimba team. Over the course of the three
days, presentations were made by invited speakers who represented
Florida social and legal service agencies, the womens' cooperative, Maya
cultural organizations in Guatemala, exiled Maya anthropologists and the
Maya community of western Canada. The seminar brought together and
recognized the individuals who are the emerging Maya leaders in south
Florida. It also provided a point of contact between the local leadership
and several sources of influence which support and encourage a Maya
cultural resurgence and a pan-Maya political agenda: indigenist
movements from Guatemala, non-governmental organizations,
anthropologists and culture brokers, among others.[2]

   This chapter examines first of all the institutional bases of Maya
power in Indiantown, which are the several agencies of the local Catholic
church, Corn Maya Incorporated, the three Protestant churches which
had Maya membership, and several Maya organizations of surrounding
south Florida. In each of these contexts, Maya leaders have found support
for the development of their claims to legitimacy. Then it shows how the
influence that comes from outside the community affects the political
agenda and the authority of these leaders or power holders, and concludes
with an analysis of the emerging process through which leadership of the
Indiantown Maya community is being constructed and legitimated.

SPACES FOR MAYAN POWER

Catholic Church

Holy Cross Catholic church in Indiantown, in addition to the spiritual
and cultic role any organized church plays in a community, sponsors four
other entities which have provided space for the development of a Maya
power base. Sharing a large wooded property with the chapel itself is
Hope Rural School, a private elementary school with more than one-half
Maya enrollment in its five grades.[3] In the center of Indiantown is the
storefront *Centro Santa Cruz* (Holy Cross Center), a walk-in service
agency providing legal aid, translations, assistance in dealing with
government offices and a clothing store for the general Indiantown
propulation. InDios Cooperative is a clothing factory employing about ten
women, half of them Maya. Finally, the Indiantown Spanish-speaking

chapter of Alcoholics Anonymous is sponsored and housed by the Holy Cross church.

Most of these efforts are the result of the presence in Indiantown of a visionary priest, who, from 1977 to 1986 focused his efforts on the needs of the Spanish-speaking migrant farmworkers and subsequently on the increasing numbers of Maya refugees. Father L. is no longer in Indiantown, but the programs have been continued by the succeeding pastors, although not without changes.

The small private school, with only a few more than a hundred pupils, is administered by two nuns hired by the church. But it serves as an institutional base and legitimating source of identity for one of the Maya leaders of Indiantown who has not yet been introduced, José Martín. An agronomist by profession, he left Guatemala as a refugee in 1981. As is true of many refugees from Jacaltenango, Huehuetenango, José Martín brought a strong tradition of respect for higher education and has indeed succeeded in sending all of his children to college, as well as learning to speak very good English himself. He serves as physical education teacher, coach, bus driver and home liaison for the school. In this capacity, he has instituted parent education classes and a demonstration community garden on the school grounds. Truly dedicated to helping his Maya people better their situation in the United States, he visits the parents of his pupils at their homes to encourage them to allow the children to stay in school. He also gathers the parents for discussion of common problems; this gives him a constituency.

The community garden is a project which assigns a small plot of land to each family who wants to plant. José Martín understands the importance to Maya farmers of having a place to work the land and grow some food for their families. He also understands how important it is for the Maya children to see their parents as experts at something in the strange new world of south Florida. Since Florida has three crop seasons, most evenings the garden is a pleasant hum of activity with entire families planting or cultivating their food crops. José Martín has brought seeds from Huehuetenango and promotes experiments with different varieties of corn, beans, peas, melons and *chipilín, flor de jamáica* and other condiments used in Maya cooking. The community garden gives José Martín a second constituency.

A third orbit within which José Martín garners support is the Spanish-speaking Alcoholics Anonymous group which he founded and directs and which meets weekly at Hope Rural School cafeteria. The first anniversary of this group was marked with a celebratory party to which the whole town was invited. The group numbers around twenty and attracts some of the activist young men who spend their free time at Corn Maya, as well as others who are not involved in any other organized groups.

From his position of leadership among parents of the school children, families who have garden plots and members of the AA groups, José Martín has expressed doubts about the credibility of the Corn Maya organization and particularly on Antonio's financial accountability. His own connection with the Catholic church provides a counterpoint to Antonio's close ties to the priest. However, José Martín has not entirely succeeded in descrediting Corn Maya for two important reasons. First, his efforts to aid the Maya community are all but cancelled out by the perceived status of his family, who are respected for their education, but seen as members of the ladino class which controls resources in Guatemala and is unfriendly to the Maya people. Second, José Martín is perceived as having made only a limited sacrifice of self, in terms of time or money, for the community. His work with the school is paid work. His work with the AA does gain him some credit, but the number of followers is limited. As an employee of the church and school, he cannot concentrate his organizing activities on the Maya community; he must be available for all. Significantly, José Martín and his family are rarely seen at the Saturday "Guatemalan" mass; they join the general Hispanic population at the Sunday service.

Maya women in typical dress occupied all the available chairs in the small waiting room at *Centro Santa Cruz* on any given day. They trusted Gaspar's daughter, Angelina, to understand and explain to them the papers that they couldn't read in either English or Spanish. Applications for food stamps, birth certificates, indigent health care qualifications, residence permits, even claims for lost money orders were brought to Angelina for an explanation in Q'anjob'al and help in filling them out, making appointments at the clinic, or just advice on how to deal with the confusing maze of government agencies in the United States. Next door, the used clothing shop is the first stop for many of the newcomers fresh from their trip from *La Huerta* (Chapter I) and Guatemala. The first Maya-speaking professional they meet is Angelina.

Centro Santa Cruz was begun in an informal way around 1981 by the priest who was pastor of Indiantown at the time, as a social service center for migrant workers. After 1982, it became the center for a gathering of North Americans, anthropologists and migration attorneys, to deal with the crisis presented by the Border Patrol arrests of numbers of Maya people in Indiantown. Alejandro, a Maya with anthropological training and José Martín, mentioned above, were also connected to the Centro, which received grant money for several years in order to prepare hundreds of political asylum cases, applications for the agricultural visas and other opportunities offered by the Immigration Control and Reform Act of 1986.[4] By 1992, the *Centro* was a store-front office attended by Angelina. A Florida Rural Legal Services worker came in once a week to attend clients. Angelina confessed to being ready for a new challenge, after five years in the job. She claimed it had been exciting when the office was filled with lawyers, nuns and social workers, but lost its appeal after cutbacks left her alone. She resigned during the summer of 1992 and was replaced by a young Mexican woman who had been a part of the team effort in former years but was not able to speak Q'anojob'al, as was Angelina. The clientele rapidly changed, as the monoligual Maya women sought help elsewhere.

The Center was orginally independent from Holy Cross Catholic church but taken under its auspices with the arrival of Father Juan around 1986. Angelina, José Martín and Alejandro all got their credibility as culture brokers through the *Centro*; after José Martín moved to the school and Alejandro moved to Corn Maya, Angelina was able to consolidate her power. Her involvement in the San Miguel fiesta was apparently intense for several years before 1992; she shared her father's and her sister Francisca's desire to open it up to all Latino people. But in 1992 she did not attend any of the fiesta events, and was no longer living in Indiantown. Her sphere of influence remained with her family and would be available to her again when she returned. Her presence at the Maya leadership seminar was a recognition by the men who issued the invitations that Angelina, her father and her sisters are indeed part of the power constellation of Indiantown.

An attention-grabbing black-and-white photograph of a clergyman's shirt draped over a chair has a stark caption: "The only clothes designed to do God's work before you ever put them on." This is the front cover of the order form for InDios Cooperative's principal product: clergy shirts. The story inside explains that the producers are former migrant workers or refugees from Central America. And indeed, there were nine women working in the small factory, four Maya women and five Mexican women. Malín and Micaela are from San Miguel, Rosa is from Soloma; Xusita, a Jakalteka, has learned Q'anjob'al in order to communicate with them. The cooperative arrangement in many ways is ideal: the members all have keys, share their lunches each day, and most importantly, do not need to worry about work permits or social security, since they are "owner-partners", not employees. The coop was begun when a nun was hired by the former pastor to start up a weaving cooperative to provide income for the Maya refugees. It turned out that the good-intentioned North Americans had assumed all Maya women weave cloth, and failed to realize that Q'anjob'al women do not. The clergy shirts were an alternative strategy; the director's desire was to provide stable year-round employment that would break the cycle of migrant labor.

The presence of traditionally dominant ladinas together with the traditionally subservient Maya women presented some difficulties, but the cooperative also became a springboard for a few Maya women to garner some influence in Indiantown. Because InDios was often the center of media attention [5] and visits by funding agencies and social service providers, these women had increased access to sources of useful information. And since they were in contact with each other, sharing their concerns as well as the latest recipe, memories of home, and news from Guatemala, they had more possibility of supporting each other than those Maya women who were isolated from each other in their separate homes. The English classes on site at the cooperative, the director's efforts to help the women and their husbands purchase their own homes and learn to use the bank, and her concern for their children's health and education all contributed to the growing sense of competence felt by all four of these Maya women. Malín played an important role in the activities of the San Miguel fiesta at the church and took part in Corn Maya organizational meetings with her husband Mekel. Xusita was involved in the Thursday night prayer group and provided room and board for visiting priests from Huehuetenango. Micaela was part of a Maya political asylum demonstration in New York harbor in 1986.[6] Although none of these women were able to attend the Maya leadership conference because of their work, they were invited.

Two other Catholic church-sponsored groups have already been described: the choir and the Thursday prayer group. Here I want to show how these groups served as both fora for and manifestations of Maya leadership. The twenty people who gathered each Thursday for Bible study and prayer included, as has been noted, a considerable number of men, at least seven, who had been *catequistas* in Guatemala. Several others had seen their fathers exercise this office. Domingo, Antonio and Lucas found the "Prayer and Friendship Group" a receptive forum for the style of quiet gentle spiritual leadership they had practiced in their *aldeas*. Domingo, in particular, had gained the respect and confidence of

Father Juan and was asked on several occasions to organize small
devotional events for the congregation or to make announcements at the
"Guatemalan mass." He was well informed about the activities of Corn
Maya, the *Centro* and the marimba choir, without actually participating
in any of them, and he served to connect the prayer group with these
other groupings. In this way he was able to exercise his office of
catequista.

It was in a very different manner that Antonio used the marimba choir
as both a constituency of followers and as a stage from which to present
his leadership credentials to the Maya community. Although he plays no
instrument, Antonio directed the choir and maintained the discipline
necessary for a competent performance each Saturday evening. The men
in the choir were all his companions and co-workers at the Corn Maya
organization, although the choir is open to all. He claims to have founded
and organized the choir in Indiantown because he thought it was needed,
and because he had exercised the same office in the Catholic church in
his home town, Soloma. It is interesting to note that none of the choir
members are from San Miguel Acatán; most of Antonio's followers are
from Soloma, Aguacatán or Totonicapán.

The choir also serves Antonio as a platform. He is able to use the
church bulletin and the song sheets to communicate messages to the
congregation, usually regarding activities of Corn Maya. He is very
frequently asked to make announcements from the pulpit or to translate
into Q'anojob'al. The name of the choir, *Peregrinos de la Cruz* (Pilgrims
of the Cross), reflects the name of the parish, but also carries the
semantic overtone of the Maya tradition of praying before large crosses
which represent the four directions. The name also connotes the
self-identification of the members as pilgrims, in exile, on the move, and
away from home.

During one service at Holy Cross church, Antonio announced to the
people that a film maker was making a documentary about the
Indiantown Maya and that the choir had decided to bar her from entering
the mass. He stated that she had declined to share the profits with the
community and was therefore exploiting the people. They could choose
whether or not they wished to speak with her, but Father Juan had told
the choir he would abide by their decision regarding her entry into the
mass.[7] On another occasion, Antonio was asked to explain the
significance of the Nobel Peace Prize awarded to Maya activist Rigoberta
Menchú; he gave a long and impassioned declaration (in Q'anjob'al)
about the rights of indigenous peoples. Father Juan also took every

opportunity to praise Antonio in public, not only for his work with the choir, but for his leadership of Corn Maya. Antonio's recognition that the church confers legitimacy on leadership, revealed in his statement: "If I am not seen at mass, I won't have a good reputation here," was actualized by his position with the choir.

Corn Maya Inc.

The first entirely Maya-operated organization in the eastern United States, Corn Maya, Inc., was founded in 1983 by Jerónimo Camposeco, a Maya refugee who is a social anthropologist, with the help of Shelton Davis and the Anthropology Resource Center, under the patronage of the Holy Cross Catholic church and its pro-migrant activist pastor.[8] The trigger event was the arrest in Indiantown and the detention in Miami of seven Q'anjob'al Maya who were unable to communicate in Spanish. By 1984, Corn Maya had a logo and letterhead, and had begun to solicit grants from funding agencies. During 1986, Campseco went to Los Angeles to help found IXIM, a sister organization, which at that time served the estimated three to four thousand Maya there. Also during 1986, Camposeco began to press for a separate identity for Corn Maya, for several reasons. First, in order to be eligible for grants from many charitable organizations, it would have to be ecumenical, that is, neither identified with nor exclusively serving members of any particular religious denomination. The possibility of obtaining money from Lutheran Immigration and Refugee Services brought this to a decision point. At the same time, the offices of *El Centro Santa Cruz* were entirely too crowded. The passage of new immigration laws in 1986 brought in many non-Maya clients to apply for legal services and the church agency could not discriminate against them. Third, the *Centro* staff was not ready to take a political stand in regard to the situation in Guatemala, whereas Camposeco and other Maya saw this as essential to their mission of advocating for the Maya refugees.

In 1989, Antonio, who had become involved in the organization after 1986, was chosen as director by the board, which consisted of several Maya residents of Indiantown and several North American professionals. One of the first acts of the new director was to begin the process of incorporation as a non-profit organization, at the same time contacting the Martin County authorities asking for a dialogue regarding the unique needs of the Mayas of Indiantown. Both efforts bore fruit. Corn Maya received its 501(c)(3) status as a non-profit corporation in 1991; the county commissioned a planning study of Indiantown.[9] With the help of many United States anthropologists interested in the plight of the indigenous refugees, Corn Maya opened a center in a rented building on Indiantown's main street, providing legal and social services for several hours each evening.[10] For the most part, Antonio and Camposeco worked as unpaid volunteers; from time to time a commissioned job would come their way. At the beginning of 1993, Antonio resigned and the membership and board elected a new set of officers, with Camposeco continuing as advisor. This led to an eventual decline of the organization until it was joined to a private legal services clinic owned and managed by Antonio.

Corn Maya had a steady stream of clients seeking services every evening. Most of those seeking help wanted to renew their employment authorization documents. But Corn Maya also provided translations, English classes, help with job applications, and a locale for meetings with immigration lawyers. During 1992, 606 different individual services were performed for clients, and at least twelve programs were implemented. Perhaps the most important service was to provide a place for the single young men to go in the evenings. Many came just to meet and talk to friends; others learned how to offer services to their compatriots, and still others came to practice the marimba. Impromptu marimba sessions often took place after meetings or activities.

The marimba saw increased use when there were difficulties and interpersonal conflicts at Corn Maya. Conflict was rarely overt. The meeting style of the Mayas is extremely polite, with careful turn-taking, silence of the group during each person's turn,and support for each speaker in the form of applause at the end of the turn. Non-aggressive intervention usually opened with a phrase like *Si me permite la palabra* (If you would allow me to speak). When the Maya speak Spanish, they use many formal stock phrases, and structure their discourse so that it can end at any point, depending on the reaction of the group or the perception that another speaker wants a turn. In spite of this charming formality, there was directness in getting to the point, which was often a questioning of financial accountability. With no paid staff, Antonio and Alberto took care of paying bills and recording income and expense, but they did not report to anyone and their decisions were often challenged. It seems that during the years previous to 1992, Gaspar and his family, backed by José Martín, used finances as the point through which to contest the credibility of Corn Maya and its leadership. Both Gaspar and José Martín are of an age to be considered elders; it is possible to interpret their opposition as a lack of confidence in the relatively young Corn Maya directorship. Among the young men themselves, there was disagreement about the structure of the organization: was it "of" or "for" the Maya community? The rivalries between persons of different municipal origins was never completely overcome.[11] Perhaps most destructive of the internal unity of the organization was the suspicion of some of the active members that the leadership used the organization for personal advantage. Yet, formal public accusations were not made. When the members believed a meeting might involve confrontation, they chose to be absent. This led to burn-out on the part of the leadership, or, as Julio put it: *Se le acaba a uno su candil* (One's candle burns out).

Yet, as a self-governed cultural maintenance organization, Corn Maya members managed to keep before the eyes of the community and of the larger world of Florida and the United States, their desire to promote Mayan-ness. One grant application states that the goal of Corn Maya is to "maintain the Maya nation in exile by providing assistance in health, education, community vitality, ceremony, language, and communication." The letterhead, in English, reads: "A Guatemalan-Floridean Organization Seeking the Unity, the Dignity and the Cultural Survival of the Maize People." The sporadic newsletter, *La Voz Maya*, explains that the unity of the Maya people and cultural pride are the reasons for the existence of the organization. Camposeco insists that their indigenous identity is what allows the Maya people to claim political asylum on the basis of persecution by reason of ethnic group and culture. He proposes and actively works for the recognition of the Maya as a sovereign nation on the model of the North American tribes: *La Nación Maya en Exilio* (The Maya Nation in Exile). "We are a new Indian nation in this land," he says. The attention that Corn Maya receives from antropologists, university programs, national and international charitable organizations and the print and electronic media is remarkable. The "external" identity of the Maya in the United States is actively promoted through these channels. The "internal" identity is promoted by the public events which Corn Maya sponsors in Indiantown, particularly the fiestas, which, in 1992, were the Copa Quetzal tournament, the Fiesta Maya Quetzal, and the *Fin de Año* celebration.[12] Many of the active members of Corn Maya were from Aguacatán or from Soloma, two *municipios* whose people are noted for being progressive, commercial-minded, and with longer access to educational opportunities.[13] But they had not formed separate groupings; their loyalties were with Corn Maya and they advocated the unity of all Maya people, without distinction by municipality or language group.

Gaspar's family found institutional support in the several agencies with which the members were connected. Angelina's work at the *Centro Santa Cruz* in Indiantown, Francisca's sponsorship of soccer teams, tournaments, dances and the San Miguel event in the park, and the work of the third daughter as a paralegal in the *Centro Guatemalteco* gave them, and through them, the Migueleño friends of Gaspar, inside information, lines of influence, and an institutional base from which to organize the Maya people in exile. A certain amount of legitimacy also came from the pioneer status of Migueleños in Indiantown. Their influence was diminished, however, by their unrelenting assimilationist stance, and by Gaspar's unembarrassed pro-Guatemalan military sympathies. The lack of help that Gaspar complained about before and after the San Miguel fiesta indicated the family's failure to capture a significant power block in Indiantown.

Protestant Congregations

There are three Protestant churches in Indiantown that counted significant numbers of Maya faithful and provided scope for the development of leadership among them. As mentioned in Chapter III, Efraín, José and Santos, three cousins from K'iché-speaking Totonicapán, were active in the Seventh Day Adventist church. This group had been founded several years prior to 1992 and met in an unfinished chapel on the property of a Maya family. They numbered around fifty adults and twenty-five children, all Maya. Scripture study groups were led by Maya assistants. Efraín was the enthusiastic and vocal leader of the youth group. His enthusiasm transferred easily to his work in Corn Maya as a member of the culture and sports committee. A larger Q'anjob'al-speaking section consisted of older men and women who had belonged to the Adventist church in Guatemala; there was no one whose influence had gone beyond the group itself.

The *Iglesia de Dios Pentecostal* (Pentecostal Church of God) had a store-front meeting room, and a non- resident part-time pastor, a Puerto Rican. Three young women, relatives of Antonio, attended this church several evenings a week; young people were a large part of the congregation of around seventy Maya. The pastor had designated two Maya assistants to lead the entire worship service except the sermon. Although they spoke in Spanish, it was in Guatemalan style. These two

youthful assistants were invited to form part of the new leadership of
Corn Maya in early 1993. Their qualities of leadership within their
congregation had been noticed by others.

The Spanish-speaking members of the Indiantown Baptist church had
services in a large classroom at the same hour as their English-speaking
counterparts met in the church. This group had a resident pastor, a
Nicaraguan, who combined his church work with a full-time factory job.
The congregation numbered around forty, the majority Mayas. Pastor
Luis had expressed his interest in promoting self respect and a sense of
ownership of their lives among his Q'anjob'al congregants, and had
indeed chosen four young co-pastors who took turns leading the worship.
Hilario, Margarito, Francisco and Caxín were being groomed to take over
the leadership of the group, and Hilario was one of those who became
active in Corn Maya at the end of 1992. Pastor Luis also promoted
community involvement, outreach and social justice projects among his
people, but felt that their illiteracy held them back. The congregation
seemed to be a promising seed-bed of Maya leadership.

Other Florida Organizations

Four other organized groups which influenced and were influenced by
the Indiantown Mayas were the *Centro Guatemalteco* of Lake Worth, the
Maya Quetzal organization of West Palm Beach, the Guadalupe Center
in Immokalee and the Q'anjob'al prayer group in Homestead. The latter
two groups were formed around religious affiliation and were smaller
than the first two. In Immokalee, a southwestern Florida town near
Naples, the Guadalupe Center, founded in 1982 by two nuns to serve the
migrant poor of the region, was the agency which supported a coalition
of around two hundred Maya from San Miguel, San Rafael and San
Sebastián Coatán. This group had organized themselves to pressure for
a mass in Q'anjob'al each week, to help their home churches, and to send
back to Guatemala the bodies of those killed in Florida. The group of
young leaders of this community, Reynaldo, Tomás and Cristóbal, looked
to the larger organizations on the east coast, Corn Maya and the *Centro
Guatemalteco*, for help when they wanted to plan activities or raise funds
for funeral expenses. Immokalee is a three hour drive from Indiantown
through miles of canefields around Lake Okeechobee, but there was
regular contact among the Mayas of the two towns. Many Indiantown
residents had lived for a period in Immokalee. The Maya organization

that used Guadalupe Center as a base had potential as a source of Maya leadership, but the transient nature of its residents was limiting.

A similar group had formed around the Catholic church in Homestead, Florida, sometime in 1991. The weekly church bulletin announced the *Grupo de Oración en Lengua Canjobal Sábado 8PM* (Prayer group in the Canjobal language, Saturdays at 8 P.M.). There was also a choir which performed hymns in Q'anjob'al. The group of about seventy-five adults and numerous children consists of Maya from Santa Eulalia, organized under the direction of a refugee who was quite involved in Catholic church leadership in Guatemala. When he moved north to Miami, a new set of leaders was elected, ensuring the continuance of the group. It has already been mentioned how the Homestead Maya were in contact with the members of Corn Maya regarding the sharing of the marimba. There were also occasional soccer matches between the two Maya groups.

The *Organización Maya Quetzal* (Guatemalan Organization of Maya Quetzal) of West Palm Beach was a group of perhaps thirty young men, predominantly from Cuilco and Jacaltenango municipalities in Huehuetenango, both near the Mexican border. These men, with a mix of ladino and indigenous members, started to meet after three of their compatriots were killed in an accident and they were faced with organizing the return of the bodies to their families. They modeled their structure on that of their Catholic parish in Cuilco, with a board of directors and committees. They asked for help from several North American sympathizers, among them a sociology professor from a local university and the priest who had been pastor in Indiantown. The priest used their request to obtain backing to start up the *Centro Guatemalteco*, but left the young men out of the planning. They resented this "take-over" of their idea and remarked, "Father L. thinks all Guatemalans are like Migueleños, wanting things given to them. We went to school, we know how to operate independently, we people from Jacaltenango and Cuilco." The result of this perceived disregard was to strengthen the resolve of the group of young men to organize themselves better, and more autonomously, than the Mayas of the *Centro Guatemalteco*. By late 1992 they had succeeded in sponsoring several activities including a dance, and collaborated with Corn Maya on a New Year party. By May 1993 they had obtained their non-profit incorporation status from the state. Their experience shows the difficulty of attempting to bring together people from different municipal cultures and also the resolve of the refugees to avoid what they consider paternalistic attempts to control them. Their desire is clearly to organize themselves according to their own past experience. This very resolve was at the root of the complicated difficulties which plagued the *Centro Guatemalteco* from its beginning.

The doors of the *Centro* opened in May 1992, in a small donated building in Lake Worth, south of Palm Beach. The newspaper announcement of its opening (Douthat 1992a:B-2) described a social service agency and community association formed and overseen by Guatemalans elected in community meetings held at churches over several weeks. From the start, the two goals of the Center conflicted. The social services role was the means by which public and private funding could be obtained and staff hired, but the reporting requirements and the drive to increase numbers of "clients" completely exhausted the time and energy of the staff. The community association goals were only weakly attempted, on their personal time. The need for tax-exempt status made it seem like a good idea for the Center to be an arm of a popular West Palm Beach non-profit shelter agency, but the director of this agency failed to see the fictional nature of his role, and insisted on overseeing hiring and services. He placed a Cuban with little cultural background for understanding the Mayas as director. The Center became less and less "Guatemalan." Even the Guatemalans on the staff were not in agreement with each other. Father L.'s ideals for a community center that would re-structure the social life of the highland Maya pueblos, with elders teaching the youth about Maya traditions in weekly *Días de Plaza* [14] and basketball teams based on village identity, was still just a dream in early 1993. The "Friends of the Guatemalan Americans," a group formed of wealthy Cubans and Colombians who wanted to help the over 12,000 Guatemalans in Palm Beach County (Holland 1992:1B, 3B), were perceived by at least some Guatemalans as extremely paternalistic: one one occasion they were confronted by the *Centro* staff and asked point blank: "Have you asked us what we want? Have you done any research to find out what our needs are?" The non-Guatemalans dominated staff meetings. One major cause of this was that their turn-taking rules were completely different from those of the Maya. The rivalry between the *Centro Guatemalteco* and the two truly Maya-initiated groups, *Maya Quetzal* and Corn Maya, was bitter.

The non-Maya nature of the Guatemalan Center's supervision created a situation in which leadership was not allowed to emerge. Several well-prepared Guatemalan ladinos left the staff after a few months of conflict. The Migueleña women on the staff, one of them a daughter of Gaspar, were not given the freedom to exercise initiative, and were only able to maintain their credibility in the Maya community through their contacts with Indiantown and by providing much needed social services to the coastal Maya community. If however these women were to wrest control of the Center from the "Friends" and from the shelter agency, the possibility of using the *Centro Gautemalteco* as a power base was real.

OUTSIDE INFLUENCES

For many years in anthropology, it was assumed that most change and what used to be called "development" came to indigenous and peasant communities from the outside world. The implication was that these communities were so entrenched in tradition that internal sources of innovation would be non-existent. In reaction to this, the ethnographers of today are careful to show that the natives, as actors, initiate change as well as react creatively to outside influence. I would like to go a step farther here, suggesting that indigenous groups and peasant communities in the late twentieth century have both the inside and the outside within themselves, in the sense that some members of most communities live outside the geographical locus of the village or tribal area. The massive migrations of the 1990s have placed former residents of the most isolated villages in the path of ideological movements as well, and they are influenced at the same time as they influence. The ongoing interactive process leads to the formation of a fluid, ever-changing ethnic identity. In the case of the Mayas of Indiantown, the presence in the United States of many men and women from the remote highlands of Guatemala has opened up for them possibilities of contact with movements of ethnic revitalization among the Maya peoples in Guatemala to which they would not be exposed in their villages. Their very situation of exile produces a readiness to hear and understand the demands for recognition presently being made by Maya activists within Guatemala. The exile or refugee identity also make the Florida Mayas the focus of attention of other groups, causes, movements and organizations which help them define their identity and find ways to obtain power. The media, the non-governmental organizations, the academy, particularly anthropologists, and others write about the exile situation; this influences the exiles and they in turn influence their home communities, thus preparing the ground for a pan-Maya political movement. Here I want to describe briefly some of these organizations which have influenced the Indiantown Maya and their agenda.

Within Guatemala, Maya activism has grown slowly since the years
of *la violencia* (1982-1983) but has gathered steam in the 1990s. In
November of 1990, the Guatemalan Congress recognized the official
status of the Academy of Maya Languages, a scientific and cultural entity
created to promote the knowledge and spread of Maya languages and
culture. A team of investigators arrived in each of twenty-one linguistic
communities in late 1992. News of their presence quickly reached
Indiantown; even before 1992, the effect of the Academy's work was seen
in the change of spelling conventions for many Maya words, the goal
being to purify the Maya languages of Spanish influence.

At the Maya Leadership Seminar held in Indiantown in June 1992,
the presence of several Maya activists helped the participants further
their contacts with the indigenist movement. Carlos from Totonicapán
was one of the presenters. He came representing the cooperative
movement in Guatemala, but also the *Casa de la Cultura*, a joint effort
between K'iché Maya and INGUAT, the Guatemalan Ministry of
Tourism. The "House of Culture" is dedicated to preserving Mayan
ritual, particularly dance and dance costumes. Carlos also brought books
of several Mayan authors, Sam Colop, Antonio Pop Caal, and Demetrio
Cojti, whose messages range from polemics against the *Cinco Siglos de
Encubrimiento* (Five Hundred Years of Cover-Ups) and assertions that
Los Mayas existen, somos nosotros (the Maya exist; we are they), to
radical calls to put aside the mentality of a conquered people, to treasure
their language, dress and customs and to avoid *mestizaje* (mixing blood).
These books published by several new publishing houses in Guatemala,
Editorial Maya Wuj, Seminario Permanente de Estudios Mayas and
Asociación de Escritores Mayances de Guatemala, remained available
at the Corn Maya office for the Indiantown community. Also present at
the seminar was Andrés López, a Mam-speaking Maya exiled in
Vancouver, Canada, who has formed the Mayan Indian Support Group
to "liase with Indian organizations" and to "maintain the Mayan identity
within the Mayan people living in exile," among other goals (Guatemala
Maya Indian Support Group 1992).

Also available to the Indiantown Maya were occasional copies of *El
Regional*, a weekly newspaper providing news of current local events and
cultural concerns from the Huehuetenango and Quetzaltenango
departments. *El Regional* publishes all articles in Spanish and one of the
Maya languages. Indiantown residents bring back this newspaper as well
as other literature from their trips to Guatemala, and share the material
with others by making it available in the Corn Maya office. Recent issues

of *El Regional* contain announcements by such groups as COMG (Council of Maya Organizations of Guatemala), the Permanent National Assembly of the Maya People (currently demanding representation in the Guatemalan Congress) and the National Maya, Garifuna and Popular Resistance Movement. Videos which show the plight and the political demands of the CPR (Communities of Population in Resistance), the internally displaced Maya who live in the jungles of northern El Quiché, and the Permanent Comissions of Guatemalan Refugees in Mexico, were seen and discussed by groups of Indiantown residents. All of these movements of reclamation initiated by Maya people could not but strengthen the resolve of the Florida exiles to maintain their culture and seek recognition of their rights.[15]

The Guatemalan Catholic church has some connection to the Indiantown community as well, in the form of visits to Florida of at least four priests and two bishops during the 1990s, all of whom encouraged the exiles to maintain their cultural traditions and their unity as Maya people, overcoming municipality and language divisions. Within Guatemala, the church has recently made several pronouncements which indicate support for indigenous self-determination, and the preservation of Maya identity and culture. Several regional bishops have promoted self-studies of local culture and have publically praised the work of the Academy of Maya Languages. In August of 1992, the Catholic bishops of Guatemala published an open letter to the Guatemalan people, *Quinientos Años Sembrando el Evangelio* (Five Hundred Years Sowing the Gospel) in which they explicitly ask pardon and forgiveness of the indigenous Maya people for the errors of the church during the conquest and colonial eras and commit the church to a serious option of supporting Maya self-determination (Conferencia Episcopal de Guatemala 1992: 54, 55). Influenced by this letter, the Fourth General Conference of Latin American Bishops, held in Santo Domingo in October of 1992, again asked pardon of "all our indigenous and afroamerican brothers" and set out a program of promoting cultural values of the Indian cosmovision (Conferencia del Episcopado Mexicano 1992: 150-151).

Another influence which has helped the Indiantown Maya, especially the emerging leaders, to shape and refine their self-presentation to the outside world, to be aware of the global dimensions of their struggle and to know where to turn for support has been the media, particularly the Palm Beach *Post* and the *Heraldo de Miami*. These papers have consistently assigned reporters to cover the situation of the Florida Guatemalan community. Anthropologists interested in Maya research have also provided support and contact with the wider world. At different times, over the period from 1983 to the present, at least ten professional anthropologists, sociologists and linguists have been present in or in contact with the Indiantown community, chiefly through the Corn Maya organization. Numerous students of anthropology have stayed in Indiantown for short or long periods to work on their research under the direction of these professors. The attention paid to Indiantown by the academic community adds weight to the perception of the Mayas that they have a tradition and language worth preserving, as well as viable claims to political rights. The active support of several of the anthropologists has been instrumental in lending legitimacy to the leadership of some of the south Florida Maya organizations, especially Corn Maya and *Maya Quetzal*.

The contributions of several "culture brokers" should not go unmentioned. In a way, one could claim that every emerging Maya leader is a culture broker, bridging the gap between United States society and its officialdom and the Maya community. But two Maya leaders have done this in an especially conscious way. Jerónimo Campseco, profiled earlier in this chapter, through his writing (1990,1991,1992) and his sustained contacts with the North American tribes and with the Indian Law Center has pushed for recognition of the Maya as a tribe, an indigenous people in exile, with their own government, tax structure and passport rights. Victor Montejo, an anthropologist who is also a political refugee from Jacaltenango, as is Camposeco, has had influence through his books. The story of his exile is a political document, and his later writings are recoveries of Maya folktales and polemics against the injustices suffered by the Mayas (Montejo 1987, 1991). All of these writings are available in Indiantown and have been read by at least some of the Maya leaders.

A large network of solidarity agencies, non-governmental organizations and support groups in the United States has also functioned to lend assistance to the Maya exiles, particularly in the areas of legal counsel and documentation to back up claims of political asylum. Many of these organizations work in cooperation with similar NGO's, as they are called, in Guatemala. At least five of these organizations have had direct influence in Indiantown (Florida Rural Legal Services, American Friends Service Committee, Carecen-Los Angeles, the Guatemala Scholars' Network and Cultural Survival) but there are many more. When proof is needed of the reasons the Maya find themselves in Florida, when facts are needed to support funding requests, it is to these organizations that the Maya leadership turns.

MEANING, MEMORIES AND KNOWLEDGE

Together, these "outside influences" have the effect of creating a field of support for Mayan claims. In this sense, and in the sense of suggesting some of the political agenda of self-determination, they have input into the development of leadership among the exiles. It would be an error, however, to exaggerate their influence. Most of the initiative for self-organization in Indiantown has come from within, from the syntheses the leaders have been able to make of their own and their communities' past experience and the needs of the present situation in exile. They have been able to use memories of the past in the highlands and knowledge of the present time and place to forge meaningful ways of organizing their followers. A great deal of this organizing has taken place around ritual, and ritual has served as the springboard for more sustained forms of structuring their leadership of the community. One of the most pressing questions for researchers of ritual is: how do the organizers of rituals gain legitimacy; why do others accept their leadership; why do their followers follow? After living in the community and observing the dynamics among groups and their leaders, I concluded that those who are claiming legitimate leadership of the Indiantown Mayas make their claim through precisely this ability to call on their own and others' memories of how things are organized in Guatemala, to adapt these styles of organization to the Indiantown reality through their superior knowledge of the North American exigencies, and to legitimate their leadership in the traditional Maya way, through visible self-sacrifice for the good of the community. I realized that this was the expected form of legitimation when I noticed that most complaints against leaders' actions were really doubts about the extent of their self-sacrifice. Some examples will illustrate this.

José Martín could call upon his memories of his work with agricultural cooperatives in Guatemala, his knowledge of agronomy, and his ability to speak English, deal with social and legal service representatives, and his status as a church worker and elder to support his claims to leadership in the Indiantown Maya community. But whatever currency these gave him was all but nullified by the perception that he worked for remuneration. His voluntary service to the Alcoholics Anonymous Organization, however, was seen in a different light. In that

arena he had earned respect and constructed a base from which to launch
his critiques of the other Maya organizations. Angelina had, in spite of
her youth, an impressive record of service to the Maya of Indiantown,
had traveled to San Miguel to get in touch with her roots, and had
intimate knowledge of social service provider agencies in Florida. Her
presence alone at the *Centro Santa Cruz*, her ability to speak three
languages and the perception that she had often gone out of her way, or
beyond her regular work hours, to serve the community, was
acknowledged by all who knew her. But her decision to return to college
postponed her consolidation of power in Indiantown. Women are not
much heard from in Indiantown; the only other woman who had
recognition as a leader was Angelina's sister Francisca. Her credentials
were similar to Angelina's, but she had not put in the long years in social
services and lacked the knowledge of ways to deal with North American
agencies. She had chosen instead to make her mark in the Latino world
of sports and rock stars, and was on the way to becoming a promoter for
both of these sorts of events. Sacrifice of time and energy was indeed part
of her ability to attract followers; but it was in an arena, according to the
opinion of many of the Indiantown Maya, that was not sufficiently
traditional. Gaspar's family as a whole had lost political capital by their
promotion of the non-Maya San Miguel fiesta at Big Mound Park. In
addition, in spite of Gaspar's status as an elder and his connections to the
Centro Guatemalteco, he had not been able to dispel the doubts of the
community in regard to his personal sacrifice. They saw him and his
family working but never saw or heard a report about the financial
outcome of the San Miguel fiesta.

    Antonio, on the other hand, had been faced with the same sort of
doubts but had presented financial reports for Corn Maya which clearly
showed that he and others had not received remuneration for many hours
and years of work in direct benefit of the community. His leadership of
the choir was entirely voluntary, and gained him status because of his
knowledge of the type of sacred music the community wanted to hear. His
work at Corn Maya had made him familiar with many government
entities in Florida, and his knowledge of English had made him able to
bridge between the Mayas and the state, which he consciously took on as
his role. Although relatively young, Antonio had carefully studied Maya
traditions and looked for ways to consult the elders in Guatemala. When
he returned there to rent the dance costumes for the Maya Quetzal fiesta,
he specifically investigated the correct way to perform the dances. In
addition, his connections with Camposeco, the anthropologists, the Maya

organizations in Guatemala and the various Maya groups around the United States gave him a unique field of support. His combination of memories, knowledge and self-sacrifice was what guaranteed that even after he resigned as director of Corn Maya, he retained a great deal of power in Indiantown.

Those who had been able to earn recognition as leaders in Indiantown, then, had done so through their experience of organizing for religious ritual in Guatemala, particularly through work with the modern Catholic church, and through their unique ability to organize similar rituals in the United States. The choice of ritual celebrations as a way to both symbolize and promote the solidarity of the Maya as an indentifiable ethnic group was both traditional and adaptive to the exile situation. But consolidation of leadership also required, according to my observations, an ability to "capture" some of the legitimacy of church organizations in Florida, to acquire intimate knowledge of the way things work in the United States, and to secure backing by forming alliances with international and national level refugee projects, Maya activist groups and the academic community.

The church organizations in South Florida, particularly the projects attached to the Indiantown Catholic church, lend legitimacy to Maya organizing efforts because of the familiarity of highland Mayas with the "human promotion" programs of the Huehuetenango Catholic diocese and their expectation that the Indiantown parish would follow the same policies. The three Protestant congregations, although not perceived as continuous with the evangelical missions in Guatemala, nevertheless were able to confer legitimacy on the leaders that emerged within their flocks by naming them as co-pastors or assistants. Furthermore, official church personnel, both Catholic and Protestant, are expected to be exemplars of the ethic of self-sacrifice for the good of the community, a key Maya legitimator of authority. The church context, therefore, was particularly appropriate as a source of Maya leadership, both in terms of the church's remembered role in Guatemala and in terms of values they are expected to promote. Leadership became power in the instances where it was joined with self-sacrifice in the Maya tradition of voluntary donation of time and labor to the community. What remains to be seen is whether or how this power will be translated into a pan-Maya political movement.

NOTES

1. This workshop took place in June of 1992
2. There were obviously different agendas and motivations present in the minds of the two organizing entities: the Martin County commissioners wanted a needs assessment of the Maya community, done by that community, and had secured a community block grant for the purpose. They also wanted to inform the Maya community about traffic and drinking laws, AIDS prevention, and other points of public interest. The Mayas, on the other hand, wanted to develop and encourage leadership among themselves, and begin an education progam about Maya culture and history. In the end, both agendas were only partially accomplished.
3. Hope Rural School also has approximately thirty percent Haitian, eleven percent Mexican and one percent Anglo children.
4. This legislation, know as IRCA, allowed legalization of those who had lived in the United States since 1982, and residence papers for those who had worked in agriculture for ninety days between 1985 and 1986. This provision was known as SAW (Seasonal Agricultural Worker). For those who did not qualify for either, political asylum was the only other way to obtain work permits, which employers were obligated to verify as part of the IRCA legislation.
5. This included a Univisión *Noticiero Nocturno* (Nightly News in Spanish from Miami) broadcast on September 9, 1993.
6. The occasion was the rededication of the Statue of Liberty. At this event, a small group of Q'anjob'al Maya people, including Micaela, asserted their rights to political asylum (Hiaasen 1986: C-1).
7. Antonio's words for exploiting the people were: *Está negociando con el pueblo* : She is using the people for commercial purposes.
8. The following information about Corn Maya was gleaned from the files of the organization, and from personal conversations with Camposeco and other founding members.
9. The study was done by Hahn and Associates, of Orlando, and is titled *Indiantown Action Plan, Draft Report*, Hahn Job No. 89122, April 6, 1990.
10. A partial list of anthropologists who have worked with Corn Maya includes Shelton Davis, Allan Burns, Duncan Earle, James Loucky, Laura Martin, David Griffith, Christopher Lutz, George Lovell, and Fernando Peñalosa.
11. An example of this is the way the Mayas tend to introduce themselves, above all in formal settings: *Mi nombre es Javier y yo soy de Aguacatán y mi dialecto es Awakateko* (My name is Javier. I am from Aguacatán and my language is Awakateko).
12. See Burns 1989b for discussion of the idea of internal and external identity among the Indiantown Maya.
13. On the other hand, people from San Miguel are perceived by other Mayas as uneducated, uncouth, and grasping. When other Mayas wish to point out how

"uncivilized" the Migueleños are, they refer to their still prevalent custom of polygyny.

14. The *Día de Plaza* in highland towns is the market day, when the streets are filled with merchants, when people come to church, and when residents of the outlying hamlets visit relatives and conduct all sorts of personal business in the municipal center.

15. There seemed to be no direct line of contact or influence between Indiantown and the more openly political movements *Rujunel Junam* and *Majawil Q'ij*. *Rujunel Junam* is a coalition of peasant villages which seek an end to the infamous Civil Patrol system. *Majawil Q'ij* is a radical indigenist movement within Guatemala.

CHAPTER VI

Toward a Mayan Renaissance and Transnational Ethnic Group

The wall behind the speakers' table was covered with a large hand-lettered sign, announcing the training seminar for Maya leaders. It was decorated with Maya glyphs and with words from the *Pop Vuh*, the Maya Book of Counsel: "Do not afflict yourselves; we are leaving but we will return. . . .It is time to sow the corn, the seed which has been left to us." "If the tree is alive, in this you will see that we are alive" (Recinos 1977:53, 68, 76). These mystical sayings had been chosen to both indicate and animate: to express the growing desire of the Maya people to recover their heritage and their self-determination, but also to encourage the participation of the Indiantown leaders in what has been called the Maya Renaissance.[1] The struggle, or *lucha*, according to the planners of the seminar, is to recover the internal identity of the Mayas, to bring the people to an affirmation of their ethnicity as a value. This is their first tactic. The invitation to the seminar announced:

We will examine aspects which correspond to the cultural identity of the Maya, the initial process of revitalization of our ancestral heritage, our Maya philosophy. We will analyze our pre-colonial, colonial and neo-colonial history. We will discuss our position regarding the 500 years since the arrival of Christopher Columbus to our continent.

Let not one or two of you stay behind, let all arise. Let no one tell you what you must do, since for that you yourselves are conscious of its importance. *Pop Vuh*.

The tactics of revitalization involve using the pre-Hispanic, pre-Christian history of the Maya, which has been mythified into a symbol of unity and cultural purity. Also emphasized is domination by others as a backdrop to the present-time urgency to resist that domination (Earle 1989:3,17). The largest indigenous group in the hemisphere, the Mayas are now the most displaced (Loucky 1991, personal communication). They find that the divisions by language, religion, and municipality which weaken their efforts at resistance within Guatemala have been carried into exile. Therefore, the second tactic is to promote a pan-Maya unity, to actualize unity by exhortations, by the use of communication and economic links, by symbolizations such as fiestas. Other strategies, in Guatemala and in the diaspora, are to promote the leadership and equality of women [2] and to seek political access through membership in the Guatemalan Congress or the formation of a Maya Nation in North America.[3] In the words of Jerónimo Camposeco, one of the urgent necessities is to "re-invent our nationality as Mayas here" (Camposeco 1991:3).

This chapter traces the nuts and bolts of the processes by which the Maya renaissance is being promoted and the transnational Maya community is being imagined, partially realized and consolidated, especially as these processes flow in and out of Indiantown. These two agendas are interwoven and are sought together, through discourse, through efforts to concretize and name a Maya identity, through forging links across national boundaries, and through seeking power and resisting absorption. The *lucha* is not without conflict and ambiguity, but movement in the direction of these agendas, precipitated by the refugee migration, is rapid and visible.

PAN-MAYAN DISCOURSE

The Maya leadership seminar was the first event in Indiantown in which the movement toward a Maya consciousness was explicit. The use of the *Pop Vuh* was just the beginning. The first speaker launched into a full-scale history-based exhortation as follows:

> Our cultures were minimalized, eliminated, reduced in value, and a foreign culture was imposed. But the Maya people, the indigenous community, tried to break with this, and when it was necessary, had to go underground. Now we are coming to the point in which this historical responsibility corresponds to us. We see ourselves despoiled once more, expelled from our own land, living in exile; during 1982, a massive exile

occurred...The cultural roots are beginning to be destroyed. The Maya culture is very old. But it has not died. It exists. And it expresses itself in each one of us. We want to take on the responsibility to revitalize, to revive our culture and to begin to extend it in a more profound way...Our work is to name ourselves for ourselves. It seems that when there is the most oppression, there is more reflection and enthusiasm for revitalization. The Maya culture that we have now is the Maya culture that we are recreating (Field notes).

The next speaker turned the focus toward Guatemala:

It is of no help to our people if we stay here. One day we are going to return. It is a struggle [*lucha*]. Now we are seeing a new dawn among all the indigenous peoples. We are struggling to value ourselves (Field Notes).

A long discussion about the different Maya languages led to this advice from the first speaker:

Our desire for unity without the barriers of language and the need to conserve our culture through our language are in tension. [But] we must insist on our language. We are a minority fighting against something more powerful than ourselves. In Guatemala, Spanish and English are languages of power, of the ruling class (Field Notes).

This astonishing self-conscious resistance discourse came, it is true, from the invited speakers and not from the Indiantown leaders. But it was those local leaders who had, again, quite consciously, subverted the aims of the Martin County officials by using county funds to bring in these missionaries of Maya renaissance. The pre-seminar planning meetings, in which the Indiantown Maya organizers provided an orientation for the guest speakers, made clear whose agenda was being promoted, as did subsequent events.

At the Festival Maya Quetzal, three months later, Genaro presented the Dance of the Conquest with these words:

May we feel that we are all together as brothers, celebrating our culture, presenting something historic as part of the life of the Guatemalan community in the United States.

Antonio moved the discourse into the theme of unity with:

Corn Maya is satisfied and pleased that for the first time we celebrate, all
Guatemalans, under this roof without distinction of race or language.

The fiesta queen reiterated:

We all unite as one single Guatemalan people. We are here in this country
becoming more like brothers and sisters [*hermanándonos*]. We walk
together.

Her speech included quotes from the *Pop Vuh* as well.

The marimba choir led by Antonio revealed its aims in the printed
program for the San Miguel mass: "St. Michael, aid us in the unification
of your people. The Pilgrims of the Cross Choir is with you." Gaspar also
spoke to his aim of unity when he explained that the San Miguel fiesta
is now a "Guatemalan Fiesta."

In all of these examples, the desire for a pan-Maya unity gets tangled
and conflated with the national identity as Guatemalans. In public speech
before an audience expected to include many non-Maya, it was important
to distinguish themselves from Mexicans and other Latin Americans; in
Indiantown, where few Guatemalan ladinos are seen, it is easier to use
"Guatemalan" as a synonym for "Maya." Nevertheless, there is confusion
and ambiguity about how far the unity that is being promoted will extend.
The politically conscious Maya abhor the indigenous/ladino division in
Guatemala, but feel the solution is the entry of the Maya into national
politics, made possible through a "Maya pride" movement.

Their public rhetoric, frequently accompanied by the visual support
offered by Maya weavings, glyphs, temples, quetzal birds, and typical
indigenous dress, could be seen as a mere sign of a desire for recognition
as an important ethnic group, but the discourse is meant to effect what it
signifies, to convince by repetition, from many different sources, that the
unity and revitalization of which it speaks is immanent and that its
realization can be hastened through signing on to the program, so to
speak. The consequences of not doing so are outlined by one of the Maya
Catholic priests who visited Florida in 1992:

We don't come here to beg; we have something to offer here. But if we
are not united, we cannot offer it. If you don't organize yourselves, if you
don't live as a community, as a people, you are going to lose yourselves
here. Each one will go his own way. But organized, the way you have
done, in groups, we can continue to grow into a community. If we don't
lose our faith, if we don't lose our customs, our language, our values, the

good things that we have there, and if we share them, if we live as brothers, we will not lose ourselves. It is the same if one day we become a people here or if we return to our fatherland, with the same values, or perhaps stronger, greater ones, through the effort we make. There are people who are interested in helping us. But they are not going to notice us if each one of you goes off on his own.

The themes of recovery and conservation of values, embodied in language and customs, are, in this exhortation, linked to the theme of unity, and both are cast into the arena of the future. But it is not just pie in the sky. Implicit is the very pragmatic realization that, as another priest, a North American, told the staff of the *Centro Guatemalteco*, the use of the Maya identity is a tactic to gain political space in the United States.

CONCRETIZING IDENTITY

Concretizing their own identity means, in Indiantown, managing the external sphere, how the Maya are seen by others, as well as inventing new symbolizations and the accompanying persuasive language to forge a unified internal identity, a community self-concept. Burns has written (Burns 1988a, 1989b, 1992a, 1993b, Burns and Camposeco 1990) about this external and internal identity. He claims that the Maya in South Florida express their identity through their residence patterns, work, leadership, religion and communications, in response to the opportunities and constraints they find in their new setting (Burns 1989b:51-54). Part of the setting involves competition with other ethnic groups, Mexicans, Haitians, Puerto Ricans, and Blacks for employment, social services and recognition as a named minority; this has meant that "their identity has evolved in the view of others in the community" (Burns 1989b:46-47).

The importance of establishing and reinforcing their identity is, according to Burns, essential to the survival of the Mayas in Florida. Legally, they must prove that they are different from, and more deserving of permission to remain in the United States than other undocumented immigrants. Insisting on court interpreters in the Maya languages has been one tactic that underscored for the Mayas themselves the usefulness of claims based on their ethnicity, as they have won many delays of deportation proceedings. Psychologically, cultural identity contributes to a sense of social belonging, and is the basis for self-confidence and success. These legal and psychological survival needs have prompted the Mayas themselves to change their attitudes toward their own Maya identity, as they respond to shifts of policy in immigration law in favor of indigenous peoples (Burns 1989b:48, 1993b:127).

Residence and Employment

In the years since Burns wrote about the internal and external identity of the Indiantown Maya, their residence patterns and work niches have become even more distinct. Since they are now a majority in the town, their housing opportunities have expanded, in the sense that many families now rent or own houses in the older central part of town (Indiantown Park), while the infamous camps where most Maya families lived in earlier years were used by the newcomers and the truly migrant Mayas until they were torn down. There is a sense in which Indiantown functions as a boot camp; after a few years, when the Mayas learn to deal with life in Florida, they disperse to other south Florida towns where employment opportunities may be greater. This allows for some grouping by municipalities and village of origin, and by religious affiliation. One finds, for example, a group of fifteen men from the San José aldea of San Sebastián Coatán municipality living in Immokalee. Indiantown itself attracts Mayas from Soloma and Aguacatán now more than from San Miguel. The San Miguel and San Rafael Mayas have collected in Lake Worth and West Palm Beach, close to the vegetable fields. The towns of Jupiter and Stuart are home to Jakaltek Mayas.

In terms of finding employment niches, Burns noticed early on that the Mayas had a hard time competing in citrus and sugar cane work and had settled into low paid fieldwork, but that they had found acceptance in plant nurseries and golf-course construction (Burns 1989b:52; 1992b:43). This concentration has increased since his work there in 1988: flower and houseplant nurseries, landscaping, golf-course construction and maintenance are the most sought after jobs by the Mayas, and they, in turn, are welcomed in these industries because of the talent and reliability shown by the first refugees to move into these jobs.[4]

Public Image

Both Burns and Earle have commented upon the deteriorating image of the Mayas held by others—their "external identity." Local residents apparently at first welcomed them as curious strangers from a world that was thought to be extinct, victims of scorched earth campaigns (Burns 1988b:20-26; 1989b:51). But as the numbers of refugees grew, the old-timers began to complain about garbage, the amounts of money sent back home to Guatemala, and the weekend drinking binges of the Mayas. They had become dangerous migrants, outside the laws of society (Burns 1989b:55-56). They are tolerated fieldworkers, no longer Mayas, but "Guatemalans" (Earle 1990b:5) or "Hispanic migrant workers" (Earle 1993a). Indeed, Hispanics often call them by the derogatory terms *Los Guatemalas* and *Chacuates*. [5]

On one occasion, a Mexican said of the Maya speakers: *Todavía no están civilizados* (They are still not civilized). Earle claims: "To the uninitiated residents of Indiantown, the reincarnated fiesta system of the local Mayas is but another rowdy example of their worthless penchant for mindless, self-degradating reverie, a typical manifestation of their irresponsibility, and their irritatingly persistent un-American idiosyncrasies"(Earle 1990b:5).

Many people have remarked about what they perceive as the Maya's tendency to lie. This is partially the result of language barriers and inadequate understanding of Spanish by those Mayas who are being interrogated, but the perception also stems from the developed ability to use multiple identities to set up a smokescreen of protection from immigration authorities and other threatening entities. During the colonial period and more recently during *la violencia*, the ability to dissimilate was essential to survival. There is also the tactic of satisfying the interlocutor only to an appropriate level. Answers to inquiries about place of origin descend through many layers: "Guatemalan," "from Huehuetenango," "from San Miguel," "from an *aldea*," "from Chimban." This kind of "segmentary lineage" self- identification reveals a sophisticated understanding of the typical Anglo's awareness. Among themselves the Mayas identify themselves and each other by municipality and language. To non-Maya Guatemalans, they use the term "natives" (*naturales*), a variant, although a slightly more palatable one, on "Indian." With social service providers, they claim to be "Guatemalans," "Mayas" or "refugees" (see Earle 1992b,1993a). But the use of "Maya" as an identifier is definitely gaining ground. It has the advantage of avoiding the divisiveness inherent in the terms refugees and migrants, and connotes a solidarity that has not existed in Guatemala until very recently. It carries the weight of a glorious past, and bespeaks pride and self-assurance. "The separate identities of different *aldeas* and municipalities from Guatemala are being submerged under the creation of this new identity as Maya Indians in a North American context" (Burns 1992b:41). "Maya" also avoids submersion of identity into the invented category "Hispanic" used in United States officialdom. Indeed, some Mayas have marked "Native American" on job applications and other forms.

Media Management

The media also informs the public about the Mayas and, at times, the Mayas use the media to establish a public identity and manage their image. The files at Corn Maya yielded a collection of newspaper clippings and local newspapers also revealed both public sentiment about the Mayan presence and Mayan proactive attempts to direct public opinion.

The views of several named Indiantown observers are made apparent in the headline: "Some residents say Guatemalans 'have ruined our town.'" In a 1989 piece, they are quoted: "They should send them back to where they came from." "I think they're 500 light years from us. It's a long, long process to acculturate. I'm not saying they're stupid. They're not. Some are very gentle, good people. But they just don't understand our ways." In the same article, the local sheriff's department spokesperson claims that ninety percent of weekend calls involve Guatemalans, in incidents related to alcohol, fights, accidents and domestic disputes (Veciana-Suarez 1989:8A). The Naples, Florida *Express* (Kidd 1991:1,4) perpetuates a stereotype even while attempting to recruit sympathy: "They are gentle and unassuming, passive almost to the point of being defenseless. Who are these 'little people'? They are direct descendants of one of the most advanced civilizations ever to inhabit the New World. They are Mayan Indians from the far Western highlands of Guatemala." The Palm Beach *Post* registered the fears of the coastal residents in an article (Douthat 1992b: B2) claiming "Hundreds of unmarried Guatemalan workers . . . are at high risk for AIDS." An attempt by "The Friends of the Guatemalan Americans" to create a cultural center for Guatemalans at an abandoned school site awoke a storm of controversy, documented in the newspaper and resulting in at least one editorial (Versteeg 1992:A-11) which claims that groups opposing the center tried to "sanitize their bigotry with plausible reasons" and quoting one official: "Guatemalans cause a hell of a problem because their culture is so different from ours. They're urinating in the streets and cooking pigs in the streets." This prompted more letters to the editor on both sides of the issue (Jarboe 1992:A-11) and a plan by the mayor of West Palm Beach to establish a city-county task force on Guatemalans (Englehardt 1992:B-6; Douthat 1992c:1-B) to "bring together other cities, such as Lake Worth and Indiantown, troubled by the influx of Guatemalans." This last article goes on to describe the "Guatemalans, estimated to number 10,000 in Palm Beach county, arrive as migrant farmworkers but live in crowded conditions and often are victimized by crime and alcohol abuse. . . . They are unique because they receive little or no education in their native country, and as Mayan Indians, have vast cultural differences from natives of more Westernized countries." A city official pleaded for help from the State commission on Hispanic affairs to deal with the urban Guatemalan refugees, who "create education, housing and health concerns." "We don't want the problem to get bigger," he told the commission. One notes the almost interchangeable use of the words "Guatemalans," "Mayans," "refugees," and "migrant workers," but the concensus is that their presence is causing problems for the receiving communities.

In the face of all this bad press, the Mayas themselves have attempted to inform the public and to present themselves in a more favorable light. In 1988, the Indiantown Mayas held a protest-cum-religious ritual at the Catholic cathedral in West Palm Beach. Using the tradition of the *Posada*, a Christmas custom which commemorates the search of Joseph and Mary for shelter in Bethlehem where Jesus would be born, the leaders from Indiantown called in the press to make public their demand for better expedition of work permits for asylum applicants. This specific demand was broadened to include a plea for rights as refugees to safe haven (*posada* means shelter) in the United States. "These people have suffered in massacres. Some were burned alive in the church. Others were chopped with machetes. We are trying to show the government that we are not economic refugees. We are Indians, not politicians," said the Maya spokesman (Brzozowski 1988, B1).

The Indiantown *News*, a free weekly, has on occasion been used to manage public opinion in favor of the Mayas. Several examples will illustrate. One edition had a brief history of Mayan civilization, the violence from which the refugees flee, and a description of the life of Indiantown Mayas (3 April, 1991:1). Another edition had a story about José Martín's daughter, who won several scholarships upon her graduation from high school (Beary 1992:1). The July 15, 1992 edition had a story (p. 1) about the Mayan leadership program which describes the event and goes on to say that a "cultural talent show demonstrated the wealth of skills and talents which the local Mayans possess." One of the leaders is quoted: "we look forward to a continuing favorable relation with the [county] commission to help the Mayan people achieve their rights and self-reliance to adapt with dignity to the U.S.A." Several sympathetic reporters from the Palm Beach *Post* have been given access to the Corn Maya operation in an attempt to educate the public about Maya history, problems and hopes. A two-part series on Indiantown success stories appeared in March, 1993 (Schifrel 1993a, 1993b), and stories regarding the effects in Guatemala of emigration to the United States have also appeared (O'Connor 1990:1E, 5E; Schifrel and Shuchman 1992b:A-18).

Jerónimo Camposeco has given numerous interviews in order to shape the external identity of the Indiantown Mayas, taking advantage of, for example, the naming of exiled indigenous leader Rigoberta Menchú to receive the Nobel Peace Prize in 1992 (O'Connor 9 December 1992:A-14). "The world has finally honored our cause. We hope that by honoring Rigoberta Menchú they will honor our right to asylum, because in Guatemala the Indian holocaust continues," he said. Camposeco is presented as "a leading spokesman for the estimated 25,000 Guatemalan Mayans in South Florida." He is quoted in the April, 1992 edition of *Hispanic* magazine as well, claiming: "Our culture will be manifested by the use of our languages, our dress, our social system, our calendar, and all the other positive values that we as a group must maintain. We are hard workers, and we help to make the economy and the wealth of Florida grow. We are not a problem to the public, but, on the contrary, we are helping" (Erdmann 1992:44).

Internal Discourse

This effort to direct public perception about the Mayas into a positive mode through hard work in selected employment niches, increasing selectivity in terms of residence, and media management accompany the ongoing "internal discourse," the exhortations and symbolizations through which the Maya attempt to concretize their identity for themselves. The pan-Maya discourse section above gives examples of public statements which encourage unity and ethnic pride; the private sphere of daily life is also an arena for this kind of self-valuation and encouragement toward unity. Some instances follow.

During the planning for the Maya Quetzal Festival, discussions about how to execute the Dance of the Conquest revealed that different municipalities have different customary ways of doing the same traditional ritual. The men from Aguacatán had to accommodate those from Totonicapán, as well as deal with the fact that many of the rented costumes proved too small, forcing them to leave out certain characters in the historic representation. Said Alberto: "Maybe we will end up with a combination of customs. That dance was our invention. The steps were authentic, but the observers noticed only the costumes, not the meaning of the dance." Antonio agreed that the fiesta was an "invention": "This is new: it is a little like a patronal fiesta, a little like a popular fiesta, but without any relation to a Catholic saint. One cannot choose, it divides the community. Not all are Catholic, not all are from the same place. We don't want to make competition for other towns." Emilio and Pablo wanted to stress the aim of their fiesta: "to make brothers of all Guatemalans, no matter what their origin, to conserve cultural values, to not forget who we are, to help our people be aware of their culture, to unite us in our memories." Both agreed that their fiesta was a pale imitation of what happens in Guatemala, but they want to do it better next year. Genaro was critical of the Lake Worth San Miguel fiesta, stating: "The fiesta in Lake Worth was a romanticism. We should have another content, more explicit, informing but also forming the people, more Maya, more explanation of the past." Antonio agreed: "If they say Indiantown is Guatemala II, let it not be like the first Guatemala, where there is division between ladinos and Mayas. Here we want to create a society without divisions; we don't want to recreate the problems we have there."

One arena in which the Indiantown Mayas freely expressed their sense of differentiation was in their talk about other ethnic groups. Mexicans were generally perceived in basically sympathetic terms, but as loud, boisterous and pushy. Blacks were perceived as dangerous and criminal. Anglos were talked about as being in charge, in a hurry, and uncomprehending of Mayan ways. The interactions among ethnic groups occurred in the work place, in the public agencies such as health clinics, and in the grocery. The rift between Mexicans and Mayan women at the sewing cooperative was real, and the Mayas resented being used as a front to gain sympathy from outsiders. The experiences of the women at the clinics and the grocery seemed to confirm their sense that people from all other groups were more aggressive in demanding service.

Another area where the movement toward a pan-Maya and even pan-Guatemalan identity was noticeable was in the women's talk and actions. When Catal said, "We are all from Guatemala. On the other hand, if some talk about being from San Rafael, from San Miguel, from Soloma, from San Juan Ixcoy, from Santa Eulalia, . . . we are all here, Guatemalans," she expresses the need to unite under conditions of exile.

Xusita says: "How am I not going to learn to speak Q'anjob'al, if we are all here together?" Malín wears a prized *corte* she bought in Jacaltenango when she passed through there on the way to the United States, even though she is from San Miguel. Xusita and Micaela share their local remedies.

Antonio went to Guatemala one fall for the funeral of a family member and brought back a video which was seen by much of Indiantown before it was sent on to the Los Angeles Mayas. He waxed eloquent in his narration on the video: "We see these five thousand people supporting our family in Soloma, be they indigenous or ladino, Catholic or evangelical. So we should be in California and in Florida."

Both Gaspar and Genaro spoke to the need for the Mayas to be self-sufficient in their exile in order to be able to command respect. Gaspar compared the Indiantown Maya to his compatriots in the *Mayab Balam* camp in Mexico: "Here we are refugees, but since the government doesn't help us, and each one has to make it on his own, we don't have the problem of being called refugees." He sees the term as implying dependence. Genaro contributed: "How is it possible that we are only going to ask for help, and not contribute our share."

The conflict experience from which the Maya fled could be unifying, but it is quite the contrary. People identified with different sides of the conflict, for one thing, but there is also the problem that many of those who have come more recently did not suffer the direct persecution experienced by the first exiles. As a matter of prudence, most Mayas are extremely secretive about their reasons for coming to Indiantown, or give superficial reasons such as: "They told me there was work here." The fear and lack of trust that the conflict has produced in the highland villages are still present in the United States; one never knows who may be a spy, or what information may find its way back to Guatemala. But the exile experience does unite them. The journey itself is grist for the conversational mill, and in the telling, most Mayas find that they passed the same landmarks, suffered similar setbacks and felt rather identical emotions. With time, these journey and exile narratives make take their place alongside the conquest stories and become a tradition, a collective memory of a communal experience, transmitted to and re-interpreted in each generation according to circumstance.

The symbolization that the Indiantown Mayas use to make their identity known to themselves and others has been discussed in Chapter IV. The fiestas themselves, with their conscious goals of unifying the Mayas and teaching themselves about themselves, is the primary symbolization. The marimba music played in almost every home and on every car cassette player, the clothing and hair styles of both men and women, and the use of the Maya languages in both spoken and written form are other ways in which people remind themselves of their common history, distinct from that of other immigrant groups.

The insistence on the Mayan languages has numerous ramifications. The Corn Maya association leaders were forced to face the fact that the business cards used by the group were no longer appropriately printed in Spanish, English and Q'anjob'al. The observation was that Q'anjob'al, although historically the first Maya language of Indiantown, no longer had primacy. K'iché, Awakateko and Jakalteko were spoken by large numbers of associates, and the Q'anjob'al speakers from Soloma also wished to distinguish their variant from the San Miguel variety, sometimes called Akateko. So the choice of which Maya language to use was up for discussion. Meanwhile, the Bible readings at the Catholic church, as well as the announcements after services, continued to be given in Q'anjob'al, although most often not by persons from San Miguel.

The publication by the IXIM organization of Los Angeles, in late 1992, of a trilingual (Spanish, Q'anjob'al and English) edition of folktales, with the help of a grant from the City of Los Angeles (Say 1992), was an eye opener for the Indiantown Mayas and was purchased by many. The legitimacy given to previously unwritten languages by their appearance in print cannot be underestimated. This is a conscious motivation in the publication of much material in Maya languages within recent years in Guatemala, and the movement has reached into the United States.

Two other deliberate motivations prompt the continued, frequent use of the Maya languages in the United States. Internally, the knowledge and use of one of the languages is a test of true indigenousness, loyalty to the Maya cause and a sign of solidarity. Those who no longer use the languages are seen as ladinos or at least as in the process of becoming ladinos. Even those women who do not wear the *traje* are accepted as Maya if they, like Xusita, use a Maya language. In addition, the use of Maya keeps the Indiantown women within the communications network. Most men speak Spanish, however incorrectly or haltingly, and understand it quite adequately. But most women will not participate readily in a conversation in Spanish and claim to speak it poorly. In fact, many have some understanding of Spanish, but do not speak it well. However, when the conversation is in a Maya language, the women hold their own in the give and take, forcefully and with none of the shame they demonstrate in a Spanish-speaking situation.[6] So the use of the Maya languages ensures the full participation of the women of Indiantown. It has become more and more a point of honor and pride and a sign of identity in recent years, and has become one of the chief symbolizations of Maya identity in the United States.

COMMUNICATIONS AND ECONOMIC LINKS

The incipient pan-Maya unity and the growth of the Maya renaissance movement are also aided by frequent and multi-level communications among United States Maya concentrations and across national boundaries, with individuals and groups in Guatemala and even Mexico. These communications are often economic connections as well, as transfers of money accompany letters and visits. We have seen how Xunik, on his way home from work, stopped by the Indiantown post office to check his box. This is an almost daily ritual for Maya people all over the United States. In over a decade of exile, increasingly sophisticated strategies for staying in touch with family members and interest groups have been elaborated. This section describes some of them and explains how they contribute to ethnic group consciousness.

Mail and Money

The notoriously unreliable Guatemalan postal service is almost never used by Mayan exiles, nor is the United States mail which feeds into the Guatemalan system. Rather, the Mayas everywhere use the courier services which advertise five-day delivery anywhere in Guatemala from the United States, and more often than not deliver on their promise. For about $7.00, King Express, Giant Express or Quetzal Express will not only deliver a letter, but provide the sender with a receipt signed and dated by the recipient in Guatemala. New companies to render this service are still springing up: Kelly Express and Intercapitales arrived in Indiantown in 1993. The companies also deliver money orders and packages for higher fees. Most of the couriers have offices in almost every Guatemalan municipal *cabecera*. The line of women waiting for these local courier agencies to open each day is reminiscent of the lines at food stamp offices in the United States, and many Guatemalan observers fear the growing dependence on remittances from the *norteños*.

Since very few Mayas have checking accounts, money order purchases in the United States are a regular feature of exile life. At the same time, a complicated money-changing black market has grown up in Guatemala in order to convert these pieces of paper into the most advantageous exchange rates of dollars to quetzals.[7] Those Mayas who have come to the United States almost always come on borrowed money, sometimes mortgaging their ancestral lands. This debt is the second to be paid, right after the typical five hundred dollar fee to the "*coyote* " who provided transportation to a work site. Men from most highland areas were obliged to pay a monthly sum to the one who replaced him in the hated civil patrols, or, as they were euphemistically called in Guatemala until their abolition in 1996, Voluntary Self-Defense Committees. These payments taken care of, the exiled Mayas can then begin to send regular remittances to parents, wife, children, siblings, or plan to buy a piece of land, electrify his house or build a new one in Guatemala.

Telephone service is not available in most Huehuetenango municipalities. Complicated arrangements are made by letter to set up times for this kind of immediate communication, in which the party in Guatemala has to travel to the department capital to use the public telephone booth. Notices of illness or death are sometimes relayed all over the United States before reaching the affected person; the caller in Guatemala uses whatever telephones he or she knows, and asks for the message to be sent on. But telephone communication between individuals and groups within the United States is frequent.

Interviews with fifty individuals in Indiantown inquired about the frequency of sending letters and money to Guatemala and about telephone communications with relatives and friends in other United States cities. Forty-six of the fifty send letters, and all but one of these sends money, in amounts from fifty to four hundred dollars a month. Some send remittances as often as every two weeks, about half send money every month, and a large number every two to three months. Many claimed to be embarrassed to send a letter without money, and wait to save a respectable amount before writing or taping an audio cassette. Those who acknowledged making telephone calls to other Mayas in "the North" mentioned the following areas: Los Angeles (six respondents), Chicago, Canada, New York, Houston (three), Arizona, and other Florida cities (four). This communication was as frequent as every two weeks or as infrequent as every three months.

New enterprises have begun to advertise the possibility of sending messages by FAX to Guatemala and money transfers through local Florida and California banks. Without doubt. the volume of communication will increase from its already astounding level when these more sophisticated methods become widespread. The amount of communication is astounding because in most cases the people doing the communicating did not write letters, tape voice messages or use the telephone before coming to the United States.

Another sort of money transfer is that sent by organized groups in the United States to similar groups back home. We have seen that Gaspar sent five hundred dollars to the parish church in San Miguel Acatán after the fiesta in Indiantown. The Los Angeles group IXIM sent money to San Miguel to repair the town basketball court. This is the most common sort of group contribution. The church buildings of San Miguel, Santa Eulalia and San Sebastián have all been enlarged and remodeled with the help of funds from the exiles. Health clinics, doctors' salaries, town plazas and other public works have benefitted from the efforts of organized groups of Mayas in the United States. In some cases, monthly quotas are levied on group members; at other times, money comes from fund-raising events. This type of remittance is an actual help to the home communities, of course, but more importantly, the senders symbolize their willingness to remain part of the face-to-face community, and signify their readiness to sacrifice their own individual interests for the common good. This guarantees their place in the community should they be deported, or decide to return voluntarily to Guatemala.

Electronic Links

The communication network is also crisscrossed with audio and video recordings. Letters are often sent by audio tape to parents or wives who cannot read or write in Spanish or Maya. A cassette recorder is one of the first purchases of a refugee who reaches the United States, and the first gift sent or taken home. It is a rare home in the highlands that does not have a battery-operated tape player/recorder. There is also a large market in music tapes, especially of marimba music and church hymns in Maya languages.

By the 1990s, many Mayas in *El Norte* had purchased video cameras, especially those who had permanent residence status and could travel by air to and from Guatemala. Videos taped at patronal fiestas and family events and local scenery were shown frequently in Indiantown. In one video taken during the fiesta in San Miguel Acatán, the procession, costumed dances, and mass were shown, but also the family sitting down to a special meal, and many scenes of the river, the mountains and the corn fields. "This is where Rambo was filmed," joked the narrator, as he panned across the tropical greenery. The video made by Antonio at his niece's funeral has been described. Another widely-shown video, seen by Mayan communities all over the United States, was of the long and solemn funeral (February 1993) of Madre Rosa, the Maryknoll nun who founded the hospital in Jacaltenango, Huehuetenango and asked to be buried in the cemetery there. Many exiles saw their friends and relatives in that video.

Just as there are group remittances to Guatemala, so there are group videos sent from Guatemala to thank the donors and to show the public works in progress. The protocol for these videos combines a stiff, formal committee report with a panoramic view of the town center and surrounding green hills, and close-up shots of the community project for which funds have been received. A spokesperson for the local project committee explains in the local Maya language how much money was received from different United States groups and how much was spent, then exhorts his viewers to remain united in backing the effort. Often these homemade videos are shot with cameras owned by the church or the town corporation, and usually include some entertainment, such as scenes from a local fiesta, a dance, or a musical number performed by a marimba band. To view such a video in the company of the community which receives it and to hear their comments is revealing of many things: the emotions of homesickness and longing, the level of intimacy of the intergroup relationships, the strict accountability for administration of funds and projects, the face-to-face quality of life in the highland *municipios*, and the breadth of familiarity with other Mayan ethnies.[8]

Visits

Visits to Guatemala are restricted by several factors: the cost, the need to take unpaid leave from work or perhaps quit a job, the desire to return with an appearance of prosperity and with generous gifts, the lack of documents to re-enter the United States, and the hardship of another clandestine border crossing. Nevertheless, fifty informants in Indiantown could account for forty-eight return trips among them within a five year period. Twenty-two of the fifty had made no visit, leaving twenty-eight informants to account for the forty-eight visits. This selectivity can be explained by a number of conditions. Although those few Mayas who have permanent resident status can purchase a round trip ticket for a flight from Miami to Guatemala City for under four hundred dollars, visits by all others may begin with a flight to Guatemala but then involve risky return trips through Mexico to Arizona and then transportation, either public or clandestine, to Florida. Those who have political asylum cases pending, the majority of the Mayas who arrived after 1986, are prohibited by the nature of their claim from returning to Guatemala. But for those men who have left wife and children behind, or whose parents are frail and elderly, or whose family members suffer illness or death, the call is too strong to ignore. The reader may remember that Xusita and Diego were anguished about their five-year old daughter, left behind with Xusita's family. This young woman made a trip in late 1993 to bring the child to the United States, traveling through Arizona as she did when her husband brought her three years earlier. Mekel had intended to go for his children at the end of their school year but was forced to make the trip earlier because of his mother's death. Visiting family members or going to bring them to the States is usually timed to coincide with Christmas (and school vacation in Guatemala) or the patronal fiesta, when it is possible to see more friends in a concentrated period. Another timing strategy is to make the trip immediately after the yearly renewal of the work permit, so that upon one's return, there are still ten or eleven months in which to find another job. Often enterprising Mayas return to the United States with items to sell to their compatriots: typical clothing items, printed material, or specialty foods. The recent returnees hold a sort of court, or salon, as neighbors stopped by to learn the latest news from home, watch a video or purchase some imported item.

Bringing visitors from Guatemala is far more unusual. During 1992 in Indiantown, one couple was able to obtain visas for the husband's parents. Official visitors included the K'iché princess, brought for the Maya Quetzal Festival; Carlos, invited to the leadership seminar; and several priests, whose travel was sponsored by their exiled parishioners. Burns relates the story of a Jakaltek practitioner of *costumbre*, or traditional Mayan religion, who visited his people because "'There are people here who we can't forget. They have to be reminded of the days and the ways to do Maya prayers, rituals, wedding ceremonies, and so forth'" (Burns 1993b:7).

Emergencies

A final communications and economic link among exiled Maya communities in the United States and with their communities of origin occurs on two occasions when it is necessary to make emergency collections of funds. The first, which happens frequently in Arizona and

California but occasionally in Florida as well, is when a relative or friend or compatriot is held for ransom by a *coyote*, or smuggler, and large amounts of money are demanded for his or her release. Often a group is held for ransom of several hundred dollars "per head." This situation triggers a flurry of phone calls around the country, door to door collections, and strategy meetings to name negotiators. Strict accounts are kept of the amount given by each contributor, in the unlikely event that the ransomees will be able to pay back their ransomers. Even when the captives are not known personally, but are compatriots from the same municipality, groups are organized along municipality lines to bail them out. *Tenemos que ayudarlos; ellos son nuestra mera gente* (We have to help them; they are our own people) is the rationale.

The second occasion which calls for emergency fund-raising and the ad-hoc organization this involves is a death of a Mayan person in the United States. This happens often in the agricultural fields and on the beaches of Florida, in inner-city Los Angeles, and in all the points between where Mayas travel. That the bodies should be returned to Guatemala for burial is taken for granted. News of the death of a member of one's language group is a signal to once again put into gear the machinery of communications links, by telephone calls or telegrams, house visits and hastily called meetings. During 1992 there were four such emergencies brought to the attention of the Indiantown community and during 1993, the need arose three times for the Arizona Mayas to collect money to send bodies back to Guatemala from Los Angeles. The need to authenticate such requests and to insure the proper use of the funds has prompted more than one Maya group to have letter-head stationery and official seals made. One Los Angeles group has a special fund for *auxilios pósthumos* (death benefits) and groups in Lake Worth and in Arizona planned to start such funds.

From this discussion of the communications and economic ties which maintain the sense of peoplehood, connection to other exiled Maya and links to Guatemala, one is able to appreciate the way in which increasingly sophisticated modern communications methods are being used to forge a transnational ethnic group. It becomes apparent that these links are at the level of households, and also at the level of organized interest groups at the municipal level, either religious—the parish, or civic—the town corporation.

CONFLICT, RESISTANCE, AND ACCESS TO POWER

The program goals of today's Maya leaders, the creation of a pan-Maya unity and the promotion of a florescence of Maya culture, are not achievable solely by the discourse of unity, the concretizing of internal and external identity and the forging of communications and economic ties across the Maya diaspora, but require direct striving for access to power. Power can be defined as the ability to influence others to obtain one's ends, and in this context it means gaining that level of credibility within the community which makes one's discourse, choices of symbols, and networking efforts authoritative. I have suggested that the traditional path the Mayan culture offers to those who seek power is the path of noteworthy self-sacrifice for the common or community good.

Within Guatemala, individual Mayas usually start out on the path of credibility and power through taking on some religious or civic organizing role on the local level. It may be as a member of a fiesta committee, or as a catechist or faith animator, or as part of a civic improvement council. If the individual is able to satisfy the community regarding his or her honesty and selflessness, and in addition, gains experience in managing government officials, achieves an adequate level of preparation or finds supportive contacts among the agents of non-governmental organizations, the person is on the way to becoming a culture broker between the Mayan people of his or her municipality and the ladino minority which controls Guatemala politically, economically and ideologically. Such persons are presently joining together into pressure groups seeking political space within the Guatemalan governmental institutions. The formation of CONADEHGUA (National Coordinating Council of Human Rights of Guatemala) on October 18, 1993, with representatives of eight activist groups is one example [9] (*El Regional* 22- 28 October 1993:21). Another is the first assembly of the new organization "Maya Defense" on October 19, 1993, with delegations from fourteen Maya ethnies; and plans to solicit economic support from the governments of Canada, Norway, Sweden and other non-governmental organizations (NGO's). It is interesting to note that the date was chosen because it was *Wajxaq' ib N'oj*, a day of wisdom in the Maya calendar (*El Regional* 22-28 October,1993:21). The naming of an indigenous Minister of Education, Celestino Tay Coyoy, in the cabinet of President Leon de Carpio was a further sign of growing Maya insertion into national level circles of power.

In the Mayan concentrations within the United States, access to power follows a roughly similar path. On the local community level, where there exists a sufficient concentration of Maya people, individuals, usually bringing some experience of group organization from Guatemala, find that organizing fiestas, both religious and cultural, is one of the most available ways to obtain credibility and eventually, authority and power. Those who take leadership in the improvement projects through which exiles' contributions are sent to the community of origin for the enhancement of the people's health, education or religious opportunities also find that they soon become nodes in the diaspora network of power. A third way is to take charge of the ransom of new arrivals or the return of bodies for burial to Guatemala. It is interesting to note that all of these strategies involve accountability for community funds as well as a donation of time and energy. This is the common thread found running through Mayan life both in highland Guatemala and in the United States.

Because there are many foundations, religious groups, human rights activists and academics who have demonstrated interest and concern for Central America's refugees in general, and indigenous Maya refugees in particular, part of the way Mayan power is strengthened and supported is through contact with these groups and individuals. If a Mayan leader is able to sustain these contacts, a world of financial aid, media support and lobbying expertise is at his or her disposal for the advantage of the community. The leader becomes a recognized culture broker, like Jerónimo Camposeco, or Corn Maya's Antonio, or Holy Cross Center's Angelica, at the intersection between United States agencies and services and the Maya people. The arenas of legal status, job information and advice, health services and television and print journalism are opened to the culture broker, and through him or her, to the Mayan community. These leaders then become the points of contact for the country-wide network of Maya efforts.[10]

Since a large part of the effort to attract supporters for a pan-Mayan entity depends on defining who the Mayas are vis-à-vis others, it becomes necessary for the nascent leadership to resist the perception on the part of the United States public that their people are part of an indistinguishable mass of uncontrolled, unwanted immigrants. Some of this self-definition is done through symbolization, as discussed above, but there are at least three areas of direct resistance: resistance to being classified as Hispanic or Latino, resistance to North American consumption patterns, and resistance to the dependency and passivity of the laity characteristic of most North American religious congregations.

Anti-Supertribalization

Although influenced by Spanish language and culture over the last five hundred years, Mayan people do not want to be grouped with Mexican, Puerto-Rican, Cuban, Dominican or other immigrant populations who retain but little of their indigenous heritage. Having been told for centuries that they are Indians, and therefore not worthy to mix with, much less govern their Spanish-speaking fellow citizens, the Mayas have turned this opprobrium back onto their interlocutors, so to speak, and insist that they are *indios, naturales, indigenas*, and most frequently, Mayas. As several leaders have pointed out, not only is the Mayan heritage a proud past but it contains elements that are valued in the postmodern world, such as a cosmovision that holds the natural world in respect, healing rituals, community solidarity and self-sacrifice. Very practically, many asylum cases are based on "persecution by reason of race," the argument being that to be indigenous in Guatemala is to be subject to elimination by a ruling society bent on ethnocide. The United States Mayas have found much in common with what are, rather ethnocentrically, called Native Americans. The Tohono O'odham reservation in southern Arizona is many exiles' first acquaintance with North American tribes, but they soon learn that some Mayas live on the Miccosukee reserve in Florida or in the Yaqui enclaves of Arizona. In fact, some Mayas are researching the cases of the Lumbee and the Yaqui, who were granted tribal status only in this century.

Anti-Consumerism

Although many Mayas buy consumer items, especially electronic goods like audio and video recorders, video and still cameras, televisions, and, of course automobiles, their choices seem to be guided more by the practicalities of work and the need to communicate with the far-flung diaspora than by considerations of comfort or ostentation. Most Mayan homes in Indiantown could be characterized as uncomfortable. Second hand sofas and chairs, with broken springs and torn upholstery, grace most living rooms. At night these same sofas and chairs become beds for some members of the swollen households. Beds are often mattresses or even just blankets spread on the floor. Chests and cupboards are improvised from cardboard boxes and milk crates. Meals are served in shifts because of a limited number of chairs and dishes. Cars are second-hand. These basic outlines of Mayan material possessions are typical of migrant groups, but the homes of long-term stable residents display the same sort of temporariness. Even after more than a decade, the *lucha* is to send money home, to invest in the community of origin, to be able to return bearing gifts.[11]

Highland Mayas are accustomed to owning their land and homes and find it meaningless to invest in property not theirs. But beyond all this practicality, there is the often-expressed dismay and distaste for what is usually termed "American materialism." The traditional self-reliance of a subsistence corn farmer is the ideal, not the accumulation of goods based on the accumulation of debt. One researcher finds the Indiantown Mayas consistently represent themselves to others as "hard workers" (Arturo 1993:5,6). Mayas use these distinctions, the indigenous identity as opposed to a Hispanic/Latino one, and the production-oriented ethic as opposed to the conspicuous consumption of North Americans, in their characterizations of themselves. The same distinctions are picked up by Mayan leaders and used in their internal discourse and in the descriptions they provide to the media of their communities.

Religious Autonomy

The third form of resistance is perhaps the most intriguing. In their religious practice, at the individual and family level as well as at the community level, Mayan people continue to produce their own prayer forms, organize their own rituals and remain semi-autonomous even within the congregations which receive them. The consumer-oriented religious scene of the United States, with its market-place competition and relatively passive laity, is not attractive to the Mayas. The same personal initiative for individual religious practice seen in the Huehuetenango towns has not been lost in Indiantown, nor in Arizona, nor in Los Angeles, where lay people relate to the transcendent without the mediation of priests or pastors.[12] They visit chapels, buy and burn candles, call together friends and neighbors to perform familiar rituals. On a larger scale, they continue to form choirs and prayer groups and to organize massive public religious fiestas, all without appreciable help or hindrance from the officially appointed leaders of their churches, whether Adventist, Assembly of God or Catholic. This resistance to the North American style of church, this energetic production of religious practice, has been little noticed in research but may be the key to cultural survival. In a situation of restricted autonomy, the exiled Mayas have discovered one area in which they have relative freedom to organize themselves. Their initiative is often welcomed by pastors who are struggling to interest their other faithful in anything beyond a weekly service. With a foothold in the religious congregations which have allowed them space or which have simply not noticed their extra-liturgical practices, the Mayas have found a base from which to exercise their autonomy and to consolidate their separate identity.

It would be erroneous to leave this discussion having given the impression that a pan-Mayan union is immanent or that any sort of international Maya renaissance movement would not be riven with conflict and ambiguity. Five hundred years of division within Guatemala precludes any easy coalition, and the seeds of division are carried across borders. The tenacious loyalties of the Maya people to their *patria chica*, the municipality level identity, is one of the first things one notices, and although in the exile situation there is more incentive for Mayas to unite across municipal loyalties, a basic contradiction remains: in order to even speak to one another, Mayas from different language groups are forced to use Spanish, which is a symbol of everything they do not want to promote. Another foundational conflict is the one between two survival strategy choices: assimilate to the dominant culture or promote indigenism. We have seen how this choice is identified with different leaders in Indiantown. Historically many new immigrants faced with this choice have assimilated; perhaps most eventually will do so. But the 1990s has opened with a new public debate about ethnic identity, cultural survival and the rights of indigenous peoples that changes the perception of where advantage lies. The contestation among leaders which is so visible in Mayan public ritual in south Florida is part of the world-wide debate.

These two conflicts affect Mayas at the level of the international ethnic group. At the household and individual level, other ambiguities are operative as well. Many households and extended families are divided by religious denominational differences. Traditional Mayanists, traditional Catholics, modern Catholics and Protestants (Evangelicals, as they are called in Guatemala) partition most highland towns and this division is carried into exile. The growing openness of the Corn Maya organization, begun within the Catholic church, to welcome Evangelical members on its board of directors is a small sign that the political advantages of a united front may outweigh religiously-based distrusts. On a larger scale, however, any movement toward indigenous pride and recovery of Mayan culture will find resistance among Evangelical Mayas, who have learned to equate "Maya" with pagan, unredeemed and given over to evil superstition. There is much more openness to Mayan religious belief and custom within the Catholic camp. But a radical indigenism that rejects the Christian confession altogether finds no welcome among Catholics either.

The strategy of calling attention to Mayan identity faces another barrier in the legal status of most Mayas in the United States. For the first decade of exile, survival depended on avoiding attention, living in the largely invisible world of migrant agriculture, small rural communities, and attempting to stay one move ahead of troublesome authorities, whether the *migra* or police or welfare officials. To stand up and demand attention based on one's Indian heritage requires some assurance that one would not be risking immediate detention or deportation.

Finally, the Mayan ethic of self-sacrifice for the good of the community can break down under the pressing need to survive and perhaps get ahead a little. Antonio resigned as director of Corn Maya because he felt that five years of unpaid service was his limit, that others needed to learn to take responsibility for the community, and that he had perhaps destroyed his chances of ever having a sufficiently good credit rating to be able to purchase a house. At some point, his immediate family took precedence over the larger Mayan community. This too, could be considered a choice for assimilation. But it could take another turn, if Antonio were to parlay economic stability into a model of Mayan potential for the host society.

These conflicts and ambiguities will not be resolved soon, and not without many trials and errors. This is precisely what makes the study of a fluctuating situation like that of the Mayan refugees such a rich research opportunity.

CHANGE HERE AND THERE

It was a sticky July night in the small church in Homestead, Florida. The fifty or so men and women strained to hear their pastor over the wails and whimpers of their children. He had come from Guatemala to visit them and they did not want to miss a single world of his counsel:

> I want to thank you for all you have done to bring me here, I know that all of you did it through a lot of sacrifice. I am happy to have come; there are so many of you here! I have learned a lot about where you work, and how. This is my worry, because, as I was saying to you yesterday, your presence here is changing the life of our towns; in one way or another, our life is changing there in Guatemala. In San Miguel, San Rafael, San Sebastián, in Santa Eulalia, in Soloma, the lives of our people are changing. And

your presence here brings good things and also negative aspects, for the
life of our communities. This is why I am so concerned; this concern
brought me here. We need to understand the changes that are happening.
I want to share with you on this last night some of the problems I am
observing in our communities, where I think you can collaborate. I see
that you send to your homes and your relatives good money. But we have
to tell them that to earn money here is not easy. There are people who
think you pick up money just like that, there is money everywhere, that
life is easy. And everyone wants to come. There are fathers and mothers
there who think it's all easy. They spend badly, they do not appreciate the
efforts you make. They do not understand that to earn a dollar you break
your necks and are working hard, suffering under the rain and the heat.
And there they don't appreciate it. I feel sad, for example, to see there, at
the King Express office, a lot of women, waiting for their check. We are
getting them used to a bad thing. Our people don't know how to use the
money. Let us invest wisely. Don't throw it away.

This homily expresses in graphic terms some of the negative effects
of large scale migration on the sending communities, from the point of
view of one observer. The irony of the situation, that flight for survival
has resulted in introducing toxic elements of the larger world into the
remote villages of origin, is not lost on scholars. If migration begins a
state of liminality, as Leo Chavez points out (1992:4,5), the limen
extends in space to encompass the highland communities as well as the
United States fields of labor and residence. It also extends in time. Forced
migration is quick and limited; in the case of the Guatemalan Mayas it
encompassed the period from 1981 to 1985 and a second intense wave in
1988 to 1990. But one of the consequences of a refugee flow now visible
is the accompanying encouragement for others to migrate in times of less
intense trouble. The networks that are created, the strategies which
become institutionalized and the conscientization of the populace in
regard to the insidiousness of a low-intensity conflict all lead to increased
migration.

The forced nature of the initial migration and supposed temporariness
of the stay in the host country lead to a psychological state of"prolonged
limen." There is no transition to the stage of incorporation, as Chavez
points out (1992:5). The psychological temporariness also reaches and
affects the points of origin, as "transnational families" await the return
of a father, a brother or a husband, grandparents bring up children whose
parents have been gone for years, young women hope their young men

will remember them, and household and civic or parish level activities are disrupted by the constant flux and lengthy absences of key members. Many analysts have pointed out that migratory labor from subsistence agricultural regions serves to preserve the domestic peasant economy (Gonzalez 1969:11, 56; Meillassoux 1981; Kearney 1986:341-344). This has been the case for over a hundred years in Guatemala, where small cash earnings on the coastal plantations have provided the means for highland Mayan families to ease their transition to a cash and labor market economy without entirely giving up the security of the *milpa*. From Huehuetenango, this migration is usually to the *boca costa*, to the piedmont areas of San Marcos and Retalhuleu, where the coffee season lasts from October to January (Pansini 1983). This three or four month absence of, in some cases, almost a third of the population, has been incorporated into the yearly cycle of civic events, school schedules and patronal fiestas. It is expected. But when the migration is to *El Norte*, it is for longer periods, necessarily, and takes a greater toll.

The toll is on family life, especially at the household level, and on the civic and religious community. As the visiting priest pointed out, the family in Guatemala often fails to appreciate the effort the migrant makes in order to send the monthly money order, and the migrant has no desire to divulge the low-pay, low prestige job in which he labors. The results are poor use of funds and the creation of a welfare mentality.

A "brain drain" effect also takes place, as young men and women cut short their studies as teachers, public accountants or health and social workers to go North. They despair of finding a job in Guatemala even were they to finish their schooling. This affects the civic community, as those with the interest, talent and self-discipline to prepare themselves for needed public and private careers are siphoned off. This in turn can discourage their younger siblings from attempting to better their prospects through education, although in many cases the migrant hopes to pay for the schooling of brother and sisters. One father in Indiantown debated on many occasions whether it would be better for him to continue sending money to keep his fourteen year old son in a private high school or bring him to the United States in order to have the advantage of his father's presence.

The religious community is also caught in this web of ambivalence about migration. On the one hand, remittances have allowed for centuries-old church buildings to be renovated, meeting halls and clinics to be built, even a hospital for one ambitious town with strong United States regional organizations of its migrant sons and daughters. But the church personnel also complain about the loss of trained catechists, faith animators and choir members. The years of investment in sending young people to training workshops are lost to the religious community when the worker comes North. But even this loss is ameliorated by the fact that many of those who were active in their Catholic or Evangelical congregations in Guatemala continue their work in the United States, becoming, as we have seen, by virtue of their preparation and experience, the rising leadership of the Mayan diaspora.

No one knows what the future will look like for the Maya. Some suggest the experience of the Kikapoo, the O'odham and the Yaqui may hold a key: these groups experienced forced migration across national borders and live at present a transnational ethnic consciousness (Burns, 1993a: personal communication). The investigations of Kearney with Oaxacan transnationals may also be instructive. Kearney describes the "transnationalization" of the new indigenous politics as Oaxacans begin to be conscious of themselves as a community for themselves, and re-appropriate the "symbolic capital of their identity," questioning the validity of nation states and attracting international allies and media attention (Kearney 1993). The continued repression in Guatemala and the difficulties of return (Montejo and Earle 1993a; Gonzalez 1993) will limit the possibilities of repatriation.[13] But years of exile have changed the identity of the Mayas, politicized them, made them aware of the notion of the Guatemalan nation, their own symbolic value to that nation, and their own possibilities (Earle 1993a). Phillips finds that Salvadorans were forced to define their identity in the hostile situation of United Nations camps in Honduras, and became self-reliant and organized. He foresees a positive effect on the areas to which they are repatriated and on El Salvador as a whole (Phillips 1993). Nancie Gonzalez also notes that those refugees who have organized themselves in exile will have a better possibility of obtaining concessions for their return and more resources to attract media attention if their rights are abused (Gonzalez 1993). Burns sees the Indiantown Mayas as part of a "new social formation that includes a great deal of mobility and communication between a series of small communities like Indiantown, both inside and outside the United States." This is a new "international indigenous community" with connections to world political movements (Burns 1993b:190; 1993c).

The growth of transnational commercial ventures and the lowering of trade barriers in the last decade of the twentieth century may find a parallel in ethnic communities, also transnational, who learn how to negotiate with and obtain concessions, such as relaxed passport and visa requirements, from the several nation-states within which they reside. This would change significantly the way everyone thinks about national boundaries, ethnicity and nationality.

NOTES

1. R. Laughlin, curator of the Smithsonian, spoke on "The Maya Renaissance" on 18 October, 1993 at Antioch College in Ohio (Morris 14 1993).

2. See Burns 1992a:9. Also indicative of growing leadership of women were the 1993 United States tours of Evangelina Rodriguez, the representative of the Guatemalan communities of the United Nations refugee camps in Mexico (CPPR, or *Comisiones Permanentes de Población en Refugio*), also representing the womens' organization *Mama Maquin*, and of Teodora Martínez, of the governing council of the organized communities of the Ixcan and the Sierra (CPR, or *Comunidades de Población en Resistencia*).

3. See *El Regional*, 15-21 October 1993:22; 22-28 October 1993:21. Camposeco (1991:3) argues that only through emphasizing the Maya identity are legal status, social services and respect obtainable for the Maya in the United States.

4. I interviewed, in December, 1992, a supervisor of an exclusive golf and residential resort in North Palm Beach, who was enthusiastic about his team of eight Mayan maintenance workers. Several had followed him from another resort where he had previously worked. He had begun with one man, then hired his brother, and then several cousins, and finally several neighbors of theirs from Soloma.

5. A discussion at the Maya leadership seminar revealed that this word is probably a combination of *Cha*, a Mayan prefix denoting familiarity, and *cuate*, Mexican slang for "guy." Evidently the term is also used by other Mayan language speakers about Q'anjob'al people.

6. Because of the Spanish inadequacy of many women, the children of Indiantown often grow up knowing Mayan and English, but not Spanish.

7. The quetzal to dollar ratio floats, but has been around Q6.00 for several years. In late 1993 it was at Q5.85.

8. This to-date overlooked method of doing ethnographic research, watching home-made videos in a group setting and asking questions, may become more important and formalized in the near future.

9. The groups are GAM (*Grupo de Apoyo Mutuo*), *Consejo de Comunidades Etnicas Rujunel Junam*, Association of Guatemalan Jurists, the Human Rights Commission, the Council of the Displaced of Guatemala, the National Coordination of Guatemalan Widows, the Interamerican Commission for the Protection of Human Rights and *Buxab Noj*.

10. As of this writing, there is no United States national level coordinating council of Mayan communities, but it seems inevitable. Camposeco is known

nationally among the Mayas, as are the organizations Corn Maya and IXIM. A temporary coalition was formed around legislative efforts to change harsh new immigration laws in 1997; its future is uncertain.

11. One area where Mayas do not stint is in food purchasing. The effect of this is an increase in girth for adults and increased height in children brought up in the States. The greatest difference in diet is that meat is eaten many more days in the week than in Guatemala.

12. The production of food in a subsistence life-style and the self-initiated production of religious ritual may be linked by the Indian cosmovision that ties the spiritual world to the material one much more intimately than Western thought systems allow. The modern Catholic Maya farmer still prays and offers sacrifice before planting or harvesting his corn.

13. Montejo notes that the major obstacle to return is the non-availability of land (Montejo and Earle 1993). Earle remarks that many return sites chosen by the Guatemalan government were in actuality buffer zones between the army and the guerrillas or are biological reserves where conflict with the international environmentalist community is inevitable. He also claims there is a deliberate government policy of alienating the receiving communities against returnees (Earle 1993).

CHAPTER VII

Conclusions

All of Indiantown was abuzz with the news about the *Rabín Ahau*. It was mid-December, 1993, and the occasion was the *Super Festival Folklórico Guatemalteco*. The *Rabín Ahau*, the Guatemalan National Maya Queen, had come to reign over the festivities. It seems that the young woman was the first ever to be chosen from the Q'anjob'al cultural area and was a native of Soloma, Antonio's hometown. When he heard that the San Miguel group of Los Angeles had invited her to their September fiesta, he quickly organized a group of men from Soloma to sponsor her trip to Indiantown and elaborated a fiesta around her visit.

The event took place under a big tent in the park, and the marimba team from Homestead came to provide the music. Father Juan said he was happy to honor the Mayan queen at his Saturday and Sunday masses but did not attend the all-day festival. He feared that Antonio's new organization was in competition with Corn Maya. The Corn Maya directors admitted they were also worried about this and wanted to coordinate future events more closely with Antonio, their former president. They had managed to organize a soccer tournament to coincide with the *Festival*.

Mekel and Malín provided more background about the event. "Yes," said Mekel, "although we are from San Miguel, not Soloma, we were proud that a Q'anjob'al woman was chosen to be National Maya Queen; it is the first time. She will visit the Mayan community in Canada next month," he said. "Our daughter," explained Malín, "took the accompanying role of the *Umial Rika Tinamit* or Daughter of the Maya People, because the Solomeros don't have any young women." After supper was cleared, Mekel's nephew ran the video of the triumphant return of the *Rabín Ahau* to Soloma after her selection. As the family watched the scenes in which all Soloma went out to the road to meet their native daughter with music, food and a parade, it was apparent that this was an important sign of recognition for the Q'anjob'al Maya, both in Guatemala and in the United States. Several versions of this video were circulating in Indiantown.

On another evening, Antonio presided over a meeting of his new organization, *Fraternidad Watzonaj T'zuluma* (Brotherhood of Soloma). Although there had been hints and allegations that the festival had not been financially successful, the members were shocked to learn that their group owed seven thousand dollars to a local bank and desperately needed to plan other activities to cover the debt. Antonio told his confrères: "We should not be ashamed; we should be proud to admit we have a large debt, because the people will see that we haven't kept any money for ourselves." This only confirmed the ethic of self-sacrifice for the good of the community observed the year before in the Indiantown Mayas. Antonio later explained that the bank had invested in the event because of his contacts with North American agencies and academics, and with movements in Guatemala, as well as his command of English, all of which assets were lacking to the directors of Corn Maya. He claimed to have organized the activity because the Corn Maya board had not done so, although he gave them the opportunity.

This festival and the political field surrounding it compresses much of the meaning of the previous data into a single symbolic event. Many of the ambiguities of the incipient Maya movement in the United States and the contested domains of leadership and symbol control are present, as well as most of the specific conclusions reached about the Indiantown Mayas. In this chapter, these observations are brought together with some more general theoretical conclusions, loose ends are tied off, and key motifs reiterated, in order to conclude this study.

At the most obvious level, the *Super Festival Folklórico Guatemalteco* confirms that a fiesta cycle is being actively elaborated in Indiantown. The San Miguel fiesta in September, the Memorial for the Awakateko accident victims in October, and the New Year party were all held; the festival in question replaced the *Super Festival Maya Quetzal*. The ethic of sacrifice as a world-renewing act as well as a method of legitimating leadership are seen in Antonio's remarks about the pride of being in debt and in his apparent need to organize a public fiesta even though he had resigned from Corn Maya completely the year before to devote himself to his family. The importance of the role of culture broker, the one who has "contacts" with the agencies, the academy and the resources of United States society is evident here also. Not to be overlooked is the proof offered by this event that there are indeed strong and active networks of communication among Maya groups in North America, and between them and activist indigenist groups in Guatemala.[1] In an even more fundamental way, this event shows how organization and the consolidation of leadership and power are taking place around ritual and symbolic action in the Mayan world of exile.

But contradictions abound in the symbolic field of this fiesta, showing that the *lucha* to construct a Mayan identity is laden with historical ambiguities and unresolved political questions. First, to choose to call an event "folkloric" is to remove it at least one level of consciousness from the customary celebrations of the highland *municipios*, which are definitely not "folklore" to their participants. The division between the secular and religious spheres, symbolized in the venues of park and church, marks this festival as well as all the others held in Indiantown. The replacement of a saint with a "queen" is symbolic shorthand for this split.

Second, the indecision and imprecision about the use of the identity words "Guatemalan" and "Maya", seen in the discourse reported in Chapter VI, continues here too, revealing the desire to differentiate the Mayas from Mexicans and at the same time claim a share of ownership in the nation of Guatemala. It is also true that in the Indiantown context, where Guatemalan ladinos are not present in any numbers, "Guatemalan" can be less confusingly conflated with "Maya." The indigenist agenda is also evident in the use of the terms *Rabin Ahau* (Maya Sovereign) and *Umial Rika Tinamit* (Daughter of the Town), K'iché terms generalized to all Guatemalan Maya.

But lest one think that this signals unity of the Maya ethnies, the fact remains that the enthusiasm this festival generated was due to the Q'anjob'al and even municipality identity of the young woman. The enthusiasm was strongest among the Solomeros, although Q'anjob'al speakers from Santa Eulalia and San Miguel were supportive of the event. The date chosen, December 12, the day of Our Lady of Guadalupe, a national and religiously significant date for Mexicans, may have been an attempt to attract Mexican residents of Indiantown, since Mexican musical groups were announced on the program. However, a concurrent event on the other side of town was billed as a "multicultural festival" and divided the populace. This second event was a sort of health and social services fair organized by Indiantown agencies involved in these efforts; Antonio clearly saw this as an attempt to homogenize Indiantown and responded with his symbolic statement of ethnic pride. But rather than continue to unpack this fiesta, let us turn to some conclusions derived from the analysis of data: first, those specific to the Indiantown Mayas, and then to other Mayan diaspora communities.

INDIANTOWN MAYAS, DIASPORA MAYAS

Five characteristics of Mayan life in exile are most salient in the Indiantown data. I identify these as the continuity of Mayan spirituality, the symbolic nature of the struggle for a pan-Maya unity, the global scope of the indigenous identity movement, the face-to-face quality of the reconstructed community and the fluidity of the process of identity formation. All of these characteristics are intertwined and interpenetrating, yet all in some sense name parts of the reality of a people with ancient roots struggling to recreate their cosmos in a new place.

Continuity of Maya Spirituality

Perhaps the theme of Mayan spiritual continuity is easiest to explicate. In the first place, Indiantown has clearly become a ceremonial center, a ritual place that integrates past, present and future time with the scattered spatial allegiances of the exiled Mayas. As such, it functions as a magnet, attracting persons, authority and other resources. As in the ancient ceremonial centers, people experience forces there which change them and their sense of orientation. It is taking on some aspects of a sacred place, where the community gathers for the patronal fiesta. As has been noted, the essence of the fiesta system in Huehuetenango, sponsorship of a public religious ritual to honor the community patron saint, offered by men and families who donate time and energy for the good of the community, in relative autonomy from ecclesiastical authorities, has been successfully reconstituted in Indiantown.

The essential ethic of Mayan spirituality, self-sacrifice for the good of the community, can be found in the *Pop Vuh*, where the creation of humans is effected through the self-immolation of the gods, and where the Hero Twins, Hunahpu and Ixbalanqué, learned in the underworld of *Xibalbá* the secret that self-sacrifice leads to regeneration (Carrasco 1990:122). This ethic is certainly continued in the colonial and post-colonial practices surrounding the cargo system, in which the leaders and organizers sacrifice time, energy and other resources. They bear the burden (cargo) for the good of others. It is noticeable in the commitment and responsibility taken on by those Christian lay leaders in Guatemala, evangelical Protestant and modern Catholic, who serve their local churches in the absence of ordained clergy. And it is one of the most obvious facets of the Indiantown ritual cycle, where organizers are judged by the amount of visible self-sacrifice they have taken upon themselves in order to provide the ritual.

The importance of ritual itself as a way to organize a community is incontestable. In Indiantown, organizing fiestas is the most available way to obtain the kind of authority, power, and credibility that the Mayas will accept. Those men who have succeeded in using their own religious organizing experience in Guatemala to create new syntheses of the group memories, the experience of forced flight and the demands of the new situation in the United States, who prove their accountability for group assets, and invent new ritual expressions of the synthesis, are the new leaders. As in Guatemala, so too in Florida; ceremonial organization offers a space from within which to develop a power base independently of civil authorities and church officials. Religious and ritual practice is one of the few arenas of autonomous action for an oft-conquered people, and the Indiantown leaders have inherited this wisdom from a long line of *mayordomos*.

But lest it seem that the choice of ritual as an organizing tool was a simple pragmatic recourse in Indiantown, it is well to remember that in some observers' analyses of the Maya cosmovision, ritual is a virtue in itself, as it strives to attune human action to the movements of the universe. Harmony among supernatural, astronomical, agricultural and social forces is the goal. When ritual is not performed, the world ends, according to this view (Edmonson 1993:70).[2] Although there is no evidence that the Indiantown Mayas plan their rituals with cosmic harmony as a goal, there does seem to be a sense in which ritual celebrations keep time and life going. The yearly round is punctuated with the four events that have become familiar axes: San Miguel, Antonio's moveable fiesta, the Memorial Awakateko and the year end fiesta. The first of these began for historical reasons in Indiantown, but is continued in part because it coincides with the return of migrant workers. The memorial for the cane-cutters who died on their way to work remembers all the Mayas who have died far from home, at a time near the traditional Day of the Dead. The *Fin de Año* party coincides with the secular year end. Antonio has planned his cultural festival for various times to take advantage of important events in contemporary

Maya life in Guatemala: independence, the election of a Q'anjob'al queen, or to balance the emphasis on San Miguel.

Two examples of traditional ritual actions which continue to take place in Indiantown and in other United States communities of the Maya diaspora are ritual costumed dancing and the ball game. Several suggestions have been advanced about the meaning of ritual masked dancing in pre-conquest Mesoamerican religion.[3] In contemporary Guatemala, the dances are usually versions of missionary-introduced religious drama (Ricard 1974, Arroniz 1979, Harris 1990) and are performed as part of a vow or promise of self-sacrifice for the community's pleasure. When the dances are performed in the United States, the meaning is, according to the organizers, to make the exile celebration more authentic, more like what happens in their villages. The ball game, now practiced in the Mayan pueblos and in the diaspora in the form of basketball and soccer tournaments, has been called a symbol of the four-sided cosmos and the struggle to bring the ball of the sun out from the underworld and into the goal/day.[4] In Indiantown, the soccer tournaments serve to bring large numbers of people together and to allow for identification of teams by municipal origin.

These ritual events provide the legitimation and the ambience of expectation that allow for the ordering of disparate objects, symbols and ideas. This clearly includes the incorporation into ritual of the key experiences of violent conflict, massacre of family and community, flight, and exile in a strange land. This is done in Indiantown through the symbolic objects of national flags, painted backdrops of familiar Guatemalan scenes, discourse regarding "making it" in the United States, talk of the conquest and resistance of Maya people, pleas for safe haven, and the inexpressibly sad music of the marimba. In important ways, fiesta ritual in Indiantown shows continuity with the world renewing role that has been attributed to it in classic period Mesoamerican religious practice and in colonial and post-colonial cargo systems.

Symbolic Nature of the Struggle

Another side of ritual is symbol. In Indiantown, the *lucha* or struggle to achieve a pan-Mayan unity is waged through the instrumentality of symbols. The pre-conquest Mayas were plagued by civil wars between territorial lineages. That heritage persists in the *municipio* and language group rivalries of the post-conquest Guatemalan Mayas. These rifts have been addressed in the exile situation through the invention of a gloriously unified past, through the widening of the patronage of saints once responsible for the well-being of only one *municipio*, through the use of common denominator symbols like the creation story of the *Pop Vuh*, the calendar glyphs, the marimba, traditional dress and hairstyles, and the honoring of heroes common to all the Mayan ethnies, such as Tecún Umán, Rigoberta Menchú, the *Rabín Ahau*, or the local "daughter of the people." The circumstances of exile have provided increased opportunity for inter-ethnie contact among Mayan peoples, and increased awareness of their commonalities. But the leadership of Indiantown consciously promotes this awareness, even while forced to do so in the only common language available, Spanish, the language of the oppressor. But imagining a future Mayan union, talking about it in public discourse, and representing it in the symbols mentioned above is meant to be effective, in the original sense of bringing about the reality so represented.

Three other rifts are also addressed through symbolic means. The separation between indigenous Maya and mixed people or ladinos is lamented, yet fomented at the same time. When Antonio says that he doesn't want the second Guatemala (Indiantown) to be like the first, with its all-pervasive social division, he is really equating the disappearance of the division with the achievement of equality by the Indians. His rhetoric does not admit of an interpretation favoring ethnic assimilation. Yet indigenous rights have never been achieved without conflict. In the events he has organized, ladinos have had a visible but minor role: witness Emilio in suit and tie as master of ceremonies at the Festival Maya Quetzal, or the ladino leaders from the coastal Guatemalan communities invited to the Maya leadership seminar. Gaspar's family has chosen to address the issue differently, with the introduction of Mexican music groups and sports teams into their San Miguel fiesta. And the Centro Guatemalteco's fiesta was a veritable dissonance experience; the speaker proclaimed the unity of all Guatemalans while presenting separate Indian and ladino queens with their respectively different marimba accompaniment.

The question of the place in, or identity within, the nation-state of Guatemala of the Maya peoples is another area of ambiguity. I read the Mayan use of the term "Guatemalan" as an attempt to distinguish themselves from the Mexicans for whom they are often mistaken, to set themselves apart and resist the supertribalization of being classified as Hispanics within the United States context, where the names of Mesoamerican tribes are not generally known. There is also, with the changes in Guatemala from military to civilian rule and the return of some refugees from exile in Mexico, a growing awareness of the possibilities of return and a desire to claim ownership of a nation that has never been responsive to Mayan people. But the term "Mayan" is used in internal discourse more, while "Guatemalan" is usually reserved for external identification.

The division by religious affiliation (traditional or *costumbre* Catholics, modern Catholics, Evangelicals) is addressed through the symbols of pre-Christian religious practice: the incense burner, the Maya priest role usually represented in the fiestas, the calendar glyphs, temple-pyramid icons, and the idealization of Mayan pre-conquest unity. In fact, the idealization of the Mayan past serves to overcome symbolically all of these divisions: ethnic, religious, language, and national identity, although it has been critiqued as romantic "essentialism" (Brown and Fischer 1996). But these attempts have not been effective yet; the struggle continues. However, the first step is imagining unity, and this is clearly in process. Whether it will lead to realization is an open question.

Global Scope of Indigenous Identity Movement

Part of the impetus and some of the models for the use of pre-conquest symbols to effect unity come from the transnational Mayan renewal movement, integrated recently into the world-wide indigenous rights movement. The global scope of the indigenous identity movement and the ties into this movement of many of the Indiantown leaders was apparent in Indiantown. An ideological agenda, that of recovering a self-conscious internal identity as members of an important ethnic group, is joined to a definite political agenda which seeks governing power, access to resources and redress for centuries of domination and exploitation. The interesting new factor in this revolution is the procedure used by resurgent ethnic groups of bypassing the national governments of their residence to go directly to regional and world level bodies such as the United Nations, the World Council of Churches or the European Economic Community. One reason for this is the non-congruence of ethnic groups with national territories. The Kurds, the Saami, the Mohawk and the Mayas all have members who live permanently in more than one nation. The refugee crisis of the 1990s only widens this phenomenon. Another reason is undoubtedly tactical: by appealing to world level agencies, the ethnic organizations expect a wider and more sympathetic response than they could hope for within the national territories where they are often seen as less than human. Making demands, declarations and deals on a world level also both symbolizes a desire to be players on a world stage as well as confers prestige and legitimacy. These observations are true of the entire indigenous rights movement, but also apply directly to the Maya renaissance movement in Guatemala. A reverse effect can be predicted. The networking done by refugees and exiles influences awareness of indigenous peoples within Guatemala, and, since 1994, in southern Mexico.[5]

Bolstered by the selection of Rigoberta Menchú as Nobel Peace Laureate in 1992, emboldened by contacts with non-governmental agencies and the media, a host of Maya rights organizations have appeared in Guatemala. We have seen how Antonio and Alejandro, in particular, have participated in these movements by inviting representatives and distributing video and print material on their behalf in Indiantown. They explicitly state their intention, first of all, of raising the consciousness of their people and recovering pride in their ethnic identity ("Let all arise, let no one remain behind"). They and others also openly discuss how they hope to enlist the non-governmental agencies, the media, and academics to further the Maya agenda. They speak of their awareness of paternalistic motivations on the part of sympathetic North Americans and plan how to use them rather than be used. Their concern extends to their external identity, how they appear to these others and how they can manage these impressions. Contacts with North American tribes, European foundations, national church administrative boards, universities, and agencies like Cultural Survival are all everyday and common occurrences at the Corn Maya office.

Face-to-Face Quality of Community

A fourth characteristic of Maya Indiantown is the face-to-face quality of the reconstructed community there, accompanied by an increasingly sophisticated effort to maintain face-to-face relationships with the communities left behind. Here it is important to remember the importance of interpersonal relationships in any small rural community. Also relevant is the common assertion that indigenous peoples everywhere hold community values over individual ones.[6]

In Indiantown, as I hope the ethnographical material has shown, the peculiar flavor of life in the highland Maya pueblos has been reproduced to the extent that among the five to eight thousand Mayan people there, common knowledge, common places, and common rituals exist, while the privacy of each nuclear family is preserved. In spite of Father L's hopes to restructure the market day activities of the municipal seats among the Centro Guatemalteco members on the Florida coast, this has not happened. But in Indiantown, residential proximity, common civic concerns and above all, critical mass have combined to provide for its Mayan residents a close approximation of life back home. The men's pick-up basketball and soccer games, the frequent visits to the church to light candles, the women's sharing of knowledge about food preparation, home remedies and child care all take place in a relatively natural way there. Visually, the numbers of Maya people walking in the street, wearing their indigenous dress, adds to the impression of "Guatemala II."

Missing, of course, at least for the moment, is the hierarchical structure by age, where elders are in charge. In Indiantown, the few elders are accorded respect but are not in charge. The men between thirty and fifty are the present leaders, and in time, will be elders. Another difference is the inability of the Indiantown Mayas to produce their own food as they do at home. However, the employment niches they have found, in plant nursery, golf course and vegetable harvest work, provide some of the work-related camaraderie among family members that used to be occasioned by work in the *milpa*. Now, fathers and sons, brothers, cousins and former neighbors are working together again, but for others. The community garden relieves some of the anxiety about production of food for the family. In some cases, cornfields back in Guatemala are still kept in production by relatives, while the exiled family member sends money for fertilizer and seed. This is a close parallel to the strategy used in Guatemala of sending part of the family to work on the coastal fincas in order to provide for cash needs. However, as we have seen, the Indiantown Maya have not given up their production of religious ritual; in this they are definitely in charge and do not wait for the initiative or even permission from church officials.

The increasingly common use of video-taped messages, now rivaling audio tapes as a means of communication between exiles and those back home, is another aspect of maintaining face-to-face relations. The excitement that is generated when a group gathers, either in the United States or in highland Guatemala, to watch a video from relatives, friends and co-villagers is proof of the importance a largely oral society places on face-to-face contact. Taking advantage of these increasingly available sophisticated means of communication is part of what is implied in creating a transnational ethnic community which shares a common

history, cultural understandings and now, an increasingly widened
territory.

Fluidity of Process

Finally, all of this process of identity formation, renewal of ethnic pride,
transnational networking and legitimacy-seeking is in flux. This is why
the foregoing ethnographic material about Indiantown can be no more
than a snapshot. The financial and legal insecurity of the Maya refugees
and the uncertainty of return are factors in the impermanence. Also, as
we have seen, the *lucha* to formulate internal and external identity and
to find adequate and acceptable symbols for it is a matter a trial and
error. The fiesta without the marimba was not satisfying. The difficulties
of self-sacrifice, the overcoming of divisions inherited from more than
five hundred years of conflict, the political strategies and the
maintenance of family and community ties are all problematic. The
situation in the United States as well as the exigencies of the rapidly
changing scene in Guatemala all call for adjustments and
accommodations. For example, the emphasis in the United States on
women's rights, the availability of programs to help women and the need
to double incomes has caused the Mayas to subtly shift their notions of
gender roles.

As Earle notes, the Mayan refugees are not just dislocated versions of
people back home. Years of exile change one, and for the Mayas it has
been a time of increased politicization, increased consciousness that they
themselves are symbols. It has also meant cosmopolitization, learning
new languages and customs (Earle 1993a). The constant flow of persons
in the two-way migration joins with increased ideological networking to
create the conditions for a renewed Mayan ethnic identity, continuous
with the old, but incorporating the new situation. It is to be expected that
this process of incorporating selected pieces of the exile experience into
the traditional Mayan identity will continue.[7]

RITUALS OF RESETTLEMENT

This study has attempted to advance anthropological theoretical
knowledge by bringing together insights gleaned from others' research
into migration issues, identity formation and the meaning of ritual and
allowing them to intersect in the microcosm of Indiantown. It is my firm
belief that a detailed and relatively prolonged microstudy is the best way
to road-test higher order theories, and to juxtapose them in new ways. It

is important to attempt to understand all the factors impinging upon a community, not just local adjustments, not just external forces, but "the intersecting force fields of both, " so as not to "swing from the myopic romanticism of the isolated little community to the facile generalizations of the all-embracing world system" (Sheridan 1988:196). Thus I have tried to situate my Indiantown findings within the larger real worlds of Mayan refugees in Mexico and the United States, political and economic conditions in Guatemala, and the international indigenous revivals, and to show how these worlds are tied together through modern communications methods.

One point on the theoretical triangle is migration and refugee studies. It is important to distinguish the two. For refugees, the time span of leaving and journeying is compressed, the spaces to which they flee are generally more concentrated, and the configurations of the groups of those who move are different, comprised of families, women and children rather than the typical young males described in migration literature. The resulting refugee communities, particularly when they reach a certain critical mass, show accelerated reconstitution of ethnic markers, including ritual and symbolic representations of their ethnic identity. Development of the new field of refugee studies in anthropology is therefore timely and appropriate. As Earle notes: "The globe has bounced unwillingly into the multiculturalist exigencies of the transnational movement of refugees, and it is largely unprepared. Now is the time to bring to bear the best of our knowledge and social theory to this current, urgent global problem. Nowhere in our vast holistic discipline is cross-disciplinary collaboration more pressing" (Earle 1993a:15).

Forced dislocation of large numbers of people from their households and towns of origin also brings unexpected effects to those who stay or are left behind. Whether the exiles return voluntarily, are repatriated, or resettle permanently, the whole people is changed, wherever they live, Thus it is important to finds ways to carry out longitudinal research on the home communities of refugees, to document these changes, and to note the methods people use to communicate across national frontiers.

A second perspective from which I triangulate what is happening with Mayan refugees is that of identity formation and maintenance. Here Burns' distinction between external and internal identity is very useful. It allows us to see that identity is clearly contextual, or situational, and is constantly and consciously managed for the external audience as well as constructed for the ethnic community itself through internal discourse. Earle has expressed this succinctly: "The use by Guatemalans of multiple identities against misidentification in South Florida is but one example. Indigenous refugees invent their Maya-ness to bridge community and language barriers [and] to resist Hispanic labels to Anglo-Americans" (Earle 1993a:15). This line of inquiry with other refugee populations would be an enormous contribution to our understanding of identity and ethnicity, and the handicaps and rewards these entail.

Ritual studies has been the third vantage point. Festival rituals in particular, and their role in identity formation and resistance, is not a new theme, but I have focused on the behind-the-scenes organization of ritual as the place from which to understand the conscious intentions of the actors. This emphasis in going beyond the performance aspects of fiesta ritual to examine the political contestation which takes place in the wings is meant to contribute to previous fiesta/cargo system analyses, which have concentrated more on the semiotic aspects of the performance or on the material functions of the system. It seems clear that self-initiated ritual, in the tradition of popular religiosity so common in Mesoamerica, provides a space of freedom from government and church influences in which some measure of autonomy can be enjoyed. This autonomy, as well as all the symbolic forms inherent in ritual events, contributes to the interlinked processes of constructing a self-understanding and a "for ourselves" stance. The gravity of ambience which attends a religious ceremony lends importance to the symbols chosen, while the organizing itself, often based on similar religious organizing in the home country, is the arena in which oppressed minorities, especially refugees, can begin to build a power base.

Another important theoretical consideration is the whole emergence of indigenous peoples as players on the world's political and economic stage. The new tactic of going directly to international fora to demand a voice and a share of resources needs to be studied in more breadth and depth. One reason is that it is an important phenomenon in itself, as indigenous groups studied in the recent past by ethnographers in relatively isolated or marginalized settings begin to send delegates to the United Nations or the World Environmental Summit. But on another level, this emergence calls into question our whole familiar way of structuring our world by division into independent nation-states and sometimes ephemeral regional coalitions. One indigenous spokesman links this structure with colonization: "Over the past 500 years, European colonialism and the emergence of the modern state as a political unit together have generated what I. Wallerstein calls the 'modern world system' as a pervasive social order" (Wallerstein 1974, 1980; Tinker

1993:116). Again, Earle sums it up neatly: "Nation-states large and small have emerged from their Cold War bunkers to discover the hegemony over ethnicity by state nationalisms unraveling, as clamors for self-determination define themselves in terms of ethnic identity" (Earle 1993a:15). Some fear retribalization, and indeed there is some evidence of that trend in the nightly news, but one would hope for better, a place for new kinds of entities, the "international indigenous communities" (Burns 1993b:190) at the world's negotiating table.[8]

REFUGEES AND RESEARCH

In a world full of refugees, the need to apply the findings of research is profound and urgent. For the receiving societies and countries of asylum, it is important to realize the practical impossibility of distinguishing "political" from "economic" refugees, when civil war in the home countries is of long duration and not only places civilians in the crossfire but disrupts most subsistence agriculture and other peasant economic strategies. Particularly in the United States, where a generalized economic downturn has historically been the trigger for harsh deportation measures, the efforts by the Immigration Service to characterize most Central Americans as economic refugees inflames a society that is already nervous about its multicultural future. Separation of an immigration policy based on solid research from both foreign policy and political expediency is imperative if our best humanitarian principles are to prevail.

For the United Nations High Commission on Refugees (UNHCR) and other administrators of refugee camps, comparative research into the long-term effects of self-settlement as opposed to resettlement in camps would be salutary. The UNHCR assists only about half of all refugees; the rest are self-settled (Montejo and Earle 1993). The incidence of self-organization, and the rate of recovering autonomy as indicated by recovered ritual practice, renewed symbolization of ethnicity, and networking with other diaspora communities, is possibly higher and faster in self-settled refugee groups, but comparative studies would make this clear.

Refugee-sending governments as well as the UNHCR must realize that the success of refugee return depends in large measure on the identity created for and by the refugees in their exile. Those designated as official refugees or asylees may be forever suspect in their countries of origin, even when international pressure protects their safety. Those who organize themselves in exile and insist on returning as already constituted communities, as is happening with the Guatemalan Mayan refugees in Mexico, may continue to have a political voice in their new identity as returnees. Non-official, dispersed or independent refugees, on the other hand, have no hope of protection, political insertion or restitution of their lands. Successful repatriations also depend on government policies toward those who stayed; if they are systematically alienated against the repatriates, peaceful resolution of a refugee crisis is made more difficult.

Until refugees can return home, social service agencies can also make use of the findings of refugee studies. In the present case, one finding is that many refugees have been able to parlay their previous training, especially religious organizing, into leadership roles in the exile community. This sort of training does not often appear on data forms and has little to do with "number of years of school completed." Leading a church youth group, organizing a choir, gathering a community weekly to reach concensus on social issues, acting as a delegate and returning with a new teaching: all of these activities are connected with modern church participation and can prepare a refugee to gather and organize others in exile. Recognition of these learned skills as important would lead to better identification of potential leaders.

Another finding is that refugees need and want, for many reasons, to keep their presence alive in their former home villages. Aid-sending agencies might find that organized groups of refugees could more efficiently channel donated resources to the major needs of their towns. In my examples, church buildings, clinics, and basketball courts have been refurbished, the salaries/training of medical workers have been subsidized, and a small hospital has been built in northern Huehuetenango through planned remittances from refugees. It could prove more respectful of what natives see as their needs to send aid through their already organized groups in exile.

Perhaps most important, the processes of internal identity construction and external identity management in crisis-constituted refugee communities are not only interesting in a theoretical way, but have consequences for the ways in which refugees are named, represented in the media and helped. The task of anthropological refugee studies is then, to provide the bases for the recognition of ethnic enclaves within nation-states, to lend visibility to their cultural riches, and to strengthen the ability of us all to welcome diversity.

As I drove down the rutted dirt road into *La Huerta* one sunny afternoon in January 1994, I reflected on the changes in Juana, in the car beside me, since our first meeting in 1985. Juana now has her own apartment in a Phoenix suburb, knows how to use a laundromat, file tax returns and use the telephone. She has recently been in frequent telephone contact with her mother, Lupe, who now lives in Indiantown. Juana's two little sons, left behind in San Rafael la Independencia in 1985 when Juana fled the dangers of a town filled with soldiers, had recently made the trip themselves, although they were only ten and twelve years old. But Mateo and Andrés have discovered that they no longer consider Juana their mother: they miss the grandmother who raised them for nine years. When I stayed at Lupe's home in Guatemala in 1991, they called her mama. So we took them, Juana and I, to *La Huerta* where a van was waiting for them, sent by relatives in Indiantown. A small cardboard box of clothing was their only luggage. The driver promised to convey my greetings to Lupe, whom I had seen in Indiantown just a few weeks previously. We watched with a mixture of sadness and hope as the van drove off.

Will Mateo and Andrés find themselves (*hallarse*, begin to feel at home) in Indiantown, as Juana has in Phoenix? Will they go to school, learn English, accompany their mother-grandmother to church to light a candle every day as they did in San Rafael? Will they attend the various events of the emerging fiesta cycle in Indiantown? Will they soon be joined by Lupe's two young sons, now with *their* grandmother in Guatemala? Or will they all return to their mountain village? Only long-term research will reveal the answers to these questions, and the larger question of what future awaits the Mayan people.

NOTES

1. This directly contradicts Hawkins' assertion that Guatemalan Indians are isolated from usable personal relations and are not interested in interconnectedness (Hawkins 1984:236,251).

2. An interesting modern parallel to this religious vision can be found in the description of a video series on mathematical cosmology, *Canticle to the Cosmos* (Swimme 1994), which states: "The universe is a sequence of creative transformations, each with its own intrinsic timing and its own store of energy. Human fulfillment rests on identifying and participating in the creativity inherent in our moment in the cosmos."

3. Ritual masked dance is said to reflect the sacredness of the human-animal relationship and the sacrifice of animals for human welfare; or to symbolize and

in some way effect the identification of the gods and their human devotees (Carrasco 1990: 29, 105-106). It carries the message that things are never what they seem (Edmonson 1993:71).

4. "In every way the Maya marked time with sacred rituals in order to both locate themselves within the great cycle of the cosmos and regenerate their smaller cycles of agricultural, social and cosmic changes" (Carrasco 1990:116).

5. One notes that in the Chiapas rebellion of January, 1994, the leaders of the Zapatista National Liberation Army went directly to the Mexican human rights procurator and also to the International Red Cross and teams of international observers and press (Reyes 1994).

6. For a discussion of this, see Tinker (1993:120ff), where he analyzes the phenomenon of New Age seekers who join Indian rites, and where "dancing in a ceremony in order 'that the people might live' gives way to the New Age, Euroamerican quest for individual spiritual power."

7. This should not be a surprise for students of Latin American native religion. The Mayas, along with many other Meso-and Latin American native groups, base their view of time and history on the model of the heavenly bodies, which disappear and reappear with regular periodicity. The pattern of order, collapse and rebirth is a mirror of the universe (Carrasco 1990:19,122; see also Sullivan 1988). If the cycle of time is long enough, it includes all change.

8. For an interesting discussion of the issues of transnationalism, together with ethnographic case studies, see Schiller, Basch and Blanc-Szanton (1992).

References

Academia de las Lenguas Mayas
    1990   Ley de la Academia de las Lenguas Mayas de Guatemala y Su Reglamento. Guatemala: Editorial Maya Wuh.

Acosta, Elías Zamora
    1985   Los Mayas de las Tierras Altas en El Siglo XVI, Tradición y Cambio en Guatemala. Sevilla: Diputación Provincial de Sevilla.

Adams, Richard N.
    1956   Cultural Components of Central America. American Anthropologist 58:881-907.

    1990   Ethnic Images and Strategies in 1944. In Guatemalan Indians and the State, Carol Smith, ed. Pp.141-162. Austin: University of Texas Press.

Aguayo, Sergio
    1985   El Exodo Centroamericano. Mexico: Secretaría de Educación Pública.

    1986   Refugees: Another Piece in the Central American Quagmire. In Fleeing the Maelstrom: Central American Refugees. P. Fagen and S. Aguayo, eds. Pp.95-176. New York: Johns Hopkins University Press.

Aguirre-Beltrán, Gonzalo
    1967   Regiones de Refugio. Mexico: Instituto Indigenista Interamericana.

Anderson, Benedict
    1983   Imagined Communities. London: Verso.

Anderson, Ken and Jean-Marie Simon
    1987   Permanent Counterinsurgency in Guatemala. Telos 73:9-46.

Annis, Sheldon
    1987   God and Production in a Guatemalan Town. Austin: University of Texas Press.

Arias, Arturo
1990   Changing Indian Identity: Guatemala's Violent Transition to Modernity. *In* Guatemalan Indians and the State. Carol Smith, ed. Pp.230-257. Austin: University of Texas Press.

Arizona Republic
1993   Asylum Seekers Flooding U.S. Arizona Republic 25 April: A-26.

Arizpe, Lourdes
1978   Migración, Etnicismo y Cambio Económico. Mexico: Colegio de Mexico.
1981   Relay Migration and the Survival of the Peasant Household. *In* Why People Move. J. Balán, ed. Pp.187-210. Vendôme:UNESCO.

Arroniz, Othón
1979   Teatro de Evangelización en Nueva España. Mexico: Universidad Nacional Autónoma.

Arturo, Julián
1993   Personal Communication.

Ashabranner, Brent
1986   Children of the Maya, A Guatemalan Indian Odyssey. New York: Dodd, Mead.

Auad, Teresa
1992   Personal Communication.

Balán, Jorge, ed.
1981   Why People Move. Vendôme: UNESCO.

Ballinger, Gene
1983   The Country Scribe (Florida). 8 December: 1-3.

Barth, Frederik
1969   Ethnic Groups and Boundaries, The Social Organization of Difference Boston: Little, Brown.

Bastien, Jean-Pierre
1993   The Metamorphosis of Latin American Protestant Groups, a Sociohistorical Perspective. Latin American Research Review 28 (2): 33-61.

Bean, Frank, J. Schmandt and S. Weintraub, eds.
1989   Mexico and Central American Population and U.S. Immigration Policy. Austin: Center for Mexican American Studies, University of Texas.

Beary, Mary
1992   Eva Silvestre Awarded Many Scholarships. Indiantown News, 13 May: 1-2.

Behar, Ruth
1993   Translated Woman. Boston: Beacon Press.

Berger, Peter and T. Luckmann
1967   The Sacred Canopy: Elements of a Sociological Theory of Religion. Garden City, New Jersey: Anchor-Doubleday.

Böhning, W.R.
1974   The Economic Effects of the Employment of Foreign Workers. *In* The Effects of the Employment of Foreign Workers. W. Böhning and D. Maillat, eds. Pp.41-123. Paris: OECD.

Booth, John S.
1991   Socioeconomic and Political Roots of National Revolts in Central America. Latin American Research Review 26 (1):33-73.

Brettell, Caroline
1977   Ethnicity and Entrepreneurs: Portuguese Immigrants in a Canadian City. *In* Ethnic Encounters. G. Hicks and P. Lies, eds. Pp.169-180. North Scituate, MA:Duxbury Press.

Bricker, Victoria
1989   The Calendrical Meaning of Ritual Among the Maya. In Ethnographic Encounters in Southern Mesoamerica. V. Bricker and G. Gossen, eds. Pp.231-249. Albany: State University of New York Institute for Mesoamerican Studies.

Bricker, V. and Gary Gossen, eds.
1989   Ethnographic Encounters in Southern Mesoamerica. Albany: State University of New York Institute for Mesoamerican Studies.

Brintnall, Douglas
1979   Revolt Against the Dead. New York: Gordon and Breach.
1983   The Guatemalan Indian Civil Rights Movement. Cultural Survival 7 (1):14-16.

Brzozowski, Carol
1988   Asylum, Work Permits Goal of Refugees. Fort Lauderdale Sun Centinelle. 23 December: B-1.

Bunzel, Ruth
1952   Chichicastenango. New York: J.J. Agustin.

Burns, Allan F.
1988a   Resettlement in the U.S.: Kanjobal Maya in Indiantown, Florida. Cultural Survival 12(4):41-45.
1988b   The Maya of Florida. Migration World XVII (3/4):20-26.
1989a   Immigration, Ethnicity and Work in Indiantown, Florida. Gainesville: University of Florida Center for Latin American Studies.
1989b   Internal and External Identity Among Kanjobal Mayan Refugees in Florida. *In* Conflict, Migration and the Expression of Ethnicity. N. Gonzalez and C. McCommon, eds. Pp.46-59. Boulder: Westview.
1992a   Maya Fiesta: Mayan Women Refugees in a Florida Community. Copenhagen: Copenhagen University Center for Development Research on Gender and Ethnicity.

1992b   El Pueblo de los Indios: Indiantown Florida. International Working Group for Indigenous Affairs (IWGIA) Newsletter (3):41-47.

1993a   Personal Communication, 14 April 1993.

1993b   Maya in Exile, Guatemalans in Florida. Philadelphia:Temple University Press.

1993c   Maya Futures: Prospects for Anthropology in Yucatán. Paper presented at the annual meeting of the American Anthropological Association. Washington D.C.

Burns, Allan and J. Camposeco

1990   La comunidad Maya en Indiantown, de la Florida, Estados Unidos. Paper presented at Conference: Los Refugiados, Diez Años Despues. San Cristobal las Casas, Mexico

Burns, Allan and Alan Saperstein

1985   Maya in Exile. Film available through Corn Maya, Inc. Indiantown Florida.

1988   Maya Fiesta. Film available through Corn Maya, Inc. Indiantown Florida.

Butterworth, Douglas

1975   Tilantongo: Comunidad Mixteca en Transición. Mexico: Instituto Nacional Indigenista y Secretaría de Educación Pública.

Cámara, Fernando

1952   Religion and Political Organization. *In* Heritage of Conquest. S. Tax, ed. Pp.142-164. Glencoe IL: The Free Press.

Camposeco, Jerónimo

1991   The Maya Diaspora. Paper presented at the annual meeting of the Latin American Studies Association (LASA). Washington, D.C.

1992   Pilín Shapín, Un Maya Contemporáneo con 500 Años de Historia. Boletín Grupo Internacional de Trabajos Sobre Asuntos Indígenas 3:48- 50.

Camposeco, Jerónimo and Allan Burns

1990   La Comunidad Maya en Indiantown de la Florida, Estados Unidos. Paper presented at Conference: Los Refugiados Mayas, Diez Años Despues. San Cristobal las Casas, Mexico.

Cancian, Frank

1965   Economics and Prestige in a Maya Community. Stanford: Stanford University Press.

1967   Political and Religious Organization. In Handbook of Middle American Indians Vol. 6. R. Wauchope, ed. Pp.283-298. Austin: University of Texas Press.

Carmack, Robert M.

1981   The Quiche Mayas of Utatlán. Norman: University of Oklahoma Press.

1988   The Story of Santa Cruz Quiche. *In* Harvest of Violence, The Maya Indians and the Guatemalan Crisis. R. Carmack, ed. Pp.29-69. Norman: University of Oklahoma Press.

Carmack, Robert M., ed.
1988   Harvest of Violence, The Maya Indians and the Guatemalan Crisis. Norman: University of Oklahoma Press.

Carrasco, David
1990   The Religions of Mesoamerica, Cosmovision and Ceremonial Centers. San Francisco: Harper and Row.

Castile, George
1981   Issues in the Analysis of Enduring Cultural Systems. *In* Persistent Peoples, G. Castile and G. Kushner, eds. Pp.xv-xxii. Tucson: University of Arizona Press.

Castile, George and Gilbert Kushner, eds.
1981   Persistent Peoples, Cultural Enclaves in Perspective. Tucson: University of Arizona Press.

Ciencia y Tecnología Para Guatemala (CTGAC)
1987   Mujer: Relaciones Sociales, Políticas y Culturales. Mexico: CTGAC.

Chambers, Erve and Philip Young
1979   Mesoamerican Community Studies: The Past Decade. Annual Review of Anthropology 8:45-69.

Chance, John K.
1990   Changes in Twentieth-Century Mesoamerican Cargo Systems. *In* Class, Politics and Popular Religion in Mexico and Central America. L. Stephen and J. Dow, eds. Pp.27-42. Washington: American Anthropological Association.

Chavez, Leo R.
1991   Outside the Imagined Community: Undocumented Settlers and Experiences of Incorporation. American Ethnologist 18 (2):257-294.
1992   Shadowed Lives, Undocumented Immigrants in American Society. Fort Worth: Harcourt, Brace Jovanovich.

Cohen, Ronald
1978   Ethnicity: Problem and Focus in Anthropology. Annual Review of Anthropology 7:339-403.

Collier, George
1975   Fields of the Tzotzil. Austin: University of Texas Press.

Comité de Vecinos
1969   Santa Eulalia. Guatemala: Instituto Nacional Indigenista.

Conferencia Episcopal de Guatemala
1992   Quinientos Años Sembrando el Evangelio, Carta Pastoral Colectiva de los Obispos de Guatemala. Antigua Guatemala: Publicaciones O.M.

206   *References*

Conferencia del Episcopado Mexicano
 1992   Nueva Evangelización, Promoción Humana, Cultura Cristiana.
         Documento de la IV Conferencia General del Episcopado
         Latinamericano (CELAM). Mexico: Ediciones Dabar.
Conover, Ted
 1987   Coyotes, A Journey Through the Secret World of America's
         Illegal Aliens. New York: Vintage Books.
Dagodag, W. Tim
 1975   Source Regions and Composition of Illegal Mexican Immigration
         to California. International Migration Review 9 (4): 499-511.
Davis, Shelton
 1983a   The Social Roots of Political Violence in Guatemala. Cultural
         Survival 7 (1): 4-11.
 1983b   Guatemala's Uprooted Indians: The Case for Political Asylum.
         The Global Reporter 1(3): 3-8.
DeWalt, Billie
 1975   Changes in the Cargo Systems of Mesoamerica. Anthropological
         Quarterly 48:87-105.
Diaz-Briquets, Sergio
 1989   The Central American Demographic Situation: Trends and
         Implications. In Mexican and Central American Population and
         U.S. Immigration Policy. F. Bean at al., eds. Pp.33-64. Austin:
         Center for Mexican American Studies, University of Texas.
Diez-Canedo, Juan
 1981   Undocumented Migration to the United States, A New
         Perspective. Albuquerque: University of New Mexico Research
         Paper Series.
Diocese of El Quiché
 1992   The Martyrs of the People of God in the Church of El Quiché.
         Working paper for the Conference of Latin American Bishops
         (CELAM) at Santo Domingo. Unpublished mimeographed
         document in possession of author.
Diocese of Huehuetenango
 1986   Plan Diocesano 1986-1991, Anexo 2. Huehuetenango, Guatemala:
         Centro de Comunicación Social.
 1987   Evangelización desde Dentro de las Culturas. Huehuetenango,
         Guatemala: Centro Apostólico.
 1990   Evangelización desde Dentro de las Culturas, Reporte. Huehue-
         tenango, Guatemala: Centro Apostólico.
Douglas, Mary
 1970   Natural Symbols. New York: Vintage Books.
Douthat, Bill
 1992a   Lake Worth Center Opens for Guatemalans. Palm Beach Post 4
         May: B-2.

1992b   Guatemalans Lack AIDS Counseling, Treatment. Palm Beach Post 25 May: B-2.

1992c   Official Seeks Help on Refugees. Palm Beach Post. 19 December: B-7.

Dow, James

1977   Religion in the Organization of a Mexican Peasant Economy. *In* Peasant Livelihood. R. Halperin and J. Dow, eds. Pp.215-226. New York: St. Martin's Press.

Earle, Duncan

1989   Maya Responses to Economic Domination: Reading a Maya Refugee Fiesta in Indiantown, Florida. Paper presented at the annual meeting of the American Anthropological Association. Washington, D.C.

1990a   Appropriating the Enemy: Highland Maya Religious Organization and Community Survival. *In* Class, Politics and Popular Religion in Mexico and Central America. L. Stephen and J. Dow, eds. Pp.115- 139. Washington D.C.: American Anthropological Association.

1990b   The Maya Diaspora, Exile in Hot Country. Unpublished Manuscript in possession of author.

1992a   Authority, Social Conflict and the Rise of Protestantism: Religious Conversion in a Maya Village. Social Compass 39 (3):377-388.

1992b   Refugees as Metaphor for the Post-Modern Condition. Paper presented at the annual meeting of the American Anthropological Association. San Francisco.

1993a   Committee on Refugee Issues. Anthropology Newsletter February 1993:15.

1993b   Realities of Return. Paper presented at the annual meeting of the American Anthropological Associaton. Washington, D.C.

Early, John D.

1982   The Demographic Structure and Evolution of a Peasant System: The Guatemalan Population. Boca Raton: University Presses of Florida.

Edmonson, Munro

1993   The Mayan Faith. *In* South and Meso-American Native Spirituality. G. Gossen, ed. Pp.65-85. New York: Crossroad.El Regional (Guatemala)

1993   Corporaciones Municipales Electas en Huehuetenango. 23-29 May:14-19.

1993   Asamblea Nacional Maya (campo pagado).13-19 June:14.

1993   Mexico: Un Fondo Especial Indígena Pide la Cumbre de Oaxtepec.15- 21 October: 22.

1993   Nace Organización "Defensoría Maya." 22-28 October: 21.

El Vocero de IXIM
    1991   No. 5, January: Los Angeles.

Englehardt, Joel
    1992   Graham's Guatemalan Plan Takes New Tack. Palm Beach Post. 15 December: 6-B.

Erdmann, Anja
    1992   New Life in the Old Tradition. Hispanic Magazine. April: 44.

Fagen, Patricia and Sergio Aguayo
    1986   Fleeing the Maelstrom: Central American Refugees. Washington: Johns Hopkins University Press.

Farriss, Nancy
    1984   Maya Society Under Colonial Rule. Princeton: Princeton University Press.

Ferris, Elizabeth G.
    1987   The Central American Refugees. New York: Praeger.

Fischer, Edward and R. McKenna Brown, eds.
    1996   Maya Cultural Activism in Guatemala. Austin: University of Texas Press

Foster, George
    1953   Cofradía and Compadrazgo in Spain and Spanish America. Southwest Journal of Anthropology 9 (1): 1-18.
    1979   (1967) Tzintzuntzan, Mexican Peasants in a Changing World. North Holland, New York: Elsevier.

Franco, René
    1993   Clinica Caminante Meeting Agenda for April 8, 1993. Chandler, Arizona: Chandler Regional Hospital.Freire, Paolo
    1970   The Pedagogy of the Oppressed. New York: Herder and Herder.

Frisbie, Parker
    1975   Illegal Migration from Mexico to the United States: A Longitudinal Analysis. International Migration Review 9 (1): 3-13.

Glick, Nina
    1977   Ethnic Groups Are Made, Not Born: The Haitian Immigrant and American Politics. *In* Ethnic Encounters. G. Hicks and P, Leis, eds. Pp.23-35. North Scituate, MA: Duxbury Press.

Gmelch, George
    1980   Return Migration. Annual Review of Anthropology 9:135-159.

Goldsten, Sidney
    1981   Some Comments on Migration and Development. *In* Why People Move. J. Balán, ed. Pp.337-338. Vendôme: UNESCO.

Gómez, Carlos Ramiro
    1993   Marinmaya de Brazo. Guatemala en USA (Los Angeles). 5 January: 8-9.

Gonzalez, Nancie L.
 1969 Black Carib Household Structure, A Study of Migration and Modernization. Seattle: University of Washington Press.
 1988 Sojourners of the Caribbean, Ethnogenesis and Ethnohistory of the Garifuna. Urbana: University of Illinois Press.
 1989 Introduction. *In* Conflict, Migration and the Expression of Ethnicity.
  N. Gonzalez and C. McCommon, eds. Pp.1-10. Boulder: Westview.
 1992 The Rise of the Not-So-Ancient Maya. Paper presented at the annual meeting of the American Anthropological Association. San Francisco.
 1993 After Repatriation, What? Paper presented at the annual meeting of the American Anthropological Association. Washington, D.C.
Gonzalez, Nancie and Carolyn McCommon, eds.
 1989 Conflict, Migration, and the Expression of Ethnicity. Boulder: Westview.
Gossen, Gary
 1974 Chamulas in the World of the Sun: Time and Space in a Maya Oral Tradition. Cambridge: Harvard University Press.
Gossen, Gary with Miguel Leon-Portilla, ed.
 1993 South and Meso-American Native Spirituality. New York: Crossroad.
Green, Charles
 1993 14% Don't Speak English at Home. Arizona Republic 28 April 1993: A-7.
Greenberg, James
 1981 Santiago's Sword. Berkeley: University of California Press.
 1990 Sanctity and Resistance in Closed Corporate Indigenous Communities: Coffee Money, Violence, and Ritual Organization in Chatino Communities of Oaxaca. *In* Class, Politics, and Popular Religion in Mexico and Central America. L Stephen and J. Dow, eds. Pp.95-114. Washington: American Anthropological Association.
Grollig, Francis X.
 1959 San Miguel Acatán, Huehuetenango, Guatemala: A Modern Maya Village. Ph.D. dissertation, Indiana University.
Groupe de Surveillance
 1992 The Right to Return: Displaced People in Guatemala. Ottawa: Central American Monitoring Group.
Guatemalan Church in Exile
 1989 Guatemala: Security, Development, and Democracy. Managua: IGE.

Guatemalan Maya Indian Support Group
    1992   Brochure. Vancouver: Guatemalan Maya Indian Support Group.
Hahn, Robert
    1990   Indiantown Action Plan, Draft Report, Hahn Job No. 89122.
            Orlando: Hahn and Company.
Halperin, Rhonda and James Dow, eds.
    1977   Peasant Livelihood. New York: St. Martin's Press.
Hamilton, Gary G.
    1985   Temporary Migration and the Institutionalization of Strategy.
            International Journal of Intercultural Relations 9:405-425.
Hamilton, Nora and Norma Stoltz Chinchilla
    1991   Central American Migration: A Framework for Analysis. Latin
            American Research Review 26 (1): 75-110.
Hansen, Art
    1982   Self-Settled Rural Refugees in Africa: The Case of Angolans in
            Zambian Villages. *In* Involuntary Migration and Resettlement. A.
            Hansen and A. Oliver-Smith, eds. Pp.13-35. Boulder: Westview.
Hansen, Art and Anthony Oliver-Smith, eds.
    1982   Involuntary Migration and Resettlement, The Problems and
            Responses of Dislocated People. Boulder: Westview.
Harris, Max
    1990   Indigenismo y Catolicidad: Folk Dramatizations of Evangelism
            and Conquest in Central Mexico. Journal of the American
            Academy of Religion LVIII (1): 55-68.
Hawkins, John
    1984   Inverse Images: The Meaning of Culture, Ethnicity and Family in
            Postcolonial Guatemala. Albuquerque: University of New Mexico
            Press.
Helms, Mary
    1975   Middle America: A Culture History of Heartland and Frontiers.
            Englewood Cliffs, New Jersey: Prentice-Hall.
Hiaasen, Carl
    1986   Miami Herald 27 June: C-1.
Hicks, George and Philip Leis, eds.
    1977   Ethnic Encounters: Identities and Contexts. North Scituate, MA:
            Duxbury Press.
Hill, Jonathan D.
    1989   Indigenous Peoples and Nation States. Latin American Anthro-
            pology Review 1 (2): 34-35.
Hill, Robert and John Monaghan
    1987   Continuities in Highland Maya Social Organization. Philadelphia:
            University of Pennsylvania Press.

Hillenbrand, Hans
1976   Algunos Aspectos de la Religiosidad Campesina. Lima: Centro
        Latino-Americana de Trabajo Social.
Holland, Grant
1992   Old School May Find New Life. Palm Beach Post. 13 July: 1-B,
        3-B.
Holland, Joe and Peter Henriot, S.J.
1983   Social Analysis. Maryknoll, New York: Orbis.
Indiantown Chamber of Commerce
n.d.   Welcome to Indiantown, Florida. Brochure. Indiantown, Florida:
        Indiantown Chamber of Commerce.
Indiantown Company
1992   Telephone Directory, Indiantown, Florida. Indiantown, Florida:
        The Indiantown Company.
Indiantown News
1991   The Corn Maya Project. 3 April: 1-2.
1992   Mayan Leadership Program Concluded at Dunklin Camp. 15 July:
        1.
Indigenous Peoples Network
1983   The Forced Migration of Mayan Peoples: a Report on the
        Situation of Kanjobal Refugees in Southern Florida. Miami:
        Indigenous Peoples Network Documentation Group.
Ingham, John M.
1986   Mary, Michael, and Lucifer: Folk Catholicism in Central Mexico.
        Austin: University of Texas Press.
Jarboe, Jill
1992   We Owe a Debt to Guatemalans Here. Palm Beach Post. 7
        December: A-11.Johnson, Tim
1993   War Forces Thousands into Life on the Run. Miami Herald. 3
        October: A-1.
Kahn, Joel
1985   Peasant Ideologies in the Third World. Annual Review of
        Anthropology 14: 49-75.
Kearney, Michael
1986   From the Invisible Hand to Visible Feet: Anthropological Studies
        of Migration and Development. Annual Review of Anthropology
        15: 331-361.
1992   Beyond the Limits of the Nation-State: Popular Organizations of
        Transnational Mixtec and Zapotec Migrants. Paper presented at
        the annual meeting of the American Anthropological Association,
        San Francisco.
1993   From Corn Fields to Force Fields: Cultural-Political Strategies of
        Indigenous Oaxacan Transnationals. Paper presented at the

annual meeting of the American Anthropological Association. Washington, D.C.

Kendall, Carl, J. Hawkins and L. Bossen, eds.
1983   Heritage of Conquest, Thirty Years Later. Albuquerque: University of New Mexico Press.

Kertzer, David
1988   Ritual, Politics and Power. New Haven: Yale University Press.

Kidd, Lucinda
1991   The Quiet Faces of Immokalee. Naples (Florida) Express. 9 January: 1,4,8.

King, Russell
1986   Return Migration and Regional Economic Problems, An Overview. *In* Return Migration and Regional Economic Problems. R. King, ed. Pp.1-37. London: Croom Helm.

King, Russell, ed.
1986   Return Migration and Regional Economic Problems. London: Croom Helm.Kirchhoff, Paul
1952   Mesoamerica: Its Geographical Limits, Ethnographic Composition and Cultural Characteristics. *In* Heritage of Conquest. Sol. Tax, ed. Pp.1-42. Glencoe, IL: The Free Press.

Kunz, E.F.
1973   The Refugee in Flight: Kinetic Models and Forms of Displacement. International Migration Review 7(2): 125-146.

LaFarge, Oliver
1947   Santa Eulalia: The Religion of a Cuchumatan Indian Town. Chicago: University of Chicago Press.

Lomnitz, Larissa Adler
1977   Networks and Marginality, Life in a Mexican Shantytown. New York: Academic Press.

Loucky, James
1991   Personal Communication of November 11, 1991.

MacArthur, Harry S.
1977   Releasing the Dead, Ritual and Motivation in Aguacatec Dances. *In* Cognitive Studies in Southern Mesoamerica. H. Neuenswander and D. Arnold, eds. Pp.3-30. Dallas: SIL Museum of Anthropology.

MacEoin, Gary
1985   Sanctuary. San Francisco: Harper and Row.

Manz, Beatriz
1983   Guatemalan Refugees: Violence, Displacement, and Survival. Cultural Survival 7 (1): 38-42.
1988   Refugees of a Hidden War. Albany: State University of New York Press.

Martin, Laura
   1992   The Cleveland State University Mayan Peoples in Exile Project,
           Indiantown, Florida. Cleveland: Cleveland State University.
Martinez, Al
   1993   When Borders Become Barriers. Palm Beach Post 22 January:
           A-15.
Maryknoll Order
   1967   Diary of San Miguel Acatán 1959-1969. Marynoll, New York:
           Archives of the Maryknoll Order.
   1969   Cuentos Folkloricos de San Miguel Acatán. Maryknoll, New
           York: Archives of the Maryknoll Order.
Maxwell, Judith
   1992   Standardization in Kaqchikel Maya and the Demise or
           Reintegration of Spanish Loan Words. Paper presented at the
           Conference on Rediscovering America. Baton Rouge: Louisiana
           State University.
McKinney, William
   1992   The Church as Community Indicator and Site of Cultural
           Preservation. Paper presented at the annual meeting of the
           American Anthropological Association. Washington, D.C.
Meillassoux, Claude
   1981   Maidens, Meal and Money. Cambridge: Cambridge University
           Press.
Menchú, Rigoberta
   1984   I, Rigoberta Menchú. Edited and introduced by Elizabeth Burgos-
           Debray; translated by Ann Wright. London: Verso.
   1992   Nobel Prize Gives Winner Hope for Guatemala Peace. Garcia,
           James. Palm Beach Post. 9 December:A-1, A-14.
Mérida-Vasquez, Cesar Julio
   1984   Huehuetenango: Historia, Geografía, Cultura, Turismo.
           Guatemala: CENALTEX.
Miralles, María A.
   1987   Some Observations of the Food Habits of Guatemalan Refugees
           in South Florida. Florida Journal of Anthropology 12 (2):11-27.
Montejo, Victor
   1987   Testimony: Death of a Guatemalan Village. Willimantic, CT:
           Curbstone Press.
   1991   The Bird Who Cleans the World: And Other Mayan Fables.
           Willimantic, CT: Curbstone Press.
Montejo, Victor and D. Earle
   1993   Realities of Return. Paper presented at the annual meeting of the
           American Anthropological Association. Washington, D.C.

Moore, Alexander
    1989   Symbolic Imperatives for a Democratic Peace in Guatemala. *In* Conflict, Migration, and the Expression of Ethnicity. N. Gonzalez and C. McCommon, eds. Pp.28-45. Boulder: Westview.
Moors, Marilyn, ed.
    1992   Unfinished Stories: Guatemalan Refugees in Mexico. Issue Brief, Guatemalan Health Rights Support Network Project USA. Washington, D.C.: GHRSP.
Morris, Brian
    1987   Anthropological Studies of Religion, An Introductory Text. New York: Cambridge University Press.
Morris, Terry
    1993   Mayan Fest the 1st Word in Tradition. Dayton Daily News. 14 October: C-1.
Nagata, Judith
    1974   What is Mayal? Situational Selection of Ethnic Identity in a Plural Society. American Ethnologist 1:331-350.
Nagengast, Carole and Michael Kearney
    1990   Mixtec Ethnicity: Social Identity, Political Consciousness, and Political Activism. Latin American Research Review 25 (2): 61-91.
Nash, June
    1970   In the Eyes of the Ancestors: Belief and Behavior in a Maya Community. New Haven: Yale University Press.
Nash, Manning
    1989   The Cauldron of Ethnicity in the Modern World. Chicago: University of Chicago Press.
NCOORD
    1993   Newsletter. 21 July: 7-9. Chicago: National Coordinating Office of Refugees and Displaced of Guatemala.Neuenswander, H. and D. Arnold
    1977   Cognitive Studies in Southern Mesoamerica. Dallas: SIL Museum of Anthropology.
Newsweek
    1990   April 9:18-20.
Nutini, Hugo and Betty Bell
    1980   Ritual Kinship, Volume I. Princeton: Princeton University Press.
O'Connor, Anne-Marie
    1989   Flight Without Freedom. Miami Herald. 6 April: 3, 28-30.
    1990   An Exodus from Fear to Frustration: Guatemalans Search for a Dream in South Florida. Palm Beach Post 24 June: E-1, E-4.
    1992   Peace Prize Vindicates Struggle for Political Asylum. Palm Beach Post 9 December: A-14.

Olzak, Susan
  1983   Contemporary Ethnic Mobilization. Annual Review of Sociology
          9: 355-374.
Palm Beach Post
  1992   Border Patrol Accused of Torture, Sex Abuse. 1 June: A-2.
Pansini, J. Jude
  1983   Indian Seasonal Plantation Work in Guatemala. Cultural Survival
          7 (1): 17-19.
Peñalosa, Fernando
  1992   Personal Communication.
Phillips, James
  1993   Repatriation: Getting Ready or Getting Nowhere? Paper presented
          at the annual meeting of the American Anthropological
          Association. Washington, D.C.
Portes, Alejandro
  1985   International Migration and Interstate Relationships. *In* Southeast
          Regional Conference on Immigration and Refugee Issues:
          Proceedings and Notes. Pp.17-24. Miami: Florida International
          University.
Rappaport, Roy
  1968   Pigs for the Ancestors. New Haven: Yale University Press.
Recinos, Adrián
  1954   Monografía del Departamento de Huehuetenango. Guatemala:
          Editorial del Ministerio de Educación Pública.
  1977   Popol Vuh: Las Antiguas Historias de Quiché. San José, Costa
          Rica: Editorial Universitaria Centro Americana.
Reina, Rubén
  1966   The Law of the Saints. Indianapolis: Bobbs-Merrill.
Reyes, Antonio
  1993   El Indio Maya Chiapaneco No Es Criminal . . ., Es La Víctima. El
          Regional 14 January: 17-18.
Ricard, Robert
  1974   (1966) The Spiritual Conquest of Mexico. Berkeley: University
          of California Press.
Roberts, Bryan
  1973   Organizing Strangers, Poor Families in Guatemala City. Austin:
          University of Texas Press.
  1981   Migration and Industrializing Economies: A Comparative
          Perspective. *In* Why People Move. J. Balán, ed. Pp.17-42.
          Vendôme: UNESCO.
Robinson, David J.
  1990   Towards a Typology of Migration in Colonial Spanish America.
          In Migration in Colonial Spanish America. D. Robinson, ed.
          Pp.1-17. Cambridge: Cambridge University Press.

Robinson, David J. ed.
1990   Migration in Colonial Spanish America. Cambridge: Cambridge University Press.

Rohter, Larry
1991   In a Florida Haven for Guatemalans, Seven Deaths Bring New Mourning. New York Times. 24 October: A-18.

Royce, Anya Peterson
1982   Ethnic Identity, Strategies of Diversity. Bloomington: Indiana University Press.

Salovesh, Michael
1983   Person and Polity in Mexican Cultures: Another View of Social Organization. *In* Heritage of Conquest, Thirty Years Later. C. Kendall et al., eds. Pp.175-200. Albuquerque: University of New Mexico Press.

Sanchez-Arjona, Rodrigo
1981   La Religiosidad Popular Católica en el Perú. Lima: Seminario Conciliar.

Santoli, Al
1988   Parade Magazine. 23 October: 16-17.

Sassen, Saskia
1992   Why Migration. *In* Report on the Americas XXXVI (1): 14-19. Washington D.C.: North American Congress on Latin America (NACLA).

Say, Pedro Miguel
1992   Ik'ti' (Cuentos). Los Angeles: Ediciones IXIM.

Schifrel, Scott
1993a   Indiantown Co. Quietly Holds Land, As Well As Martin Town's Destiny. Palm Beach Post 7 March: A-1, A-20.
1993b   Migrant Makes Good in Indiantown. Palm Beach Post 8 March: A-1, A-6.

Schifrel, Scott and Lisa Shuchman
1992a   Migrants Still Face Hazards.Palm Beach Post. 27 December: A-1, A-18.
1992b $1000 Connection Funnels Guatemalans to Indiantown. Palm Beach Post. 27 December: A-18.

Schiller, Nina Glick, Linda Basch and Cristina Blanc-Szanton
1992   Towards a Transnational Perspective on Migration: Race, Class, Ethnicity and Nationalism Reconsidered. New York: New York Academy of Sciences.

Schirmer, Jennifer
1993   Whose Rights Are They Anyway? The Guatemalan Military's Looting of Human Rights Discourse. Paper presented at the annual meeting of the American Anthropological Association. Washington, D.C.

Schwartz, Norman
    1983   The Second Heritage of Conquest: Some Observations. *In* Heritage of Conquest, Thirty Years Later. C. Kendall et al, eds. Pp.339-362. Albuquerque: University of New Mexico Press.

Schwartz, Theodore
    1978   Where is the Culture? Personality as the Distributive Locus of Culture. *In* The Making of Psychological Anthropology. George Spindler, ed. Pp. 419-441. Berkeley: University of California Press.

Segundo, Juan Luis
    1976   The Liberation of Theology. Maryknoll, New York: Orbis.

Sheridan, Thomas
    1988   Where the Dove Calls. Tucson: University of Arizona Press.

Siegel, Morris
    1941   Resistance to Culture Change in Western Guatemala. Sociology and Social Research 25: 414-430.

Smith, Carol A.
    1988   Destruction of the Material Bases for Indian Culture: Economic Changes in Totonicapán. *In* Harvest of Violence. R. Carmack, ed. Pp.206-231. Norman: University of Oklahoma Press.
    1990   Social Relatonships in Guatemala Over Time and Space. *In* Guatemalan Indians and the State. C. Smith, ed. Pp.1-30. Austin: University of Texas Press.
    1992   Indigenous Identity as Ideology. Paper presented at annual meeting of the American Anthropological Association. San Francisco.

Smith, Carol A., ed.
    1990   Guatemalan Indians and the State: 1540-1988. Austin: University of Texas Press.

Smith, Waldemar
    1977   The Fiesta System and Economic Change. New York: Columbia University Press.

Spicer, Edward
    1969   Introduction. *In* Handbook of Middle American Indians, Vol. 8. R. Wauchope, ed. Pp.777-791. Austin: University of Texas Press.
    1980   The Yaquis: A Cultural History. Tucson: University of Arizona Press.

Spring, Anita
    1982   Women and Men as Refugees: Differential Assimilation of Angolan Refugees. *In* Involuntary Migration and Resettlement. A. Hansen and A. Oliver-Smith, eds. Pp.37-47. Boulder: Westview.

State of Florida
  1989   Department of Human Resources and Services (HRS), Martin
          County Public Health Unit 1989 Report. Cited in R. Hahn.
          Indiantown Action Plan. Orlando: Hahn and Company.
Stephen, Lynn
  1990   The Politics of Ritual: the Mexican State and Zapotec Autonomy,
          1926-1989. *In* Class, Politics, and Popular Religion in Mexico
          and Central America. L Stephen and J. Dow, eds. Pp.43-60.
          Washington D.C.: American Anthropological Association.
Stephen, Lynn and James Dow, eds.
  1990   Class, Politics, and Popular Religion in Mexico and Central
          America. Washington D.C.: American Anthropological
          Association.
Stoll, David
  1990   Is Latin America Turning Protestant? The Politics of Evangelical
          Growth. Berkeley: University of California Press.
Sullivan, Lawrence
  1988   Icanchu's Drum, An Orientation to Meaning in South American
          Religions. New York: Macmillan.
Swimme, Brian
  1994   Canticle to the Cosmos. Video Series No. 10: The Timing of
          Creativity. Livermore: Tides/New Story Project.
Tactaquin, Cathi
  1992   What Rights for the Undocumented. *In* Coming North, Latino and
          Caribbean Immigration. Report on the Americas XXVI (1): 25-28.
          New York: North American Congress on Latin America
          (NACLA).
Tax, Sol
  1983   Forward. *In* Heritage of Conquest, Thirty Years Later. C. Kendall
          et al., eds. Pp.vii-xvii. Albuquerque: University of New Mexico
          Press.
Tax, Sol, ed.
  1952   Heritage of Conquest. Glencoe: The Free Press.
Tedlock, Barbara
  1982   Time and the Highland Maya. Albuquerque: University of New
          Mexico Press.
  1983   A Phenomenological Approach to Religious Change in Highland
          Guatemala. *In* Heritage of Conquest, Thirty Years Later. C.
          Kendall et al., eds. Pp.235-246. Albuquerque: University of New
          Mexico Press.
Tedlock, Dennis
  1985   Popol Vuh. The Definitive Edition of the Mayan Book of the
          Dawn of Life and the Glories of Gods and Kings. New York:
          Simon and Schuster.

Time
  1993   The New Face of America: How Immigrants are Shaping the
          World's First Multicultural Society. Special Issue on Immigration.
          Fall: 10-12.
Tinker, George
  1993   Missionary Conquest: The Gospel and Native American Cultural
          Genocide. Minneapolis: Fortress Press.
Trueblood, Marilyn
  1977   The Melting Pot and Ethnic Revitalization. *In* Ethnic Encounters.
          G. Hicks and P. Leis, eds. Pp.153-1167. North Scituate, MA:
          Duxbury Press.
United Nations
  1993   Common Threads- Indigenous People and the Modern World.
          New   York: United   Nations   Department   of   Public
          Information/Centre for Human Rights (UNDPI).
Univisión
  1993   Noticiero Nocturno Broadcast of 9 September.
  1994   Noticiero Nocturno. Broadcast of 10 March.
Van den Berghe, Pierre L.
  1981   The Ethnic Phenomenon. New York: Praeger.
Van Kessel, Joop and André Droogers
  1988   Secular Views and Sacred Vision: Sociology of Development and
          the Significance of Religion in Latin America. *In* Religion and
          Development. Van Ufford and P. Scoffeleers, eds. Pp.3-65.
          Amsterdam: Free University Press.
Van Oss, Adriaan
  1986   Catholic Colonialism: A Parish History of Guatemala 1524-1821.
          Cambridge: Cambridge University Press.
Veciana-Suarez, Ana
  1989   Guatemalans Find Florida a Mix of Hope, Hostility. Palm Beach
          Post. 1 October: A-1.
Velasco-Rivera, Pedro
  1983   Danzar o Morir: Religión y Resistencia a la Dominación en la
          Cultura Tarahumara. Mexico: Centro de Reflexión Teológica.
Versteeg, Jac Wilder
  1992   A Bad " Good Neighbor" Policy. Palm Beach Post 13 July: A-11.
Vogt, Evon
  1967   Zinacantán. Cambridge: Harvard University Press.
  1976   Tortillas for the Gods. Cambridge: Harvard University Press.
Wagley, Charles
  1949   The Social and Religious Life of a Guatemalan Village. Memoir
          #71. Washington D.C.: American Anthropological Association.
Wallerstein, Immanuel
  1974   The Modern World System I. New York: The Academic Press.

1980   The Modern World System II. New York: The Academic Press.
Warren, Kay
    1978   The Symbolism of Subordination: Indian Identity in a Guatemalan
                Town. Austin: University of Texas Press.
Watanabe, John M.
    1990a   From Saints to Shibboleths: Image, Structure, and Identity in
                Maya Religious Syncretism. American Ethnologist 17 (1):
                131-150.
    1990b   Enduring Yet Ineffable Community in the Western Periphery of
                Guatemala. *In* Guatemalan Indians and the State. Carol Smith, ed.
                Pp.183-204. Austin: University of Texas Press.
    1992   Maya Saints and Souls in a Changing World. Austin: University
                of Texas Press.
Wikan, Unni
    1992   Beyond the Words: The Power of Resonance. American
                Ethnologist 19 (30): 460-481.
Williams, Brackette
    1989   A Class Act: Anthropology and the Race to Nation Across Ethnic
                Terrain. Annual Review of Anthropology 18: 401-444.
Williams, Peter
    1989   Popular Religion in America, Symbolic Change and the Modern-
                ization Process in Historical Perspective. Urbana: University of
                Illinois Press.
Yinger, J. Milton
    1985   Ethnicity. Annual Review of Sociology 11: 151-180.

Index

For Product Safety Concerns and Information please contact our EU
representative GPSR@taylorandfrancis.com
Taylor & Francis Verlag GmbH, Kaufingerstraße 24, 80331 München, Germany

www.ingramcontent.com/pod-product-compliance
Lightning Source LLC
Chambersburg PA
CBHW050706280326
41926CB00088B/2684